A Thousand Pieces
of Paradise

Wisconsin Land and Life

ARNOLD ALANEN

A Thousand Pieces
of Paradise

Landscape and Property in the Kickapoo Valley

LYNNE HEASLEY

THE UNIVERSITY OF WISCONSIN PRESS
PUBLISHED IN ASSOCIATION WITH THE CENTER FOR AMERICAN PLACES

The University of Wisconsin Press
1930 Monroe Street
Madison, Wisconsin 53711

www.wisc.edu/wisconsinpress/

3 Henrietta Street
London WC2E 8LU, England

2   4   5   3   1

Printed in the United States of America

Library of Congress Cataloging-in-Publication Data
Heasley, Lynne.
A thousand pieces of paradise : landscape and property in the
Kickapoo Valley / Lynne Heasley.
p. cm.—(Wisconsin land and life)
"Published in association with the Center for American Places."
Includes bibliographical references (p.) and index.
ISBN 0-299-21390-0 (cloth : alk. paper)
1. Kickapoo River Valley (Wis.)—History. 2. Kickapoo River Valley (Wis.)—
Geography. 3. Kickapoo River Valley (Wis.)—Environmental conditions.
4. Landscape—Wisconsin—Kickapoo River Valley—History. 5. Property—
Wisconsin—Kickapoo River Valley—History. 6. Land tenure—Wisconsin—
Kickapoo River Valley—History. 7. Land use—Political aspects—Wisconsin—
Kickapoo River Valley—History. 8. Landscape protection—Wisconsin—Kickapoo
River Valley—History. I. Center for American Places. II. Title. III. Series.
F587.K4H43   2005
977.5′74—dc22   2005011171

Small portions of material have appeared previously in *Who Owns America:
Social Conflict Over Property Rights*, edited by Harvey M. Jacobs (Madison:
University of Wisconsin Press, 1998), and "Shifting Boundaries on a Wisconsin
Landscape: Can GIS Help Historians Tell a Complicated Story?" in *Human
Ecology* 31 (2003): 183–211.

Contents

Illustrations

Acknowledgments

I owe countless debts to the people who helped make this book possible. I was fortunate to have two extraordinary mentors at the University of Wisconsin–Madison. Ray Guries took what must have sounded like an unwieldy project when I proposed it and helped mold it into a nearly ideal interdisciplinary collaboration. I owe much to his genius in translating the ecological history of a landscape for people who know less of the natural world than they should and to his uncanny ability to spot surprising trends, contradictions, and errors in the most complex GIS maps. Ray's generosity and warmth set the tone for my time at Madison.

Bill Cronon's guidance and intense curiosity inspired me to be braver in my ideas than I was naturally inclined. His remarkable graduate seminar on the history of the American West became a turning point for my scholarship, which, though unabashedly interdisciplinary, had been in need of some discipline. Bill's real gift to his students lay not in introducing everyone to brilliant ideas (though he did this) but in welcoming each of us into a family of scholars.

I cannot express enough appreciation to Keith Rice and Hawthorne Beyer, my research collaborators at the University of Wisconsin–Stevens Point. Not only did they steer the GIS work from that end, Keith cheerfully smoothed the bureaucratic feathers that get ruffled when two campuses share a research project. Keith produced the GIS maps for this book. Over two summers Mike Stanek, Matt Dahlen, and Ben Gramling provided invaluable field assistance. My good friend Mike Barrett provided both research assistance and astute comments on many chapters. I am thankful that he never visibly tired of talking with me about the complexities of land tenure, a topic our families could not long endure.

Nancy Langston has been a strong supporter, a tough critic, and at all times a good friend. I am grateful to other people at the University of Wisconsin for their support and counsel, including Matt Turner, Steve Ventura, Don Field, Jess Gilbert, and David Mladenoff. Harvey Jacobs reviewed the entire manuscript, and his suggestions improved the book a great deal. I owe a special thanks to Wolfgang Hoffmann, who allowed me to use his stunning photos in the book and on the cover.

Over the years, many colleagues have commented on chapters, articles, and papers; directed me to resources; and made time for long discussions. For their mental labor on my behalf I thank Marsha Weisiger, Brian Donahue, Don Worster, Rebecca McLain, Thomas Andrews, Tim Bawden, Mary Eizabeth Braun, Joe Cullon, Jim Feldman, Paul Hirt, Neil Maher, Jared Orsi, Bill Philpott, James Pritchard, Louise Pubols, Volker Radeloff, Greg Summers, and Jay Taylor. I was fortunate to find a small but enthusiastic group that applies GIS to history, including Geoff Cunfer, Julia Haggerty, Anne Kelly Knowles, and Ken Sylvester. At Western Michigan University, Michael Chiarappa, John Cooley, Nora Faires, Buddy Gray, Sarah Hill, Dave Lemberg, and Kristin Szylvian all provided helpful feedback on my research. Mike Swords will see the results of our extended conversations about the amazing course we shared, "Values and Sustainable Society."

I cannot go far down my list of debts without thanking the terrific people who work and live in the Kickapoo Valley. They made my research possible. Department of Natural Resources forester Jim Dalton opened up his files, cleared away a desk, and even agreed to supervise field assistants. Marilyn Dalton went still further by opening the Dalton home to an assortment of researchers who traipsed in and out over the summer. Phil Hahn offered his help and technical skills throughout the project, and on one snowy Sunday morning at the Common Ground Café he impressed a group of my students with an inspiring talk on the conservation history of the Valley. County conservationist Jeff Hastings authorized a collaboration with us in the first place, while early on Jim Radke helped me make sense of the confusing system of local, state, and federal agricultural extension programs. Solving the historical maze of the Kickapoo Valley Reserve would have been exceedingly difficult without the professional perspectives of John Anfinson, Marcy West, and Glenn Reynolds. Along the same lines, Susan Lampert Smith assisted me with her unique professional perspective on Woodland Farms. Editor Terry Noble encouraged me to offer early versions of this work for public comment in his newspaper, *The Vernon County Broadcaster*. I thank them all for their time and openness.

One of the most heartening aspects of working in the Valley is the passion and intelligence with which residents approach their own history. Judy Daily, Danny Deaver, Rosanne Boyett, Joel Swanson, Eddi Blakley, Brian Turner, and Clifford Turner provided so much useful information that they will immediately spot their great influence. I must also thank Judy Wilmes, Bill Putze, and Senn Brown for their enthusiasm and encouragement while I was writing the book. Bob Djerdingen gave me a tour of his ranch, and in so doing gave me the benefit of his keen insight into thorny environmental issues. Lonnie Muller turned the tables on a researcher and asked me all the questions. Every academic should have someone like Lonnie ask: Why does your work matter? Who funds you? And most importantly, do you realize that academic research is not just an objective exercise as far as we who live here and love this place are concerned? Ben Logan understood these questions well. On a panel we developed together, he offered me gentle guidance on how I might become a more effective storyteller. I'm afraid I have not shed what Ben considered the most tiresome academic tropes (summary conclusions, for one), but my work is still better for his wisdom. Ken and Chris Stark always brought me back to the sense of place and beauty that binds people throughout the Kickapoo Valley. With his kind permission, Ken's line art appears in chapter 4.

I could not have written this book without the archival resources and professional assistance available in Wisconsin at university, state, and local levels. Collections at the Wisconsin Historical Society, the University of Wisconsin–Madison Archives, and a number of university libraries—Steenbock, Memorial, Wendt, Water Resources Institute, and Environmental Studies—allowed me to examine virtually any facet of rural midwestern history. Just as essential for researching the Kickapoo Valley were University of Wisconsin–La Crosse's Murphy Library and the Vernon County Historical Museum archives. Museum curator Judy Gates gave me a desk in the attic (very romantic for a historian) and free rein to go through dozens of boxes of historical materials, while Judy Mathison kept an eye out for the eclectic information I was searching for. Sandy Vold-Brudos saved historic township tax rolls from permanent destruction or relocation long enough for me to enter them in my database. During long weeks in the Vernon County Register of Deeds, Betty Bolton and Konna Spaeth offered me their lovely company, and also their sympathetic labor in lifting heavy volumes when I was nearly nine months pregnant.

The commitment of George Thompson and Randy Jones at the Center for American Places launched this book in the first place. The Center's vision of bringing scholarship about land and people to the broadest possible audience has never been more important. It has been a pleasure working with Steve Salemson and Adam Mehring, my editors at the University of Wisconsin Press. I am also honored that series editor Arnold Alanen included this book in the Press's new series on Wisconsin land and life. Generous support for research and writing was provided by a United States Department of Agriculture McIntire-Stennis research grant, the Environmental Protection Agency's Science to Achieve Results (STAR) program, the American Association of University Women American Fellows program, and the College of Arts and Sciences at Western Michigan University.

My parents, Dick and Judy Loofboro, together with my husband and son, have seen me through this Valley journey. I dedicate the book to Phillip and Jacob.

A Thousand Pieces
of Paradise

Introduction

I began this study with the ambition of bridging two areas of inquiry, one national in scope and public attention, the other decidedly local (and locally idiosyncratic). I planned to examine the historical roots of modern property debates in the United States. The prism of property has become a powerful lens in the American political consciousness. It has fundamentally shaped national policies on agriculture and the environment. I wanted to explore how these debates intersected with processes of rural transformation in the twentieth century. In what ways did rural change and emerging ideologies of property influence each other? At what levels in American society did they intersect—primarily nationally, with the consequences trickling down to local places? Or locally as well, with national institutions responding to the grassroots? But beyond property as an idea, or a debate, I wanted to look more closely at land ownership. It was important, I believed, to reexamine dichotomies that we assume apply to real people in real places—the environmental steward (*homo environmentalist*) and the environmental exploiter (*homo economicus*)—or alternatively, the ecologically educated, civic-minded environmentalist and the leave-me-alone-on-my-*own*-land libertarian property rights enthusiast. Underneath the dichotomies lie assumptions about who makes a good or bad land manager. Yet I wondered, given my own family history in the rural Midwest, where motivations are complex to say the least and even schizophrenic at times, would these assumptions hold up if you tracked environmental outcomes rather than environmental sensibilities? What would patterns of environmental change in local landscapes tell us about different kinds of land management? About different kinds of landowners?

Bridging the national and the local (the larger idea and the individual action) was conceptually simple and practically very difficult. To my mind, the land itself was the ideal bridge. Though passionately debated, competing philosophies of property rarely come down to earth. They can only partially address questions of environmental outcomes because they don't demonstrate those outcomes in actual places. Property rights debates, for example, are bound up in a still deeper tension in American agrarian history. This tension centers on the interplay between individual interests and what a community (or society) defines at the time as the common good. The fault line runs along the question of whether deference is given to the prerogatives of the individual landowner over any given parcel of land or whether some larger, negotiated vision prevails for a whole landscape and its uses. My plan was to trace this tension on some small area of land over several decades. I hoped to render different ideas of property visible in the changing fields and forests of rural landscapes.

As a corollary, I decided to trace the emergence of cultural narratives about property in the histories of local communities who occupied the land. This would address one of my primary concerns about national discourse today: the tendency to reduce people's ideas and motives to ahistorical sound bytes, such as "property rights versus the environment." (Even academics can fall into this trap by taking proclamations at face value, or by assuming that a person's position on a subject is more static than contextual.) Rather than focusing primarily on what people say in the present, it seemed just as important to probe when they started saying it, to whom, why, and in what context.

As I began the research for this book, it became clear how oblivious many of us are to the full shape our system of property has taken in rural communities and landscapes. Rather than clarifying matters, the way we talk about environmental debates acts like a veil. In one moment a reporter describes the latest controversy over a development proposal that threatens an endangered nesting bird. In another moment a family conversation around the kitchen table turns to a neighbor forced to remove the trash piling up in her yard. In both cases we are focused on an individual and on a clearly demarcated piece of property. In both cases we are weighing our sympathy for the landowner or lack thereof on a very specialized scale: whether we believe the particular situation warrants some economic cost to the owner or some imposition on her personal freedom. No matter where the scale in our mind's eye falls, we have a vision of property that is extraordinarily isolated. We see a single landowner facing down a few disgruntled neighbors or an environmental group. That small group of people is standing on land so circumscribed that it occupies most of our field of vision.

There is an alternative vision that extends the boundaries of these disputes. In this vision, a vast landscape swallows up any one parcel, integrating it into a complex mosaic of landcover types, soil regimes, and hydrological networks. And far from standing in relative isolation, the landowner is part of an intricate social web (loosely called a democracy) that has not only negotiated the terms of holding land but also of distributing that land in the first place.

These different ways of seeing local land disputes—the first much more common than the second—are surface manifestations of deep philosophical divides over how our property system should accommodate individual and collective interests. Historically, three areas of disagreement have been especially powerful in shaping the politics of land use: the function of property, the fluidity of property rights, and models of property in U.S. law. Together these recurring themes provide a useful reference point for understanding an array of environmental controversies. For this reason I hope that readers will feel free to return to the synopsis I offer here as they make their way through the book's diverse stories.

The first disagreement concerns the function of property—who or what it serves. One tradition goes back three-hundred-plus years to English philosopher John Locke's famous theory of private property.[1] The contemporary version of Locke holds that property is primarily a means to increase the wealth of individual citizens and thereby to assure their personal freedom.[2] Another tradition, inspired by the ideas of Thomas Jefferson, argues that property is a tool for ensuring the public good and, ultimately, for securing democracy.[3] An addendum to this second position is that democratic societies have a fundamental interest in moderating the influence landowners have over public policy; otherwise, their disproportionate, or concentrated, power puts democracy itself at risk.[4] Both philosophical traditions have enduring places in U.S. history.[5] The problem arises when these two sets of values come into conflict. Then we have to decide which are the deeper values, which ones to privilege.

To make the point more clear we need only look to a book that Alan Gottlieb edited in 1989 called *The Wise Use Agenda*.[6] The *Agenda* articulated a number of principles that marked the debut of the antienvironmental "wise use" movement of the 1990s. The name itself—wise use—co-opted an expression that Gifford Pinchot, famous conservationist and first chief of the U.S. Forest Service, had popularized early in the twentieth century: that the wise use of natural resources should be "for the greatest good of the greatest number for the longest time."[7] *The Wise Use Agenda,* however, did not share any of Pinchot's deep-seated mistrust of corporate monopoly over land (which he considered to be at odds with his own ideal of equitable land distribution in a democratic society as well as with effective resource conservation).[8] Among its specifics *The Wise Use Agenda* called for monetary compensation to landowners for any public action that restricted land use.[9] This was a clear statement that the primary function of property is an economic one. In effect, Gottlieb and Ron Arnold, cofounders of the wise use movement, were arguing that when conflicts arise the default should be to economic values. Where land is concerned, they implied, all other values are subordinate.

The second area of disagreement turns on whether the terms of holding land are static or fluid over time. Those who argue for a static reading do so on the grounds that assuring an economic return to an individual landowner is a core function of property. This can only be accomplished, they assert, if property rights are constant, so that individuals can make decisions with no fear that the rules of the game will change.[10] Those who argue that property is fluid contend that the concept of fixed property rights is mythological, not historical, and furthermore that it is antidemocratic. Society's values will evolve, finding their way into policy and remaking property relationships. This is not a problem, they stress, but rather one of the virtues of living in a democratic society. The citizenry should be able to respond to new conditions, to advances in knowledge or changes in values.[11]

More difficult to grasp, but fundamental nonetheless, is a third area of disagreement involving models of property in American law. Most orthodox is the ownership model of property, which depicts property as a relationship between a person (or a corporation) and a thing.[12] The central relationship here is between the landowner, who holds title, and the land or resource the owner controls. Property law is supposed to support the relationship: first, by defining the legal rights of individual owners, and second, by placing a heavy burden of proof on nonowners who challenge those rights for whatever reason.[13] Today this "classical" idea of property (as property theorists call it) would seem self-evident to some people, whereas others find it hopelessly flawed. According to legal scholar Joseph Singer, "the ownership model of property utterly fails to incorporate an understanding of property rights as inherently limited both by the property rights of others and by public policies designed to ensure that property rights are exercised in a manner compatible with the public good."[14]

The basic premise of the ownership model is wrong, say Singer and other theorists. The central relationships in our system of property are those negotiated among members of society. Property rights are therefore *contingent,* or dependent, on the social *context* in which someone wants to assert those rights.[15] Singer calls this a social relations model of property. Property law in this model referees conflicts between people. It decides the merits of competing claims by judging between their effects, not by judging the superiority of a property right over some other right.[16] Matters of property rights are a triad, explains economist Daniel Bromley: "My dreams for a piece of land I claim to control, your disgust at the thought that I may actually be able to realize my dreams on that land to your detriment, and this third part called 'government.' The dispute is between the two of us, with government as the arbiter of our conflicting and mutually incompatible interests."[17]

Contemporary property debates involve all three areas of disagreement—its function, its terms (whether fixed or fluid), and the best legal model to represent it. But most prominent in public discourse are ways of talking about property that honor the individual landowner. Much less audible is discourse that proclaims the prerogatives of a larger community whose values are not wholly economic. Questions about whether or not a particular land use regulation represents a "takings" of your private property correspond to the deeper premise that property's primary function is to offer you an economic return.[18] When some change in public policy results in heated discussion over its fairness, the underlying assumption is that you hold property under terms that are primarily static, not fluid. Language that you have been prevented from "doing something with" your land assumes a model of property in which the primary relationship is between you and a thing, rather than between you and other members of society. Notice how easily one philosophical perspective on property can frame the conversation. Around the kitchen table we tend to speak of property in terms of the individual owner and his rectangle of land, no matter where on a given issue we actually fall. Willingly or not, it would appear that we defer to the classical view of property.

My argument in this book will not be that individual and economic notions of property are false; to the contrary they have held powerful sway culturally and politically, and I will show their influence ecologically as well. My argument instead is that this vision has coexisted alongside a democratic and fluid vision of property, less visible, to be sure, but equally powerful. Interesting things can happen when this alternative vision finds expression. This I will also show on the land itself. My aim, then, is to uncover histories of property that are less well known and to place them alongside the histories we think we know well. I aim to both clarify and complicate the property relationships that have shaped great stretches of the country.

In southwestern Wisconsin, the Kickapoo Valley offers an ideal site to consider the ecological dimensions of property. Like many rural regions, the Valley has experienced land concentration and fragmentation, absentee land ownership, agricultural decline, and seemingly unpredictable changes in land use. More than once it has been a staging ground for contentious new environmental policies. This is the land of Aldo Leopold, who helped draw the region's farmers into one of the nation's earliest efforts at soil conservation. The Kickapoo Valley hosted the first Army Corps of Engineers dam project in the country to be halted—midstream and three-fourths of the way through construction—because of the National Environmental Policy Act of 1969. Two decades later the defunct dam project became the means by which the Ho-Chunk Indian Nation successfully regained some of the land the federal government had violently evicted it from more than 150 years earlier. The Kickapoo Valley has also become home to both the Old Order Amish and to the Coulee Region Organic Produce Pool (CROPP), one of the country's most influential organic cooperatives. Both groups thrived in the Valley landscape, and they gained a national audience for reasons we will explore at length later. These stories and others will unfold in the chapters that follow. I highlight them because they speak directly to our most intractable debates over the persistence and well-being of rural communities, over environmental degradation, and over who controls land and to what ends.

And then there is the sheer passion that emanates from the place. For 150 years, maybe longer, residents have been passionate about the Kickapoo Valley. People have stewed over it, like Gertrude Frazier and Rose Poff, who toward the end of the nineteenth century wrote in a huff, "The Kickapoo Valley and its inhabitants have an established unsavory reputation, extending throughout the state of Wisconsin and even beyond that it is a territory some fifty miles long, wild and undeveloped, inhabited by illiterate people who are designated timber thieves, horse thieves and desperadoes." To correct "such statements" that were "wholly false," the two undertook a whole book extolling the virtues of their landscape and their community—*The Kickapoo Valley: The Gem of Wisconsin.*[19]

People have suffered from their gem's sharp edges: "We look around to see what is around us and our thoughts come fast as we ask our sephs . . . who will meet disaster and death some by flods and that by the hundreds on the home near a river or rivers and traped like rats in a trap to drown," quoted from the 1913 diary entry of longtime resident Mattie Dawson.[20]

They have rhapsodized about "our enchanted Coulee land, this friendly and hospitable paradise"—this from one of the Valley's nature lovers, Ralph Nuzum, in 1955.[21] Nuzum was a local lumber baron who self-published four books about the place and established a large endowment at the University of Wisconsin–Madison to "support a model comprehensive land use forestation, conservation, and rehabilitation project" in the Kickapoo Valley.[22]

People have fought over the Kickapoo Valley. Fought to stay in it. Fought to come back to it.

I believe that this passion, this constant engagement with a changing world that is only partly human, resonates throughout rural America. Where land is concerned, strong emotions make sense.

The Valley landscape itself provides an exceptional primary document for reconsidering how historical processes have interacted *in space* to transform rural America. Its story—at once cultural and ecological—provides the framework for this book. There is a question, though, of how to do justice to the very nature of this place. How to excavate processes that are both social and ecological? Environmental historians struggle with this question all the time.[23] It is built into our field. The answer varies with the particular slices of history under consideration and the particular interests and talents of the historians writing them. Nevertheless, such a simple explanation masks how strong feelings can run on the question. In 2001, historian Stephen Pyne wrote a provocative essay condemning the strong influence of "humanist history" and "postmodern cultural analysis" in environmental history. According to Pyne, environmental history risked losing its way if environmental historians did not get outside and study real ecosystems. In a now-famous line (at least among environmental historians), Pyne said that, otherwise, environmental history "will be shrunk into body studies, surgically transgendered, strip-mined for environmental justice, dissolved into a misty sense of ethnic place."[24] Although my own work may prove guilty of one item in Pyne's catalogue—the "misty sense" part—I view this statement as a distraction from the more valuable point he makes. Like Pyne, I believe that my research has demanded intimacy between me and the fields and forests of the Kickapoo Valley. For a historian who, like Pyne, *is* on a "search for a usable place," the Kickapoo Valley is a fine hunting ground. My own answer, then, has been to write an ecological history of property and a cultural history of ecosystems. Saying all this requires a clarification of methods, because like the Valley's own residents, I have engaged the environment there in very specific ways.

When I began this study I immediately faced two problems. With local archival sources I could develop a historical profile of land ownership in the Valley. By foraging more widely I could establish chronologies for controversies like the Corps of Engineers dam, a real estate development gone awry, an intense dispute with the Amish. By digging deeper I could even unearth a cultural mosaic of how different groups, in different contexts, thought about property and the environment. What I could not do was flesh out in similar detail an environmental mosaic of the landscape and its ecosystems. I could generalize the landscape to field and forest, hill and dale. I could summarize what ecological literature there was for the Kickapoo Valley and the wider Driftless Area. The most relevant research showed that oak-hickory forests, a major component of the region's landscape for over one hundred years, were having trouble regenerating.[25] This was suggestive but limited for my purposes. I could not analyze with any credibility the impacts different property regimes had on the land, or the impact the land might have had on them. I could only *suggest* those relationships. Thus I was in no position to synthesize social and ecological phenomena. Those were the two problems: ecology and synthesis.

There was also a related matter of the spatial dimension inherent in my inquiries. Geographers occasionally charge historians with being spatially naïve or spatially crafty. This means that we do not understand how critical spatial dynamics are in people-environment interactions or that we move up and down scales without saying so, for example, fitting secondary sources on spatially specific ecosystem dynamics into whatever regional unit the narrative calls for.[26] Whether or not such charges have merit, their cautionary note is useful. If I wanted to track how property systems played out on the ground over time, I needed to understand how the ground itself had changed. I needed to be able to explain: Here is how the landscape mosaic of field, forest, pasture, lowland, slope, and upland looked around 1940, and again in 1955, and still later in the 1960s, up until the

1990s when forests covered much more area than they had in the 1930s, and fields covered less. Here also is how the finer mosaic of forest ecosystems lay in the 1930s, but not for long: See where some older, sun-loving oak-hickory stands gave way to shade-tolerant sugar maple and basswood?—and how still more of the oak gave way each decade, up through the end of the century? A historian could really do something with this kind of detail. She could explore patterns and processes, causes and effects, land ownership and the environment. Inconveniently, no ecologist had carried out an ecological history of the Kickapoo Valley.

So I turned instead to doing ecological field research and to using a favorite spatial tool in ecology and geography—geographic information systems, or GIS.[27] I also moved back and forth between solo work in the archives and work with a multidisciplinary team of collaborators. Over several years we traversed the Valley's landscape, compiling information into what eventually became a huge GIS database. During our analyses we felt a sense of discovery whenever the spatial histories of forests and agriculture intersected in some important way with property histories. Especially exciting were connections we found between land ownership and forest succession from oak to maple. Some of these dynamics would have been extremely difficult to discern without both the GIS and the historical perspective. The maps in this book are the artifacts of these analyses. They make for a compelling historical narrative in their own right.

Like everything in the academic enterprise, GIS-based research entails workaday choices that will profoundly affect the outcome of a study.[28] The hardest choice in this project involved how much to scale down coverage of the Kickapoo Valley. A GIS could not represent all of its 766 square miles in any kind of meaningful detail, not with the resources we had. So I decided to concentrate on a few of the Valley's townships.

For a long time I had been fascinated by the role of townships in shaping rural life. My own family history in northwestern Wisconsin includes a Byzantine network of extended relations and friendships, with lines of the network leading directly into township government. As an adult visiting the family homestead I began to see (or rather, to hear) how this network came into play during land use disputes. When, in the middle of the night, a neighbor blew up a beaver dam on my uncle's lakefront land, the network pulled its strings. Strange as it might sound to an outsider, the incident had occurred because someone imagined that the rising water level of my uncle's lake from the dam was responsible for lowering the water level of a neighboring lake. The demolitionist was closely related to the town chairman, with whom my uncle (the chair's good friend) spoke, and who spoke, in turn, to the young man. The network was both informal and official. As land tenure specialists would say, it involved both customary relationships and statutory ones. In his treatise *Democracy in America,* Alexis de Tocqueville saw townships as the origin of American political life.[29] The township, said Tocqueville, "at the center of the ordinary relations of life, serves as a field for the desire of public esteem, the want of exciting interest, and the taste for authority and popularity; and the passions that commonly embroil society change their character when they find vent so near the domestic hearth and family circle."[30] Although my study was not primarily concerned with town governance, I knew that township boundaries made a difference on the landscape. (In Wisconsin, townships are formally called "towns," but for consistency and clarity I will use the term township throughout the book.) At the least, townships made logical units for depicting broad swaths of land and landownership in a historical GIS.

My criteria for selecting townships were not complicated. The townships should represent changes that had affected the whole Valley—both the well-publicized, spectacular types of change and the modest adjustments that accumulate year after year into major transformation. I also wanted the townships to be situated near to each other. This runs counter to the scientific method of random sampling, but my sample would not have been random anyway. I thought comparing townships that share a small space might be more telling than comparing townships that lie far apart. Finally, I wanted townships where both farmland and forests are prominent on the landscape (nearly all of them). Rural scholarship tends to focus on either forests or agriculture, yet this is an artificial division.[31] As historian William Cronon demonstrated so superbly in *Nature's Metropolis,* even nineteenth-century farmers on faraway western prairies depended on forests in the Upper Midwest.[32] In the Kickapoo Valley, fields and forests have lain side by side for just as long, so surely the interplay between them had an important part in the regional property system. In the end I settled on three townships, Liberty, Clinton, and Stark, in retrospect an incredibly fortunate choice.

The histories of Liberty, Clinton, and Stark are often difficult and conflict ridden; they can cut many ways. Together they epitomize the Kickapoo Valley in all its complexity. I have organized the rest of the book around them, much as William Least Heat-Moon was inspired to do in his reflection of a township's "deep maps," *Prairy Erth.*[33] In the chapters

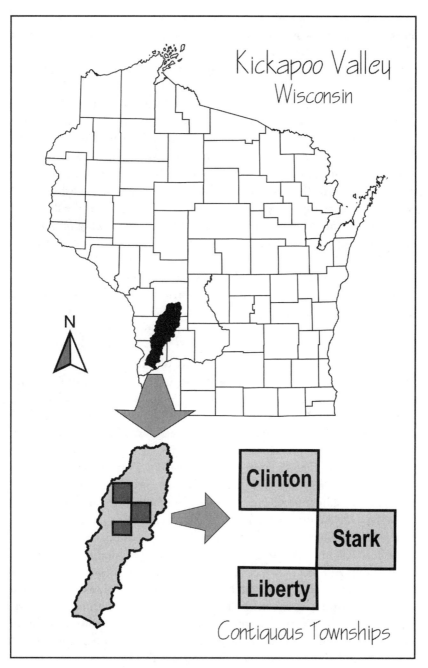

Figure 1. Study townships in the Kickapoo Valley, Wisconsin.

that follow, each township is a touchstone for larger themes. The themes are of three sorts. First, in each chapter I narrate a historical trend or event that reveals some important facet of property. In effect, I want to bring property theory to life by grounding it in real situations. Second, each township as a whole—all the chapters therein—speaks to particular cultural narratives about property and the environment that would sound familiar anywhere in this country. These narratives are the lenses through which people have come to see the world around them.[34] As an example, the narrative of local places against the federal government is a common one. The township of Stark will show how that narrative emerged from the ground up in the Kickapoo Valley. And third, each township represents a counterpoint to the other townships. They represent the divergent outcomes possible when communities submit to a governing principle of individual landowner prerogatives, or when some larger, negotiated vision prevails.

In the first three chapters, Liberty is the touchstone. Chapter 1 uses a history of soil conservation and contour strip cropping to show just how fluid the terms of holding private property have been in rural America. Chapter 2 looks at concentrated landownership and absentee corporate beef ranching. Chapter 3 follows the saga of Woodland Farms, a real estate agency that brought wave after wave of city dwellers to the Valley looking for their own piece of paradise. In Liberty, the overarching cultural narrative is that of the "invisible hand" of market forces. The narrative posits that far-reaching changes in land ownership and land use arose from thousands of individual decision makers, each responding to the logic of the market. Hence those changes were outside the ability of communities to influence. But Liberty's own history of soil conservation belies that narrative. Liberty also shows what can happen when the common interests of residents are submerged beneath those of the individual landowner.

The fourth and fifth chapters move six miles north, to Clinton township, where the dominant cultural narrative is of ethnic conflict and accommodation. In chapter 4, a large Amish settlement begins buying up farmland, even as non-Amish farmers are having a difficult time holding onto their farms. In the process, the Amish bring to the fore territorial dimensions of property. Chapter 5 looks more closely at ways in which the Amish interact with their landscape. By contrast with Liberty, the Amish in Clinton realize a community ideal for the kind of life their members should lead on the land. The results raise the question: Do the Amish offer us a model for sustainable agriculture and sustainable land ownership?

The last three chapters take us to the Kickapoo River and to one of the townships it runs through—Stark. Chapter 6 examines the long genesis of a contested piece of federal land. Local communities, the Army Corps of Engineers, environmental groups, and the National Environmental Policy Act all had a hand in its birth during one of the nation's most bitter dam controversies. Deer management, the ostensible focus of chapter 7, is also a jumping in point for exploring the social and ecological spillovers of the La Farge dam. Finally, chapter 8 witnesses the return of the Ho-Chunk Nation to the Kickapoo Valley. The Ho-Chunk play an extraordinary role in bringing about new and visionary property relationships, which transcend all previous boundaries.

Prologue

Weekend Drive, Summer 2002

Driving due west of Madison, Wisconsin, on U.S. Route 14, you soon leave behind a glaciated landscape of lakes and rolling terrain. You enter a different kind of land, hillier and surely more dramatic if you prefer topographic relief. Unbroken acres of corn and soybeans give way to small fields or pasture on ridges and valley bottoms; mixed hardwood forests lie on the steep slopes in between. A line of white pines appears high up on sandstone outcrops, like a column of weathered soldiers. You have entered the Driftless Area, a region the glaciers never reached.[1] Without glaciers, whose advances and retreats sculpted a lake country across the rest of Wisconsin, the Mississippi River and its tributaries and their tributaries were unimpeded in carving the hills and valleys that characterize the region. One of these tributaries is the Kickapoo River, which glides through the landscape with so many twists and turns that its very name means "one who goes here, then there" in Algonquian. Turn north off 14 to meet one of the twenty-seven thousand people who call the Kickapoo Valley home—perhaps someone who lives on a ridge far above the river—and she will probably tell you that she loves the panorama of fields and forests unfolding like a verdant patchwork quilt. She might add that her neighbors who live down deep in the Valley's hollows enjoy their dark green solitude just as much, but this can be downright claustrophobic to visitors. "Coulee country," they all call it, because of these narrow, haunting valleys. Such sensibilities are not recent either. "No matter in what direction one sets his face a new scene presents itself at each turn of the road and each seems more beautiful than the last," wrote two sisters in 1896 in homage to the Kickapoo Valley.[2]

16

Still, on a first drive you might not mark this place as one of the most fascinating and important valleys in the Upper Midwest. The Kickapoo Valley is among the poorest parts of Wisconsin, a fact the pretty scenery will not hide. Old cars with For Sale signs by the road, droopy farmhouses with weeds in front and household junk piles around back, abandoned barns lying in charred ruins (used for practice by the fire department when they were no longer safe to keep standing)—these are all part of the view too. Like rural communities around the country, the Valley lost thousands of farmers during the twentieth century. The land did not make it easy to grow a farm there. Short of leveling hills and filling in valleys, Kickapoo Valley farmers could not plant unbroken miles of cash crops, so they could not use large farm machinery at the industrial scale necessary to pay it off. Dairy farming faced the same crisis of scale, dependent on a flimsy pyramid on which the land must sustain the herds necessary for producing larger volumes of milk and the returns per volume (no matter how marginal) must support the capital investment. With a shrinking and aging farm population, and an adjusted gross income only 55 percent of the state average in 1990, economists labeled the Valley "underdeveloped."[3] Others called it Little Appalachia. The Kickapoo Valley could be any hardscrabble place where farmers are having a hard time holding on to land, where teenagers are bored and talk about leaving, and where local officials are praying for economic development.

But stay longer and baffling sights and sounds intrude on first impressions. Even people who have lived in the Valley their whole lives marvel at the shifting scene. For example, just north of a speck of a village called Liberty you will come upon a motocross racetrack. Dusty and filled with motorcyclists bobbing in and out of view, it looks like a strange twist in the proverbial road that goes ever on. How did *that* get way out *here,* you might wonder. And how do the neighbors—or the neighbors' cattle, poor things—feel about all the *noise?* Still, from a cyclist's perspective, this would certainly be an exciting landscape. Not five miles further north, the whining of the machines has ceased and once more the land has morphed into a new vision. As motorized traffic fades away, a clip-clop, clip-clop, clip-clop takes its place. A black horse-drawn buggy sedately rounds a bend in the road. A kind of signature house dominates miles of landscape now—large, rectangular, entirely white, a black buggy posted in front. A plain-clad signature person stands out as well. Coulee country, it seems, is also Amish country. All these Amish farms send a pretty strong signal that agriculture is not dead in the Valley (notwithstanding the motocross), but how have the Amish done it? Why do they look so prosperous when other farmers have obviously not prospered?

A mere three-mile detour southeastward and the Rockton Bar provides a pleasant rest stop for a cold Bud, if you want one. The bar appears blessed with its location near the Kickapoo River. Stretching north and south is a vast deciduous forest whose rippling light green surface is smudged and streaked in places with darker stands of white pine. No Amish land this, but an 8,500-acre natural area called the Kickapoo Valley Reserve. If you mused that it must be absolutely gorgeous here when the leaves turn in the fall, you would follow in the reveries of thousands of tourists who came before you. You might even dream for a moment about buying a little piece of land in the area: What a great place to take a family on weekends. In this, too, you would not be the first—to dream or to buy. On the patio of the bar sit picnic tables, slyly inviting you to hang out. This is clearly a place trying to make customers feel at home. And right there with the tables sits a tombstone. (Yes, a granite tombstone.) The rear end of a horse is etched on the tombstone, which reads: "In Memory of Those Who Sold Us down the Kickapoo River."

A racetrack, an Amish farm, a tombstone at a bar. Together they make no sense. But there they are, in just a fraction of the Valley's 760 square miles. *In memory of those who sold us down the Kickapoo River.* Only a person with absolutely no curiosity could resist asking what this is about. The tombstone expects your questions; it demands them. How did it get here? What stories is it hinting at? With so much happening round every bend, where do you start?

PART I

Landscape Succession

I

Intended Consequences
Soil Conservation

Sometimes research data confirm a story that many people know well.
The GIS maps in figures 2 and 3 look like just such a case. The maps
themselves come out of a quantitative study of the Kickapoo Valley's
history, which my colleagues and I carried out in the late 1990s. Based
on data for six dates at intervals of roughly ten to fifteen years, they show
land ownership trends and landscape change in the township of Liberty
since 1930.

Figure 2 shows that local residents owned almost all of Liberty's land
up to 1955. The few exceptions involved out-of-town heirs (usually children of deceased landowners) or banks holding property on which they
had foreclosed. This is not to say that land ownership was static in Liberty
or in the Kickapoo Valley. Land turnover was a fact of rural life before and
after 1955. A majority of the land in Liberty went to new owners at least
once every ten to fifteen years. But the picture in Liberty changed during
the 1960s, almost imperceptibly at first. Someone from outside the Valley
bought 249 acres from two local families. Then a second couple, not from
the area, consolidated five parcels totaling 950 acres in the northeastern
part of the township. This same couple, along with five more local landowners, later sold a combined 1,800 acres to an Illinois buyer. By 1965,
absentee owners had made inroads in Liberty; by 1978, they had bought
nearly half the land there; and by 1995, they controlled the majority of the
township. These are data that rural areas around the country might take
to be their own. They know firsthand the trend from local to absentee
land ownership.

Figure 3 represents Liberty's landscape from 1939 to 1995—its dynamic
pattern of agricultural fields, pasture, and forest. The eye will naturally

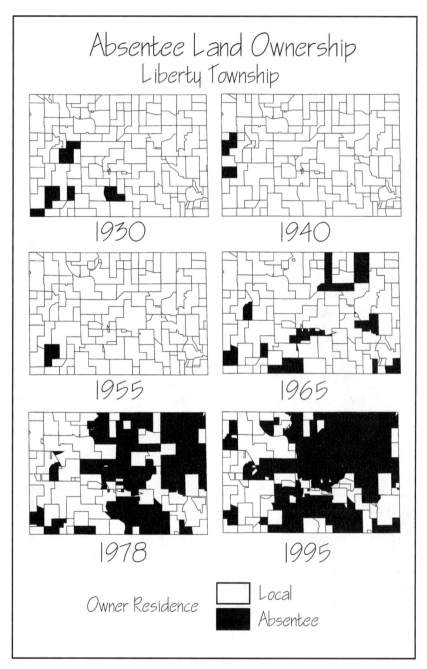

Figure 2. Trends in absentee land ownership in the township of Liberty, 1930–95.

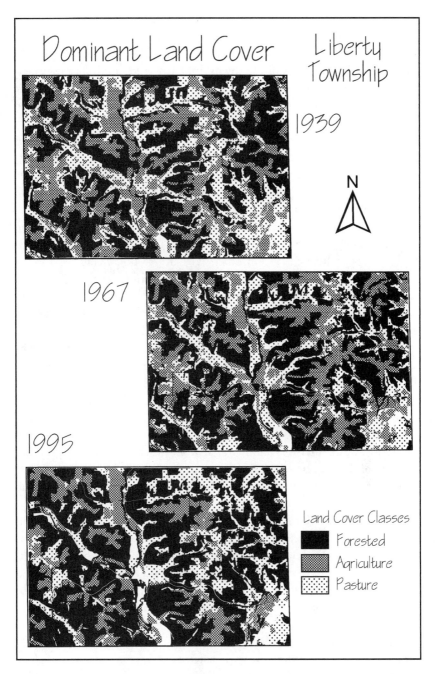

Figure 3. Township of Liberty land cover, 1939–95. Note the decline of cropland (the "agriculture" category), while forest cover expands. In the early 1950s, cultivated land was at its peak in the township, but by 1995 it had declined by nearly 60 percent.

pick out changes in the figure from one date to another, with forests increasing in some parts of the township, pasture expanding or contracting in others. Putting actual numbers on the changes complicates the picture considerably. For instance, from 1954 to 1967 cropland decreased by 425 acres. Some of this land went into pasture, while an additional 375 acres of pasture regenerated to forests. Like land ownership, farm systems in the Valley were never static. So a shift in cropland, pasture, and forest between any two dates could have been a typical fluctuation. But the virtue of looking at a place over several dates is that you can distinguish normal fluxes within a landscape from long-term changes across the landscape. In the Liberty of 1967, agriculture was clearly on the wane. A drop of 425 acres by 1967 became a drop of nearly 1,875 acres by 1995. From a high in 1954, cultivated land in Liberty fell almost 60 percent.

In many rural places, changes in land ownership are bound up with what has become their overriding story, the decline of farm communities. In its most generic form, the story explains the relationship between the two sets of maps as follows: During the twentieth century, national and global market forces clasped an ever-tighter grip on rural America. Farmers had to meet international market demands or get out of agriculture. By the 1960s, local real estate markets were also changing. Farmland went cheap in many places—an attraction to investors and speculators—while recreational land (rising in popularity) went more expensively. Increasingly those who could or would pay fair market value were neither local nor farmers. An "invisible hand" was at work in which thousands of independent real estate buyers and sellers inexorably reshaped rural America. This is the big story, the narrative with which these first three chapters are concerned.

There is an interesting puzzle in the data, however. Land turnover in Liberty actually decreased from 1955 to 1965, the very period in which agriculture began its decline. Only 44 percent of Liberty's land changed hands during that period, by comparison with a turnover of 52 percent from 1930 to 1940 and 68 percent from 1940 to 1955. Afterward, from 1965 to 1978, turnover spiked to 72 percent.[1] This particular juxtaposition raises questions. Many people would associate agricultural decline with stress. Wouldn't this be the most likely time for farmers to sell their farms? Yet more farmers were holding on to their farms, at least for a time.

The remainder of this chapter will set the historical context for Liberty after 1955. It will fill two gaps in Liberty's free market narrative (and in the maps themselves). The first gap is the federal government, and more specifically its efforts to unite two kinds of national policy—soil conservation and agricultural commodity output. The second gap is public policy on the ground, in the Kickapoo Valley, where the dynamics of private land ownership come into play. "There's a story here," said Liberty town chair Danny Deaver, as we talked about data and maps and the changes he had seen during his lifetime.[2] Deaver's family had farmed in the Kickapoo Valley since 1877. "It was all brought about," he said, "because government offered the free money."

Few agricultural problems were more pressing to the federal government in the 1930s than the loss of rich, fertile topsoil to the erosive forces of water and wind; and no culprit appeared more obvious to policymakers than the farmer.[3] Prominent officials thought the nation was committing "suicidal agriculture."[4] Many decades earlier, George Perkins Marsh had sounded a general alarm with his landmark work, *Man and Nature; or, Physical Geography as Modified by Human Action.*[5] Marsh had despaired of the degradation he saw everywhere settlers had cleared forests for crops and livestock. In the history of western civilization, he had divined a connection between deteriorating environments and declining societies.

Marsh might have despaired indeed had he visited the Kickapoo Valley seventy years later. By the 1930s, farmers had cut most of the region's mature forests: first white pine in the Valley's pineries, which made a small contribution to the enormous nineteenth-century timber cutover that swept through Michigan, Wisconsin, and Minnesota; then hardwoods—oak, hickory, and maple—which supplied local lumber needs and made way for cropland and pasture, or became part of a farmer's back forty woodlot or "grubs." Photos from the era show sheep and cattle making their way along steep hillsides, grazing among scrawny trees. Because of logging, excessive burning, and overgrazing (and also because the region's rough topography exacerbated the effects of these practices), the Valley had endured some of the worst soil erosion in the country.[6]

Since the publication of *Man and Nature,* upwards of 60 percent of the Valley's cropland had lost one plow depth of soil or more.[7] Massive gullies sliced through farms in southwestern Wisconsin, at times moving a thousand feet in a single storm.[8] At depths of fifty feet, some gullies seemed to swallow whole fields. University of Wisconsin soil scientist F. H. King lamented that "storm by storm and year by year the old fields are invaded by gullies, gorges, ravines, and gulches—until the soil of a thousand years growth has melted into the streams, until the fair acres are converted by hundreds into bad lands, desolate, and dreary."[9] Soil erosion and sedimentation had touched a national nerve about the catastrophic influence of agriculture on nature. This was when rural communities first started to grapple with environmental problems typical of the twentieth century. This was also when the country's ideas about property became inextricably linked to regional environmental controversies.

In the 1930s, soil erosion was vivid in the national consciousness and obvious to every farmer in the Kickapoo Valley. The first two maps in figure 4 provide a clue about how farmers eventually responded. The figure depicts an agricultural practice called contour strip cropping, in which farmers cultivated fields in narrow alternating strips of grain and hay running along the contour of the land. Together the maps show a shift in the practice, which in turn reshaped landscape patterns throughout the region.

Plowing along the contour was a technique that had only a sporadic history in the United States up until the 1930s. Most farmers plowed straight rows. But Thomas Jefferson had once suggested cultivating corn along the contour to keep the soil in place.[10] He saw that rows of crops running across a slope might act as miniterraces, keeping raindrops in place where they fell. Jefferson aside, southwest Wisconsin claimed for itself August Kramer, an obscure German immigrant in the mid-1880s. Today many soil conservationists laud Kramer as the pivotal innovator in contour strip cropping. Kramer farmed a few miles west of the Kickapoo Valley. He carried out what soil conservation agencies now consider "the earliest known definite action to control erosion and prevent gully formation on cropland."[11] Kramer's novel technique was to lay out his fields along the contour in alternating bands of different crops and hay. Kramer believed his approach would result in less runoff and erosion than planting rectangular fields to the same crop every year.[12] In a 1948 inventory of Kramer's farm, his fields had five inches more topsoil than other comparable fields. The technique evolved so that today many midwestern farmers combine contour strip cropping with complicated rotations of grasses, small grains such as oats, and row crops, especially corn and soybeans. But more than one hundred years later, the basic concept remains intact. Soil scientists and agricultural engineers in Kramer's time seized on his method and began promoting contour strip cropping in their publications.[13]

The maps of Liberty represent a succession of sorts—agricultural succession. But was contour strip cropping the inevitable outcome of an environmental problem? That individual farmers shifted from one practice to another reasonably suggests good risk management at a time when soil

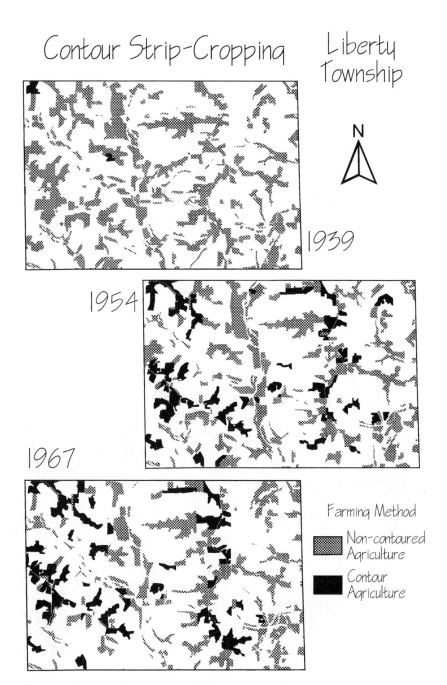

Figure 4. Contour strip cropping in Liberty, 1939–67. Contour strip cropping spread noticeably between 1939 and 1954, but not between 1954 and 1967.

erosion was of local and national concern. This would have been a logical response to an environmental crisis in agricultural production. Alternatively, the shift from noncontoured to contoured fields might have resulted from the local adaptation of farm communities to their physical environment. By then they had many decades of experience with the Valley's steep hillsides, narrow valley bottoms, and rolling ridge tops. Either explanation makes sense, lending an air of inevitability—which environmental scholars sometimes call "environmental determinism"—to the phenomenon I euphemistically called agricultural succession. But it is difficult to avoid the actual timing of the change in Liberty. Consider figure 4 again. It shows that only two fields had contour strips in 1939, despite their earlier indigenous introduction only a few miles away, and despite technical advice on their virtues going back over forty years.

My argument is that contour strip cropping was not preordained; it was instead the result of powerful government programs aimed at influencing private landowners, primarily farmers. Such programs, moreover, fostered a number of entirely new land tenure relationships: of agriculture to science-based conservation techniques; of landowners to government and

In the Kickapoo Valley, a rectangular field alongside fields in contour strips. Since the 1930s, soil conservation agents in southwestern Wisconsin have encouraged farmers to use contour strips on slopes. (Courtesy of Wolfgang Hoffmann)

university extension agents; and of private property to public interests in private land. "Can we permit one generation to waste natural resources that belong to all generations?" asked Melville Cohee in his 1934 study of soil erosion on thirty farms in a township adjacent to Liberty. "Aside from these philosophical considerations, what about the right of one farmer to damage the land of another through neglect or mismanagement of his soil? What about the cost to local governments when roads have to be cleared of rocks and earth after every heavy rain and bridges have to be replaced after being torn away by floods? What about the spoiling of trout streams, riparian erosion, and silting of rivers? Erosion within the line fence of a given farm affects the interest of individuals and governments from the township all the way up to the Federal Government."[14] Cohee's passionate questions presaged the changes to come. Contour strips spread across the Kickapoo Valley because the federal government made a concerted effort to create new public prerogatives on private lands.[15]

Contour strip cropping in Liberty was part of the larger national setting of erosion control in the 1930s. In 1928, Hugh Hammond Bennett, then with the Bureau of Chemistry and Soils, cowrote with W. R. Chapline *Soil Erosion as a National Menace.*[16] This article created a sensation, putting Bennett center stage, from where he later convinced the Roosevelt administration of the need for a more active federal approach to reduce erosion.[17] Department of the Interior secretary Harold Ickes strongly supported his idea of a new soil conservation program, which would fight erosion from the high ramparts of national policy down to the local front lines of the farm field. Erosion control might have ended up as little more than a collection of modern engineering and land use techniques—best management practices in today's conservation language—had it not become a central strand running through Franklin Delano Roosevelt's New Deal programs.[18]

The National Industrial Recovery Act of 1933 authorized creation of the Soil Erosion Service, placing it within Ickes's Department of Interior and under the direction of Bennett. In 1935, after a jurisdictional tussle between Interior and the Department of Agriculture, Roosevelt transferred Bennett and the Soil Erosion Service to Agriculture, where it became the Soil Conservation Service, or SCS.[19] The transfer meant more than a change in home and a new name. The initial mandate of the Soil Erosion Service had been to prevent soil erosion through technical assistance to farmers, Civilian Conservation Corps labor, free lime, fertilizer, tree seedlings, and fencing wire. The Soil Conservation Service was still responsible for these tasks, only now, in 1935, its mandate encompassed a new national policy for soil conservation. The law to "provide permanently for the control and prevention of soil erosion" also authorized the secretary of agriculture to "acquire lands, or rights or interests therein, by purchase, gift, condemnation, or otherwise, whenever necessary for the purposes of this Act."[20] The terms under which people managed agricultural land were about to change.

The SCS did not remain the only soil conservation kid on the block. A 1936 amendment to the Soil Conservation Act charged the U.S. Department of Agriculture's Agricultural Adjustment Administration (AAA) with administering the Soil Conservation and Domestic Allotment Program. This made soil conservation one of its primary thrusts.[21] The rationale for a second program was straightforward. The U.S. Supreme Court had just declared unconstitutional the original Agricultural Adjustment Act of 1933, under which the Agricultural Adjustment Administration used price supports to control the output of agricultural commodities.[22] The AAA had made direct payments to farmers who reduced their acreage in certain surplus crops, a policy the court declared illegal. The new program bypassed the court decision. It would now make payments to farmers who carried out soil conservation practices, defined as reducing acreage in certain soil depleting crops. Many years later, Wisconsin soil scientist Leonard Johnson wrote critically of the AAA's twin mandates in the 1930s: "Thus there was conceived an attempt to combine in a single program under a single agency two kinds of public policy objectives that differ fundamentally in their most efficient and effective modes of achievement."[23] At the time, erosion control and commodity control seemed more symbiotic than competitive. What's more, hard cash had the potential to influence land use to an extent no previous government initiative had achieved.

The commitment to reduce soil erosion raised a mountain of government agencies and programs from the federal to the local level. The Soil Conservation Service and the Agricultural Adjustment Administration became the base of the mountain. To the public these were not faceless bureaucracies. What is important to understand is that soil conservation gained momentum not as a series of programs but as a peculiar hybrid, a sociogovernmental movement. It is hard to exaggerate the zeal, personal commitment, and sheer force of personality that permeated this movement in the 1930s. Epic metaphors abound in both the literature of the time and in later retrospectives. Early prophets like Hugh H. Bennett became revered leaders, preaching the gospel of soil conservation. Everyone concerned—

politicians, bureaucrats, public extension agents, university professors and yeoman farmers alike—made emergency preparations for the war on erosion. One SCS employee in the Kickapoo Valley attended a Bennett sermon and described the performance this way: "There he stood, a big man, probably six-foot-four and big all over. He had a round face with heavy jowls and was quite bald. His large chest continued right down to a large stomach, which, for all its bigness appeared to be solid. He stood before us in a full suit, vest and all, with a gold watch chain draped across, looking like an evangelist prepared to preach at us. And preach he did."[24]

If Bennett was the bishop of soil conservation, Aldo Leopold and Otto Zeasman were two powerful and charismatic Wisconsin priests, sometimes at odds in their tone and approach, but always fighting the same holy war to save the land. Zeasman was a land drainage specialist with an engineering bent, a real problem solver. His soil conservation career began in 1922 when he traveled to Buffalo County in southwestern Wisconsin to advise on highway maintenance, only to be confronted by gullies over a quarter of a mile long.[25] From that moment, Zeasman dedicated himself to the practical challenges of gully control. At first this involved grass waterways and diversion terraces, but Zeasman's expertise expanded into permanent gully control structures such as the drop-inlet dam. In 1936, he took a joint position with the Soil Conservation Service and the University of Wisconsin Extension. Zeasman participated in nearly all aspects of soil conservation in Wisconsin up until his retirement in 1956. Numerous Wisconsin publications still refer to him as the "Dean of soil conservation."[26]

Yet some of Zeasman's colleagues thought he was not holistic enough. "While responding to farmers' requests for help in solving their newly-realized erosion problems," explained Leonard Johnson, a soil conservation specialist in university extension, "and in the spirit of evangelists eager to confirm a conversion while both flesh and spirit were willing, it was quite natural and reasonable that Zeasman and the workers under his direction would take a direct problem-solving approach and aim to heal the most evident, open and bleeding wounds of cropland erosion at the points of injury as quickly as possible."[27] The problem, however, was that halting the progress of a single gully did nothing to change the wider farming practices that caused the gully in the first place.

Aldo Leopold was skeptical of wholly technical approaches to conservation. Today Aldo Leopold is famous for his environmental treatise, *A Sand County Almanac*.[28] In 1933, he was a professor of game management at the University of Wisconsin and deeply immersed in most of the conservation issues of his time, including soil erosion. That year, Hugh Bennett requested proposals from around the country for soil conservation demonstration projects. Raymond H. Davis, superintendent of the Upper Mississippi Valley Erosion Control Experiment Station, put together the Wisconsin team, which included the station's associate director, Noble Clark; E. R. Jones, who was chairman of the University of Wisconsin's Department of Agricultural Engineering; Otto Zeasman; and Aldo Leopold.[29] The plan they developed was so impressive that Bennett brought Davis and Clark to Washington to work with him on a "Tentative Program for the Control of Erosion on the Watershed of Coon Creek in Southwest Wisconsin, Upper Mississippi Valley Region."

What exactly attracted Bennett to the Wisconsin plan? For one thing, it included the problem-oriented detail that was so much a part of Zeasman's work. The demonstration would synthesize current science on the physical processes of soil erosion and the techniques that could successfully retard them. Goals 3 and 4 in the tentative project, for example, were "to install certain improvements such as dams, strip cropping, terracing, planting trees and other vegetation"; and "to erect fences to protect areas devoted to forests and pasture, to conform to the new layout." Framing the details, however, was a comprehensive philosophy that appealed mightily to Bennett, and this philosophy bore the unmistakable signature of Leopold: "Erosion control is not a challenge to technical men to work out methods which will permit farmers to continue any and all present land uses. Rather it is a challenge to define and secure the basic changes in land utilization which must precede and accompany control works. We can not get very far on a plan which consists entirely of applying public palliatives to private abuses."[30]

The distinction between Leopold and Zeasman is critically important on two levels, one philosophical, the other social and institutional. Zeasman felt that individual landowners did not have the capacity to prevent erosion; primarily they needed public technical support to relieve the problem.[31] Zeasman's ideas were more limited than Leopold's, and he placed less responsibility on landowners to radically alter *their* ideas. According to Leonard Johnson, "Zeasman's approach did not explicitly encompass the notion that quite possibly a farmer's whole economic enterprise as well as the physical arrangement of his farm should be revised to relieve stresses on soil and water resources, and perhaps even to accommodate the needs of song birds, game birds, deer and other useful and desirable creatures."[32]

This difference in viewpoint is crucial to the history of environmental thought; however, an equally important distinction underlies Johnson's insightful comment. The plan that Bennett enthusiastically supported was not a technical plan, but one that expressed a social and institutional vision of the government's place on private land. "An erosion control program to be effective," said the plan, "must recognize and reconcile (1) the private ownership of most eroding land, and (2) the public nature of the considerations which require that erosion be prevented and checked." The demonstration project that Bennett envisioned was not a plan to work with clientele landowners who needed their help. It was a plan to reshape to the greatest extent possible the way those owners used land. "It will probably take another decade before the public appreciates either the novelty of such an attitude by a bureau, or the courage needed to undertake so complex and difficult a task," said Leopold in a 1935 essay on the project.[33] Though generations of soil conservationists have since worked to achieve politically palatable regulations, Leopold saw even then that their very presence on the land could bring about a fundamental shift in the public-private dynamic of property. The year 1933 arguably marked the beginning of a new set of social and environmental relations with respect to rural land tenure and the more specific institution we call private property.[34]

It takes a sharp picture of what the public presence entailed to fully understand the evolving property dynamics. What was happening on the ground while Bennett, Leopold, and Zeasman were organizing and firing up the troops? For SCS personnel, the initial answer was that working the fields was not so easy. Roy Dingle was one of those agents. Dingle is not a celebrated figure in soil conservation history (you will not find his name alongside Bennett, Leopold, or even Zeasman in sweeping histories of the movement). But he was a participant and keen observer on the ground. Dingle spent much of his career working with the Soil Conservation Service in the Kickapoo Valley.[35] There he developed a powerful regional perspective on soil conservation. Dingle's commentary in the pages that follow offers a striking, albeit one-sided, conversation with Leopold, Zeasman, and Bennett.

Roy Dingle would not have been surprised at the dearth of contour strip cropping in Liberty by 1939. Liberty was no fluke because farmers were reluctant to try new methods, especially contour strip cropping. In those early days, Dingle remembered, contour strip cropping "immediately branded a farmer." Neighbors would tease, "Here was a crazy man going to that 'rainbow farming,' that crooked farming." They would jest, "That President Roosevelt—he's laughing up his sleeve at those crazy farmers plowing in circles as if they followed a heifer around the hill with the plow." Dingle always had to restrain himself from retorting, "The heifer has more sense than you."[36]

For the farmer, laying out new contour strips was terribly hard labor. According to Roy Dingle, even "the old straight fences—'you could shoot a rifle straight down that old fencerow'—had to be completely removed and changed."[37] After that, establishing the crops in successful rotations could take several years. The first strips of hay, for example, always included a mix of qualities from good to very poor, so the earliest yields might be low.

There was cultural labor involved in contour strip cropping as well. The professional consensus was that "deeply ingrained habits brought over from Europe" created a barrier to modern practices.[38] To make his point, Dingle offered the intriguing example of tenant farmers. Even today, conventional land tenure theory generalizes that tenants will do more damage to land because they have less of a stake in its long-term health.[39] Economists and tenure specialists refer to this stake as "security of tenure." The idea is that a tenant is less secure in his or her land because an owner can evict her at any time. A tenant will therefore be reluctant to invest financial resources, personal labor, or immovable capital (e.g., trees) in long-term conservation. The owner rather than the tenant might realize the profits from these investments, either through an increase in rents or by evicting the tenant. Making the same point with less sympathy, an early book on soil erosion stated, "A tenant operator, in general, has no specific interest in keeping up soil fertility, as he is ready to move to another farm any time he sees fit."[40] If this statement were put in the form of a hypothesis, it would posit that a tenant's field should have a higher rate of erosion than an owner-operator's.

The experience of Roy Dingle and his contemporaries did not support the hypothesis. They found "that a renter was more concerned about protecting the fields than was the owner." Their explanation was that owners were often older than their tenants, and thus more suspicious of "this crooked farming business."[41] Soil scientist Melville Cohee did not see a clear difference either way. His 1934 study of soil erosion in the township of Webster (adjacent to Liberty) showed that tenants and owners used the same methods to control gullies. "This is not without significance," noted the author, "since 38 percent of the farmers in the Driftless

Area are tenants and 35 percent of the farm area of Webster is operated by renters."[42] Regardless of the virtues or vices of the two groups, erosion control specialists like Dingle felt strongly that contour strip cropping was a revolution.[43]

Reduced erosion and better crop yields were not sufficient lures for adopting soil conservation measures. Yet an expanding network of state and federal conservation agencies would eventually induce change among landowners. Brute assertion of governmental authority would not be the means. Instead these agencies would lay new groundwork for expanding public prerogatives on farmland. They would further their goals by (1) creating new social relationships on the farm; (2) providing financial incentives to landowners; and (3) integrating formal conservation plans into the farmer's working life. All three strategies converged in a place called Coon Valley, which lay in Wisconsin's Driftless Area just one watershed west of

Dairyland Contour Plowing Contest, La Crosse, Wisconsin, October 8, 1941. The beginning of an agricultural revolution that transformed the landscape. (Courtesy of the University of Wisconsin–Madison Archives)

the Kickapoo Valley. After meeting with the Wisconsin delegation, Hugh Bennett named Coon Valley his agency's first demonstration project. As a prototype for national soil conservation efforts to come, Coon Valley would become one of the nation's great experiments in soil conservation.[44] As its close neighbor, the Kickapoo Valley would become one of the first places to replicate this pioneering work. To really understand contour strip cropping, you have to look deeper than the technique; you have to look at Coon Valley and the paradigm shift in land use it catalyzed.

The scale of the project was enormous—experimenting on and rehabilitating 91,000 acres of privately owned farmland. In eighty years of farming since European settlement, Coon Valley had lost three inches of topsoil.[45] Under Bennett's plan, the SCS would work jointly with the University of Wisconsin. Yet even with the combined resources of the university, the state, and the federal government, modifying the behavior of hundreds of landowners was daunting. Future publications would call Coon Valley the "birthplace of soil and water conservation in the nation."[46] It could also have been called the birthplace of modern agricultural land tenure.

Forging new social relationships on the land became the first order of business (though SCS agents probably did not think of it in such terms). Technical consultants descended on the watershed, advising farmers on every detail of their environment from the overall farm layout of crops, pasture, woods, and even wildlife habitat to fertilizers and land use practices, such as contour strip cropping. One can only wonder how many cups of coffee or tea these newcomers shared with longtime residents around the family table. Or how many acres of land they walked with farmers. The Civilian Conservation Corps (CCC) provided laborers for the heavy work. Local farmers helped train and toughen these young men.[47] It is hard to imagine a more physical federal presence than that on Coon Valley farms in the 1930s and '40s. The SCS, the CCC, and the university represented an unprecedented public incursion onto private property. The relationships they forged among landowners, state, and landscape became stronger over time.

Financial incentives were also part of the program. Cooperating farmers received fifty cents per acre. This was a modest sum in comparison to payments future conservation programs would make. Even so, Noble Clark complained that, "To pay every landowner fifty cents an acre on all of his land regardless of how much of this land is a public menace due to erosion is directly contrary to all precedent and to the equities involved."[48]

Shouldn't a landowner use environmental, social, and moral considerations to decide the right course of action, rather than cash in hand? Clark implied. Is there no ethical responsibility to one's neighbors and to one's land that makes financial payments unnecessary? Clark was not alone in these complex sentiments, then or now. But the cash did give the state a new lien on Coon Valley: limited property rights purchased from farmers to help direct future uses, and even the look, of the landscape. In complicating and redirecting a farmer's decision about how to manage his or her property, the demonstration project began to shift the relationships inherent in all private rural land—economic, ecological, social, and moral, as well as individual and collective.

The most potent tenure mechanism of all—the enforcer—was the "Agreement for Demonstrational and Experimental Work in Soil Erosion Control." This was a formal erosion control agreement tailored to the site conditions of each farm. The Agreement marked the real revolution, not only for agriculture but also for private property. When a farmer signed on, he committed his labor and his farm for five years. What had been advice from technicians became required practices. What had been public help with particular fields or single gullies became a new agricultural system covering the entire farm. A farmer could not request lime one day without also mapping out next year's contour strips and compiling a timeline for the next five years' crop rotations. Coon Valley was the first of 147 sites around the country. Of the three Wisconsin projects, 1,253 farms had the agreements.[49] That was quite a reach.

There was real power involved in putting agents and CCC workers on private land, providing payments for cooperation, and enforcing farm plans. One result was that contour strips started to change the face of the landscape. By the early 1940s, they had become popular throughout southwestern Wisconsin. Roy Dingle and his fellow conservationists were responsible for laying out the strips for farmers. Spring became hectic, he said, "as we struggled in the short time that we had to reach all requests before it was too late."[50] This was perhaps a conservationist's equivalent to the accountant's tax season, because Dingle would have as many as three hundred jobs to complete before farmers began planting, and farmers were always eager to plant as soon as possible. "They get a disease in spring," said Dingle, "and they've just got to get out and *plow*. . . . If we didn't get to a stripping job before the plow itch set in, we lost that job for the season." The hurry of the season was only one part of the physical labor, Dingle recalled with humor. Laying contours required a farmer to follow closely with his tractor, which allowed him to test the physical prowess of his friendly agent: "Some of them thought we city slickers knew nothing about hard work. This would sometimes be reflected in the speed with which they operated a tractor. . . . When that happened, we ran to stay ahead."[51]

Science was also helping Dingle's work. A 1936 book titled *Soil Erosion and Its Control* spoke favorably of contour strip cropping while also saying that "its effectiveness has not yet been thoroughly established either by field practice or experimentally."[52] By the 1940s this data-poor situation had changed.[53] The Upper Mississippi Valley Erosion Control Experiment Station (twenty miles west of the Kickapoo Valley) had begun publishing important results. Unlike Coon Valley, the Experiment Station was a single farm on which scientists carried out long-term controlled experiments on the physical processes of erosion.[54] The station made one of its most significant theoretical advances when it found that only a few intense rains each season caused most of the erosion. This gave credence to the notion that farmers who used methods from Europe did have some adapting to do in southwest Wisconsin. In Europe rainfall was higher in some places, but the rain fell more gently.[55]

The Experiment Station produced data of immediate use throughout the region. Where corn was continually planted along the contour, fields lost an average eighty-nine tons of soil per acre per year. Soil loss was thirteen tons per acre per year on a four-year rotation of corn, followed by barley, then hay, then more hay. On a corn, barley, hay, hay, hay rotation, the loss was eight tons. For a corn, barley, hay, hay, hay, hay, pasture, pasture rotation, it was five tons. Scientists reached their optimum soil loss of three tons with the lengthy rotation of corn, barley, hay, hay, hay, hay, hay, hay, pasture, pasture, pasture, pasture.[56] It is easy to see in this last rotation how farmers looking at such data might have decided that they could not afford to conserve the soil. Yet the Experiment Station did show economic benefits from contour strip cropping. A 1943 article entitled "Soil Management: Does Soil Conservation Pay? It Did Here!" documented a one-third increase in soybean yields after the installation of contour strips. The explanation? Rainwater remained on the fields instead of running down slope, so soil moisture content stayed high.[57] Soil science strengthened the new tenure relations taking hold in southwestern Wisconsin. The changing patterns of the landscape rippled out as each additional farmer drove Roy Dingle and his cohorts faster along the contour.

From their respective positions of policy and implementation, Leopold and Dingle were deeply engaged in the next phase of the agriculture-property revolution: the conservation district. Just a few years of experience in Coon Valley had convinced the Soil Conservation Service that it needed better ways to enforce agreements with individual farmers. More broadly, the agency had come to see that states and land grant colleges could hinder SCS objectives.[58] Hugh Bennett outlined one possible collaboration when he suggested that states should enact laws "authorizing: (a) cooperation with the federal government in erosion control; (b) the organization of conservancy districts or similar legal sub-divisions with authority to carry out measures of erosion control; and (c) the establishment of state or local land-use zoning ordinances where lack of voluntary cooperation makes such ordinances necessary."[59] The eventual result of Bennett's proposal was the Standard State Soil Conservation Districts Act, which Congress passed in 1936.[60] The act created a model law for states to enact in some form if they wanted to retain federal dollars for conservation.[61]

The conservation district became the third institutional framework for soil conservation, after the Soil Conservation Service and the Agricultural Adjustment Administration. The conservation district would put individual landowners under close though sympathetic scrutiny from county and town governments. It would make landowners more responsible for the environmental consequences of their land use choices. Wisconsin enacted soil conservation district legislation in 1937.[62] Chapter 92, as it is still known, made districts special-purpose local units of state government, and formally linked them to general-purpose county units of state government. The federal government and the state of Wisconsin would now work through local districts to control soil erosion. The township of Liberty became part of Vernon County's Soil Conservation District.[63] A conservation district's ability to draw on county taxing and regulatory authority assured a powerful local base from which to influence the environmental behavior of private landowners.

When it came to implementing conservation districts at the county level, Roy Dingle had his problems with Aldo Leopold. "Leopold loved the law of Wisconsin Soil and Water Conservation Districts which gave Districts power to regulate land use, to legislate soil and conservation within their boundaries," said Dingle (somewhat critically). "He hoped that Soil Conservation Districts would legislate a set of laws that would enforce conservation on all farmers within their District boundaries. This would be Utopia in Leopold's mind. And he was bitter about Districts because they weren't using the power that they had."[64] Dingle was referring to the fact that county conservation districts did not enact land use regulations, although they had the authority. The differences Dingle perceived with Leopold were about the level of public input possible on private land.

Leopold had once directed a revealing study, "The Erosion Problems of Steep Farms in Southwestern Wisconsin," a survey of 348 farms.[65] Leopold and his coauthor Joseph Hickey found a number of problem farms where erosion control would be difficult to accomplish. "Erosion, like poison-ivy, is spread by its own irritations," said Leopold and Hickey; "one sore spot begets another."[66] As they physically stood, certain farms would certainly continue a process of degradation—sore spot begetting sore spot—for three reasons. To begin with, the authors explained, "Modern dairying requires a heavy investment in buildings and machinery. This cost is easier to pay off when spread over more cows." Related to this, they continued: "Dairying requires much corn and grain. When the farmer extends his plowland uphill to raise this feed, he pushes his hayland uphill into the pasture, and his pasture uphill into his timber." And finally, Leopold and Hickey addressed the actual property boundaries that made erosion control all but impossible on some farms: "A third reason is the quadrangular land survey, which was and is misfit for rough country."[67]

"Thus we have," Leopold and Hickey concluded, "two economic trends plus an historical accident combining to distort the landscape of 'America's Dairyland.'"[68] Their recommendation was that a land readjustment board should purchase these problem farms; that the board then fragment or consolidate parcels into more appropriate units for the landscape; and that it resell the land under contracts requiring new owners to implement strong erosion control measures. They also suggested that county boards establish conservation covenants on lands they acquired from tax delinquency.[69] These proposals were too far-reaching for rural counties in the twentieth century. Yet the ideas were practical. They made sense as a way of honoring private land ownership while accommodating society's evolving values. "The crux of the land problem," said Leopold in 1935, "is to show that integrated use is possible on private farms, and that such integration is mutually advantageous to both the owner and the public."[70]

Leopold approached land ownership in much the same the way that property theorists approach it. He recognized the legal boundaries so prominent in our American system of property (more formally, a cadastral system for recording land titles). He also saw beyond those boundaries in ways that will become clear. Most people, though, focus on the boundaries; history justifies this. Like Leopold, we can see the Ordinance of 1785 literally carved in the landscape. The ordinance deployed the U.S. rectangular survey, in which surveyors mapped much of the country in township plats of thirty-six square miles divided into sections of one square mile (or 640 acres). The mathematical logic of the survey's squares—their simplicity and divisibility into smaller and smaller units—provided the foundation for later federal acts to dispose of land in the public domain to private owners.[71] By this process, said geographer Hildegard Binder Johnson, the 160-acre quarter section became "an American institution," while 40 acres, or the forty, eventually became "the modular unit" of the Upper Midwest.[72] Hence the rectangular shape of most ownership parcels in the Kickapoo Valley, no matter how curvilinear the contours of its landscape.

Order upon the Land, Johnson's study of the rectangular land survey, has special significance here. Regionally, she showed the ways in which the survey changed and was challenged by the physical landscape of the Driftless Area. Nationally, she demonstrated how the survey became one of the foundations of private property as we know it today. The rectangular survey is intuitively familiar, even to people who do not know its history. We observe the survey every day in the rectangular yards of our neighborhoods. We also derive one of the survey's basic premises: that owning a piece of land gives us the right to use it, to keep other people out of it, and to sell it if we choose. To many people, property itself is merely a set of categories that describes land ownership in slightly more detail, primarily "public" or "private." Yet this general sense of land ownership is not adequate for understanding soil conservation districts the way that Leopold understood them. Property boundaries alone do not explain a highly complex system of property like ours, nested as it is within a democratic society.

Leopold's approach to farmland recognized property boundaries, but it also embraced the complexity within and across those boundaries. It is this complexity that legal and economic theories of property try to capture or influence. Perhaps the theories easiest to visualize are those that conceptualize land ownership as a "bundle of rights." Within the bundle are individual sticks, each one representing a discrete right. Bearing the fruits of one's own labor on the land (the usufruct right), kicking someone off of it (the right of trespass), and bequeathing or selling it to someone else (the right to alienate), are important sticks in the bundle. Other sticks include the rights of eminent domain and taxation, both of which reside in the government's bundle. The bundle metaphor gives us a way to visualize what freehold property means to most people: a full set of rights gathered together in the sack of the landowner.[73] Yet the metaphor also helps us to envision how multiple parties can hold rights in the same piece of land. For instance, my father-in-law holds title to his farm in Michigan. But a natural gas company owns the below-ground rights to exploit any gas there, a stick his father sold some fifty years ago; a neighboring farmer rents twenty acres for corn, so that person has temporary usufruct rights; the Natural Resources Conservation Service (formerly the SCS) prevents my father-in-law from cultivating his marginal land, because he has enrolled in the Conservation Reserve Program; and a nonprofit land trust owns the development rights, a stick that my father-in-law donated for a generous tax break and the satisfaction of keeping his land intact after he dies. The state of Michigan reserves to itself the right to regulate deer on the land, while my father-in-law controls access to any deer there. The bundle of sticks shows us how rights are spread out among many parties, how private land always has public dimensions.[74]

The federal Standard State Soil Conservation Districts Act and Wisconsin's subsequent Chapter 92 may not have achieved the complete transformation that Leopold had hoped for. Counties and districts did not claim all of the sticks that they might have under the law. For the time being they chose to leave those in the landowner's bundle. Yet Chapter 92 did accelerate the threefold tenure changes first visible in the Coon Valley project: financial incentives for action, new social relationships on the land, and compulsory farm-level conservation plans. Financial incentives helped increase the number of farmers who participated. Payments for establishing contour strips went from fifty cents an acre to five dollars an acre. Conservation agents still felt ambivalent about the subsidies. "What often bothered us," said Roy Dingle, "was that there were actually farmers who signed up for strips just to get the payment." Such farmers were unworthy, he believed. "Five dollars per acre was damned poor pay for such as these. These people were the ones who, after they got their payment, would goof up their strips at the slightest excuse."[75] In practice, tenacity made for successful contour strips. In theory, good farmers would have plowed along the contour without the extra money. Nevertheless, Roy Dingle thought that the results justified the payments.

Conservation districts solidified a convergence of federal, state, and local governments on the farm. Farmers themselves could not always keep track of the confusing mix of programs, rules, agents, and agendas that increasingly influenced their farm systems. To understand how intricate the links among federal, state, and local agencies were, consider that a 1953 interagency agreement for community watersheds included the Soil Conservation Service, the Wisconsin Conservation Department, the Agricultural Extension Service, and the Wisconsin Soil Conservation Committee. An updated agreement in 1961 added the Agricultural Stabilization and Conservation Agency and the Farmers Home Administration.[76] The important point is that farmers came to accept these new relationships as the norm. The conservation plan continued to be everyone's focal point, and this became even more powerful. Conservation agents began using detailed soil surveys to develop plans for individual farms. From these surveys they produced complicated capability maps. Each capability class determined the suitability of a field for particular uses.[77] By incorporating a formal scientific rationale for a conservation plan, agencies further reduced the latitude a farmer had in managing his land. Yet more and more, farmers agreed to carry out such plans. By 1964, thirty thousand Wisconsin landowners had developed conservation plans. What is striking is the everyday quality these plans came to exude. When farmers started taking it for

A classic Driftless Area scene. (Courtesy of Wolfgang Hoffmann)

granted, the farm plan did indeed become "the basic ingredient" of public-private cooperation, as one state publication described it.[78]

Most of this soil conservation history falls between the first two maps of Liberty in figure 4. This was a period when contour strips expanded onto nearly one-third of Liberty's cropped land. Contour strips covered 52 acres in 1939, whereas in 1954 they covered 1,395 acres. There is a third date to consider, however. From 1954 to 1967, the area in contour strips increased by only 105 acres. Approximately two-thirds of Liberty's agricultural land showed no contour strips at either date. Even accounting for flat land, where contours strips were unnecessary, there were surely farmers to influence and fields that could benefit from conservation measures. Given the momentum of the 1940s, it seems strange that the effort would stall.

Otto Zeasman had his own thoughts on where soil conservation stood in the 1950s. In 1955, Zeasman's colleague E. O. Baker asked for his perspective on the profession. "I have been asked to serve on a panel to discuss 'How We Do Extension Work in Soil Conservation,'" wrote Baker. "Since you are a veteran Extension Soil Conservationist in this state I am coming to you for help. . . . I am especially interested in your very early work since much of what you did has served as a guide for many through the years."[79]

"The popular viewpoint now," replied Zeasman, "seems to be that lots of bally hoo about what we owe future generations, and the contributions soil conservation makes in controlling floods to help the other fellow and availability of planners to help farmers with farm plans is all that is needed to create a rush of farmers toward soil conservation farming."[80] Soil conservation extension had always been different from other extension work, continued Zeasman: "Most projects deal merely with solutions of problems of which the farmer is acutely aware. Method demonstrations of effective solutions readily convert farmers to the adoption of the practices. Not so with soil conservation. Seeing special soil conservation practices such as terracing, contour strip cropping does not make the farmer yearn to go home and do likewise. Mere observance of practice does not make him want to adopt them, but may even bring forth ridicule unless his thinking and convictions have undergone revolutionary changes from the habitual and traditional methods of land management acquired from previous generations." Zeasman went on to say that still more emphasis was needed on "damage to the physical condition of the soil" and on "immediate benefits" to the farmer with improved methods. He was restating a long-standing argument over approaches to rural landownership.

Had he seen the Liberty data on contour strips, Hugh H. Bennett, too, would surely have agreed that federal policy could accomplish more on the farm. But in the 1950s he was concerned with another long-standing policy argument. During a commemoration of the Coon Creek Demonstration Project in 1954, Bennett reiterated a justification for federal soil conservation efforts that harked back twenty years to the Agricultural Adjustment Administration. "We could cure most or all of the difficulties which have plagued our production and marketing operations in recent years through use of the land according to its capability," he said.[81] Bennett was emphasizing a persistent theme in national policy: that with the right approach, control over agricultural commodities and control over erosion could walk hand in hand.

In fact, though, conservation policies had not stalled. Both the twin goals that lay behind them and their actual implementation persisted into the 1950s. It was only that Zeasman and Bennett were not in a position to see the pivotal historical moment at hand. Thus they could not see the implications of evolving soil conservation programs. Just two years after Bennett's speech, President Dwight D. Eisenhower renewed the long union between markets and soil conservation with the Soil Bank Act of 1956.[82] Stated simply, the Soil Bank paid farmers to take land out of production, and it paid them more if they converted that land to forest.[83] The Soil Bank, moreover, encouraged farmers to put their entire farms in the program. This meant that farmers took whole farms out of production, not just marginal land. Earlier policies had indeed changed patterns of land use. The Soil Bank, however, would change patterns of land ownership. The Soil Bank set the stage for a great demographic shift upon its end in 1965.

Returning to the paradox that began this chapter: land ownership between 1955 and 1965 was stable by comparison with the dramatic increase in land turnover after 1965. In light of the Soil Bank, the two periods now make sense. A 1961 study of the program for all of Wisconsin observed precisely this decrease of land turnover after 1956. As study authors R. C. Buse and R. N. Brown Jr. explained, one large group of older farmers used the Soil Bank to keep their land while they prepared for retirement. A second, younger group worked off the farm, but supplemented their incomes with Soil Bank payments.[84] So, too, did Buse and Brown foretell a surge of farm sales when the program ended: "It is highly unlikely that, when the contract expires, farmers will come out of retirement or quit their non-farm jobs and return to farming." Likewise they predicted a rapid concentration of land "into larger, more efficient units."[85] As agricultural economists, the researchers judged this outcome favorably. They believed that consolidation would help modernize the agricultural sector. Residents in Liberty were not so sanguine. Farmers did not want to sell, recalled a few who stayed, but they could not afford to get back into farming.[86] According to historian David Danbom, the cumulative result was that the Soil Bank helped empty the American countryside. The program, he said, "allowed farmers to remove their entire farms from production and induced tens of thousands to move away."[87] For this reason primarily, the Soil Bank explains some of what happened in Liberty during the 1960s.

The Soil Bank must have seemed like a comprehensive means to finally accomplish twin economic and environmental ends. (Incidentally, with land out of production contour strip cropping becomes moot.) But the program sat on the cusp of widespread upheavals in American agriculture. Soon to follow was a concentration of both land and production. Included in this trend would be rising capital outlays for equipment and buildings, heavier reliance on fertilizers and pesticides, a shift in cropping systems to monocultures, and a corresponding shift in national agricultural policies toward production for export. The Soil Bank signaled this turning point for many rural communities. Its special role was not to speed all communities—or all townships—toward the same destiny, but to send them veering in different directions as the agricultural economy changed.

The conservation programs that grew out of the New Deal and found new life in the Eisenhower-era Soil Bank had worked for a while as policy makers had intended. Most notably they expanded public prerogatives over privately owned land. Conservationists like Hugh H. Bennett were therefore able to make progress toward national and regional goals of erosion control. Contour strips provided a visual marker of the progress. By some measures the Soil Bank advanced the same objectives. Farmers curtailed their overall agricultural output. Production in Wisconsin fell by 4 percent during the first four years of the program.[88] As for soil conservation, many working farms became fallow farms in waiting. But close on the heels of such intended consequences came unintended consequences—a wholesale turnover of rural property, and a shift from local to absentee ownership.[89] Many of these new landowners would find soil conservation programs irrelevant. While the Soil Bank had achieved some of its aims, the Soil Bank also failed, not because it ended, but because it helped eliminate its own clientele.

2

A Midwestern Ranch

Bulldozers roared, woodlots were dozed into ditches, buildings were smashed and burned and soon scores of the small family farms were gone forever. The land that had produced poets, dreamers, willing hands for industry, friends and neighbors were soon all gone to be replaced with a pasture for a herd of beef cattle. Cattle whose owners didn't give a hoot whether they made a profit or just returned a deduction on their income tax.

Who are these men who have destroyed the beauty spots, the bubbling springs, the prized woodlots, the ethereal little coves where the lady slippers and trilliums grew in profusion?

—Kickapoo Valley weekly newspaper,
The La Farge Epitaph, May 17, 1978

In their 1961 study of the Soil Bank, economists R. C. Buse and R. N. Brown Jr. did not foresee that absentee ownership would accompany land concentration. They saw probable patterns emerging when the Soil Bank ended, but not particular kinds of new owners from particular places. In Liberty, the pattern assumed the form of out-of-state family corporations that specialized in beef production. In other places the details would have been different; there might have been another kind of landowner, another specialization, or an even higher concentration of property. Regardless, you could produce maps similar to figure 5 for countless rural locales. This map and others like it are significant because of the larger patterns they show.

They are also significant because they provoke local questions. "Who are these men?" asked the nearby *La Farge Epitaph,* in a passage that was speaking specifically of the changes in Liberty. Media usually focus on the local and the personal. Television, radio, and newspaper alike scrutinize individual contenders in land use debates: the rural landowner versus the government agent, the rancher versus the environmentalist. Academics ask the same question—who are these people? A wide sociological litera- ture has looked for answers, parsing landowners by livelihood, income, educational achievement, and numerous other measures of a person's demographic place in the world. Hundreds of surveys have tried to tease out a link between socioeconomic status and environmental attitudes, values, and beliefs. Many researchers then take a leap, attempting to pre- dict future behavior of different types of owners.[1] One study concluded that highly educated absentee owners were more likely to be good forest stewards than poorer, less-educated local landowners.[2] As we will see, such a study does not capture the everyday complexity of owners in places like the Kickapoo Valley. Inevitably though, people will personalize the property lines.

Beef Ranching
Liberty Township, 1965–1995

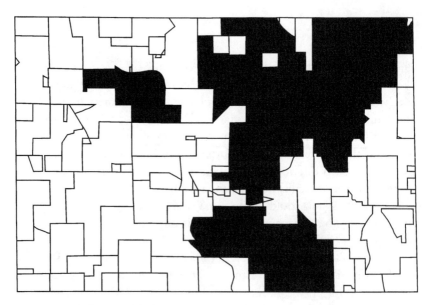

Figure 5. Land shown in black was converted to beef ranches between 1965 and 1995. Representative parcel lines are from 1978.

Both the impersonal patterns and the personal questions miss the elemental reality of landownership. Woodlots *dozed,* lamented the *Epitaph*—*family* farms gone, friends and *neighbors.* These are all relational images, concerned with neither the pattern nor the individual but with relationships. Landownership does not exist outside of the relationships that define it. Neither can landowners, even absentee landowners, be understood apart from the local landscapes and people with whom they have interacted. An environmental history like this one offers a counterpoint and alternative to landowner surveys: first, by looking closely at how the landscape changes as land changes hands; second, by contrasting different cultural perspectives with the change, instead of assuming the connection; and finally, by returning to the larger historical and ecological contexts within which people and their landscapes have reshaped each other. While the first chapter was a macrohistory of soil conservation and property dynamics, this chapter will be a brief microhistory of land ownership in Liberty. My aim is to place absentee beef ranchers within the community and ecological relationships that gave meaning to their tenure.

After 1965 small locally owned farms like this one in Liberty became surrounded by absentee land ownership. (Courtesy of Wolfgang Hoffmann)

As Liberty's largest landholder in the 1990s, Bob Djerdingen could have challenged the interpretive abilities of the most meticulous survey giver. Djerdingen called himself a rancher, because of his beef cattle. Likewise he called his place a ranch. The exception was when he talked about the dairy herd he also owned. Then he called himself a farmer, and his place became a farm. Like most ranchers and farmers in the Kickapoo Valley, Bob Djerdingen had another job off the land. But his job was one that neighbors took special note of. For most of the year he was a music history professor at Northwestern University. Bob Djerdingen was in the most highly educated echelon of absentee owners in the Kickapoo Valley. His own identity was a shifting mosaic, a complicated midwestern quilt.

One late August day he gave me a tour of his ranch—all four square miles of it (2,600 acres). He had quarter horses for getting around the property, but on my visit we used an all-terrain vehicle to cover the rough ground. At one point we stopped under the shade of a lovely maple forest. He was an excellent host—enthusiastic and gracious—so it wasn't surprising to me that foremost on his mind was the recent party he and his wife had hosted in Liberty. They had tried, he said, to bring together some of the farmers, hippies, and tradespeople in the area. The community in Liberty was not so close as he would have liked. After many years in the township he had not even met his nearest neighbor, another absentee beef rancher. He interacted primarily with his on-site manager, who oversaw work on the ranch in his absence.

Bob Djerdingen's neighbors, it would turn out (not the absentee landowner but those who lived in Liberty), also saw the scene in terms of relationships. But their time frame was considerably longer. They looked across a thirty-year history of beef ranching in the township. The new intensity of production had not by itself been an issue. At the turn of the twentieth century in fact, Liberty and its surroundings had boasted the highest density of sheep in the state.[3] So livestock were not intrinsically a problem. The problem was the fences. The first thing these modern ranchers did was to take out all the fences. Then they tore down many of the dairy barns on their new property. Finally, they burned or abandoned some of the farmhouses they had inherited.

Beef corporations wanted neither the buildings nor the property taxes and maintenance costs that accompanied them. At the same time, individual landowners like Bob Djerdingen wanted a close community. The problem was, the infrastructure undergirded community relationships.

When the buildings came down, residents said, Liberty's tax base was decimated. Farmers had been seeking barns to rent because there was a real shortage in the area. Now there were fewer. This part of the Valley faced a severe housing crisis. Rental houses were so scarce that the destruction of several such possibilities caused a real stir. As for the old fences, in a way that loss was the hardest because of what it portended. New fences were extremely expensive, so there was little chance the land would revert to other types of agriculture when landowners like Bob Djerdingen decided to sell their property. What would become of the land? What would become of the community? That the new landowners *didn't give a hoot* was indeed the local consensus. "They were all take and take some more," said Hugh Lieurance, who had farmed in Liberty since 1949. "They never gave anything."[4] Feelings were so intense for a while that the family of a fifth-generation local man was ostracized when he went to work for Djerdingen as resident manager. "Everyone was uniformly angry," said Liberty town clerk Judy Daily.[5]

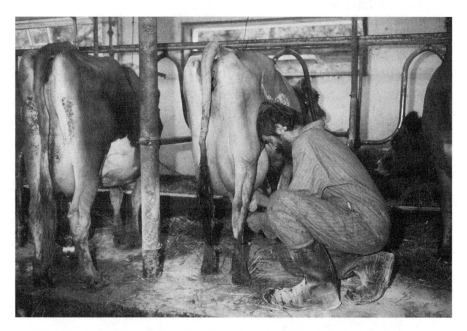

When the Soil Bank ended, small and medium-sized dairy farms became rarer in the Kickapoo Valley. Many of them gave way to large beef ranches. (Courtesy of Wolfgang Hoffmann)

In destroying the infrastructure of earlier farms, ranchers had a more profound effect than they may have realized. They had transformed what geographers call the vernacular landscape. In a vernacular landscape, physical signs of a community's culture and economy are integral elements.[6] The vernacular landscape includes houses, barns, tobacco sheds, milk houses, wells, fences, cemeteries—any evidence that people have gathered in a particular place to live, work, and die. The vernacular landscape is the visible historical evidence of the relationships that make up a community. Though residents would not have used the term, it was nonetheless the vernacular landscape they saw when they looked around and considered the impact of beef ranching on Liberty.[7] The ranchers had rewritten this landscape. As a result, they had altered human relationships in the landscape.

The simple truth was that social relationships were not a priority for ranchers, no matter how much they influenced or were influenced by them. On the other hand, environmental relationships were a topmost priority. After racing up and down hills and bullying our way through loitering calves (no doubt causing erosion), Bob Djerdingen and I rested in a cool spot by the bank of a stream. We talked about land. It was precisely the *bubbling springs, the prized woodlots, the ethereal little coves where the lady slippers and trilliums grew in profusion* that had drawn ranchers to Liberty. Abundant sources of water, excellent pasture, shady woods on sweltering days, and cheap real estate prices—all these had converged in the township.

In particular, we talked about forests. Ranchers had torn down the old fence lines in order to integrate forests into their pasture system. This ran contrary to conservation efforts going back to the 1930s. Since that time, forests had expanded across the Driftless Area because many farmers had taken some advice from people like Aldo Leopold, Otto Zeasman, and Roy Dingle. Farmers had largely given up plowing the steepest hills, while conservation programs had taken still more land out of cultivation. Gains in forestland were not large year to year, but cumulatively they were impressive—600-plus acres of additional forest in Liberty from 1939 to 1954, another 265 acres by 1967, and 182 acres more by 1978. Overall, forests had increased from 43 percent of the township's landscape in 1939 to 54 percent in 1995. Forests had always held a prominent place in conservation programs. As early as the pilot program in Coon Valley, owners could not qualify for some conservation payments unless they fenced their forests from livestock.

Nonetheless, foresters always had their hands full coping with livestock. In the Kickapoo Valley it is nearly impossible to map the spatial extent of grazing through time because cattle and other domesticated animals have been ubiquitous on the landscape since European settlement. "Our hogs and cattle all ran in the woods," wrote J. L. Barto of pioneer life during the 1860s and 1870s. "I can remember mother telling us kids to hear a hog squealing on the hill in the big woods, Mr. Bear was getting his supper."[8] "The farmer," said soil scientist Melville Cohee in 1934, "somehow feels that every acre of woodland pasture is an acre gained irrespective of the damage to the woodlot or the increasing danger from erosion, in spite of the fact that the wooded hillsides of 30 percent or more slope have very little desirable pasture grass."[9] "The superficial observer, motoring through this region, sees much timber still growing on the slopes," said Aldo Leopold and Joseph Hickey.[10] "What he does not see is that 87 percent of it is pastured, therefore it cannot reproduce, therefore it must disappear as the mature trees are cut, or blow down, or die of the drouths and diseases that all wood is heir to." Livestock have moved in and out of

Beef ranching in the Kickapoo Valley. Note the landscape of pasture and forests. The latter were of special concern to foresters, who wanted ranchers to fence their livestock from forests. (Courtesy of Wolfgang Hoffmann)

Valley forests as farmers have moved in and out of government programs, or responded to drought, or sold their farms, or simply said yes to a neighbor who wanted a little extra pasture one year.[11] For a sense of the magnitude, consider that as of 1967 Vernon County and Crawford County (encompassing most of the Kickapoo Valley) had 188,000 acres of grazed forest.[12] Consider, too, that cattle grazed in fifty million acres of the nation's eastern forests.[13]

Embedded in this forest history are multiple environmental relationships. One way to imagine these relationships is as a series of triangles: field/pasture/forest, landowner/cattle/forest, and then, landowner/forest/forester. For foresters these relationships could be frustrating, a fact to which forty-five years of correspondence with landowners attests. For example, in 1965 Department of Natural Resources (DNR) county forester Robert Roach tried to convince Liberty landowner Irving Ludlow of the pitfalls of woodland grazing. "We all know that there is no pasture in the woods for livestock," he coaxed, "and that many dangers lurk there for cattle, falling trees, lightning, poisonous plants, acorns and many more. Actually you are doing yourself a favor by keeping stock out of the woods."[14] Close on Roach's heels, forester Alan Jones cautioned another Liberty farmer, "It is critical that the woodland be protected from grazing. Grazing will destroy young trees which comprise the reserve growing stock. Grazing can retard the growth of larger trees because of soil compaction. Grazing breaks down the leaf cover on the ground; the cover acts like a sponge to reduce the amount of runoff."[15] And in 1981, forester Don Streiff delivered the same warning to Jerald Ahrens. "The first step in forest management is to protect your woodlands from grazing," he wrote. "Grazing is very destructive to woodlands in that livestock not only browse off young seedlings and cause mechanical breakage on existing trees, but also cause soil compaction. Soil compaction results in less air, water, and nutrients available to the feeder roots of the tree near the ground surface. This causes stress on the tree. This stress may cause increased susceptibility of the tree to infection, disease, and possibly death."[16] Scientific data buttressed the case foresters made to landowners. A 1959 study in southwestern Wisconsin showed that when cattle grazed in oak and pine forests, the rate of water infiltrating forest soils declined by 93 percent.[17]

But when it came to cattle, foresters were not entirely without influence. They were aided by the mixed farming system typical of the region, in which cropland lay alongside pasture and forests. Their own pragmatic approach also aided them; for foresters did not vilify cattle so much as

cajole farmers to put cattle in their proper place on the land. "It is important to understand that there is nothing inherently destructive in . . .
cows," said Leopold and Hickey. "Cows, in fact, are inherently conservors
of the soil, for they give back most of what they take. Cows become
destructive only when there are too many, or when their pasture is too
steep."[18] Eventually, farmers did establish an extensive network of fences
that kept cattle away from forests as well as crops. Beginning in the 1950s,
moreover, forestry incentive programs in Wisconsin, such as the Forest
Crop Law, the Woodland Tax Law, and its modern incarnation, the Managed Forest Law (MFL), required landowners to keep livestock out of
woodland. Drastically reduced property taxes—as little as $1.20 an acre—
enticed landowners to enroll. To offset the expense of the livestock provision, the programs provided cost sharing for fences. Between 1955 and
1995, Liberty landowners enrolled forty-one tracts of land, each of which
covered anywhere from 10 to 260 acres. One of these was the forest in
which Bob Djerdingen and I stood.

He admitted that the previous owner had enrolled this forest in the
MFL program. Briefly he invoked his own private property rights and
called resource managers enemies, but he quickly retracted the comment.
The problem was really the government agencies, he said—the DNR
and USDA—not their agents (who were nice people). Mainly he needed
the forest as a corridor for running his cattle from one part of the ranch
to another. The forest also gave them shelter in the winter. So he had taken
80 acres out of MFL. County forester Jim Dalton was furious with him
for it, having marked some timber for logging a few years earlier. Unfortunately it was the wrong type of timber harvest if livestock were to return
to the woods. Djerdingen could only concur that his cattle might inhibit
regeneration. He was also suffering from prickly ash and raspberries—
tough competition for his twenty-foot brushhog. But the woods were not
valuable in themselves (he wouldn't benefit from new timber for most of
his lifetime anyway), and he liked the clean look of his grazed woods.

Absentee ranchers like Bob Djerdingen knew that their operations
could put them in conflict with a new generation of conservationists like
forester Jim Dalton. The soil conservationist of the 1930s, '40s, and '50s
had slowly metamorphosed into a natural resource manager. Whereas soil
conservationists had most likely come out of agronomy, soil science, engineering, and forestry backgrounds, natural resource managers came to
include ecology and wildlife or stream biology in their résumés as well.
Whereas erosion control had guided the thought and actions of people

like Otto Zeasman, by the 1970s a whole host of environmental concerns had come to the fore, reflecting the holistic ideas of Aldo Leopold. Fertile soil, healthy forests, and abundant wildlife—the health of the land demanded all of these; and to them had been added water quality, biodiversity, endangered species protection, wilderness preservation, population control, clean air, livable cities, and an old idea in new words, sustainable agriculture. Indeed, of Earth Day in 1970 soil conservationist Roy Dingle said, "I listened and read about Earth Day, but it has nothing to do with soil conservation. Does Earth Day refer to a different kind of earth? It seems that nobody cares about the soil. . . . Like Elijah of old, I feel that 'I alone, even I only, am left' to preach our complete and total dependence upon topsoil."[19]

Right alongside forests, resource managers worried that Djerdingen's large herd would degrade water quality and endanger trout habitat in the stream we stood beside. If he saw a trout he would be tempted to strangle it. The trout lobby (Trout Unlimited) was so strong that it might force him to remove his livestock.[20] Yet he had been willing to let a stream biologist use this stream as one of her study sites. She ultimately chose other sites. Still, he supported her work in spirit because she was looking at whether rotational grazing was less harmful to trout streams than conventional grazing. Besides, he joked, his cattle tended to stay on the bank, putting just their heads in the water to drink, so how much manure actually got in the stream if their rear ends stayed onshore? (To that I had no answer.)

On a first hearing you might conclude that some kind of ideological American West had expanded back east. Like his counterparts out west, landowner Djerdingen openly resented certain relationships that he could not entirely avoid—with foresters, disapproving neighbors, Trout Unlimited volunteers, and so on. At the same time, he lamented the absence of tight community relationships (forgetting perhaps that county foresters were themselves long-standing members of Valley communities). But Djerdingen's environmental perspective was much more nuanced than his initial comment about trout suggests. To his mind critics overlooked much of what beef ranching was accomplishing in the Kickapoo Valley. To begin with, he was one of many ranchers who practiced rotational grazing as an alternative to concentrated feed operations. University extension agents had come to regard the Kickapoo Valley as a model region for innovative, grass-based systems. The University of Wisconsin study he had supported was just one example.

As it happened, this research later bore out some of Djerdingen's optimism. It showed that rotational grazing "is nearly as good as grassy buffer strips and is an improvement over continuously grazed strips." The study also found better habitat, but not more trout, with rotational grazing. The conclusion was that landscape-level management was needed. "If you're going to have a big influence on fish it will take more than 5 or 10 percent of farms in the watershed to make a difference," investigator Laura Paine said.[21] Paine even chastised an environmental organization for its efforts to expand regulation of livestock waste in Wisconsin. She worried that new state laws on nonpoint source pollution would hurt rotational grazers. "Banning livestock access to surface waters would have a profoundly negative impact on a group of farmers who are arguably some of your greatest allies within the agricultural community," she contended in a letter to the group. "I strongly urge you to re-evaluate your position on this issue."[22]

In his own defense, Djerdingen continued, he avoided the chemical inputs (pesticides and fertilizers) that the previous landowner had used. He

Trout fisherman on the Kickapoo River. To improve stream quality and trout habitat, university scientists and groups like Trout Unlimited studied grazing patterns along the Kickapoo River and its tributaries. (Courtesy of Wolfgang Hoffmann)

was seeing a great increase in bird species as a result. It was true that cattle caused erosion on hillsides, but he grazed his cattle less intensively when this happened. What's more, erosion control had made spectacular gains since the 1930s, to the extent that few modern farm systems, including beef, were as devastating as those earlier in the century. Just look at old photos of the place when sheep were dominant, he suggested. "I might not walk with the angels," Djerdingen said, "but in my line of business I've tried to be a good steward."

Bob Djerdingen's point about erosion was a fascinating and important one. It was a useful reminder that his relationship with the land was not a solo affair. Rather, he was the latest in a long line of landowners. Looking at each owner independently of the others risked taking all of them out of historical context. Fears about soil erosion had not ended with the death of the Soil Bank. Valley residents and extension agents continued to follow the evidence on erosion rates in the region. Not everyone would have agreed with Djerdingen. In 1981, the dean of the University of Wisconsin's College of Agriculture worried that southwestern Wisconsin continued to lose one inch of topsoil every seven to ten years. "With only twenty inches of soil to bedrock," he calculated, "it's not too difficult to predict that in the foreseeable future some of these thin soils could be rendered largely useless for agriculture."[23] One explanation was that farmers were planting ever-larger areas of corn and soybeans, upwards of 50 percent of the cropland in the Kickapoo Valley alone.[24] Because row crops like these posed the greatest risk of heavy soil erosion, agriculture was as environmentally risky as ever.

Another study told a different story. Back in Coon Valley, geographer Stanley Trimble disputed assertions that erosion was as high in the 1990s as it had been in the 1930s. His field data showed that soil erosion peaked in the 1930s then declined to a mere fraction of the highest rates by 1993.[25] Trimble had no doubt about the underlying causes. "This decrease was due to improvements in land use and not due to a change in climate," he said. To scientists whose work contradicted his, Trimble replied, "the burden of proof is on those who have been making these pronouncements about big erosion numbers. . . . For one big basin, I've measured the sediment and I'm saying, I don't see it."[26] Roy Dingle and his successors might have taken comfort in Trimble's study, for they played their own part in the achievement.

Despite its importance, natural resource managers and other environmentalists counted soil erosion as only one of many concerns with large beef operations. By the 1980s they saw the landscape very differently than either their conservation predecessors or present-day ranchers. No longer was erosion the primary measure of degradation.[27] Drawing on new ecological insights into watershed dynamics, ecosystem fragmentation, and presettlement vegetation patterns, critics saw a lot to worry them. Forests may have expanded, but grazing created forest fragments, taking a toll on wildlife and rare plants, some endemic to the Driftless Area. Livestock disturbance facilitated the spread of invasive exotics and early successional species, including buckthorn, honeysuckle, prickly ash, and raspberries. Grazing aspirations were at odds with environmental aspirations to restore forests, grasslands, and streams to the richness of presettlement ecosystems. Science backed up ranchers, who looked to the Valley's recent degraded past and saw improvement in the present, and also environmentalists, who gazed farther into the past and envisioned a more pristine future.[28] The negotiations between them—the relationships with the land that also bound them to each other—would continue.

In any tapestry there will be loose ends. Despite the best efforts of social scientists, people are hard to characterize independently of the whole fabric. Moreover, the threads of their lives continue after the brief moment of a conversation. The environmental history of rancher-professor Bob Djerdingen came to include a postscript. A few years after we talked he put his land on the market. Local wisdom held that he would not get his highest offer from another rancher and definitely not from a farmer. Local wisdom was right. Thirty plus acres went to a young man who converted the land into a motocross racetrack. In 2001 and 2002, landowners adjacent to the racetrack brought out members of the town board to hear the volume of noise they now had to endure. In a twist that many Liberty residents found droll, the most irate complaints came from another absentee beef ranching outfit. The owners had planned to retire on their land, their peaceful land now next to a racetrack. "There is a remnant of the community," remarked a neighbor at the time dryly, "who has no sympathy for them." A real estate developer purchased most of Djerdingen's ranch, calling it the "Djerdingen Estate." This was the first step in its destiny to become a montage of smaller recreational parcels.

The bystander feel of the changes in Liberty is striking. Relationships so central to the condition of landownership *while* someone owns land are peripheral during the transition *between* landowners. In the end, property moves from one individual owner to another individual owner. The community watches with curiosity, or anxiety, from the sidelines. The result is paradoxical: the community, which will enmesh any new landowner in a whole web of relationships, asserts little input in the rate or direction of change. The landowner, who instantly encounters a long history of relationships impossible to escape (where land is concerned, no slate is ever clean), experiences isolation and weaker ties to the community than he would like. It is no wonder that the relationships break altogether when markets change, or when demands elsewhere weigh heavy. In Liberty, both sides experienced some measure of disempowerment, though the largest share went to the community. Each turn of events seems abrupt when it happens, but in the world of rural land markets nothing is really surprising. If concentration is one historical theme, so is fragmentation. In this kind of transformation, Liberty would also prove a microcosm. The Soil Bank, it turned out, did not lead to a single, linear outcome. It led off a kaleidoscopic pattern of change.

3

What the Real Estate Ads
Don't Tell You

Turn the kaleidoscope of Liberty once more and its historical mosaic changes completely. Onto this new stage two entirely different characters move forward. For them, neither Hugh Bennett, Aldo Leopold, farmers, ranchers, foresters, nor the Soil Bank would hold any meaning; their concerns were far too different. These two were intensely focused on real estate, the engine that drives our system of property. They ramped up the engine in Liberty, so real estate must be our focus as well. Yet their presence in the township was as much a consequence of the Soil Bank (and the larger rural trends it represented) as were contemporary ranchers. With its low human density on the land, its high concentration of property in outside hands, and its sensitivity to shifts in markets or the physical environment, ranching created ideal conditions for real estate speculators to enter the scene, to steal it almost.

Sometime around 1970, the year of the first Earth Day, realtors Thomas White and James Smith saw southwestern Wisconsin through different eyes. Though White and Smith lived there in coulee country, they could imagine what a crowded, harried, tense Chicago couple might see on stepping out of their car and taking in the valley vista for the first time. After inhaling slowly, deeply, the couple would surely gaze with delight at a generic folk country of fields and forests. The thrill of discovery would be intoxicating: Here was a lifelike landscape painting—rolling hills as far as the eye can see; shimmering streams wending through the valley; crops and trees forming seasonal mosaics of green, gold, and red. An idyllic drive would add detail with quaint villages and the occasional black-and-white cow by a fence. Every angle, every moment would offer a world utterly charming, utterly peaceful. They could imagine themselves returning to this place, perhaps settling in. A practical image might hover in the back of their minds as well: property at a bargain—lots of cheap rural space if you were smart enough to grab some before everyone else discovered this little piece of paradise. Land, after all, was safe; land held its value. All this White and Smith surely saw. Then with the clarity of prophets, they envisioned an empire: not one built on land, but on the landscape.

White and Smith formed a partnership called Woodland Farms. Figure 6 shows the fragments of the Woodland Farms development in Liberty, the product of a distinctive vision of property and nature. This vision is worth being precise about because Woodland Farms had counterparts throughout rural America. The township of Liberty was but a local chapter in a national book of rural land speculation and fragmentation. In its basic form, the speculative method is to buy cheap land, subdivide it, advertise the new parcels in promising markets, and sell them at a profit. Woodland Farms accomplished this by bringing property and nature together in ways that their urban clients would never have anticipated. The buyers simply did not have all the relevant information in front of them, which was exactly what everyone involved with Woodland Farms intended.

Few people understood property as well as White and Smith. They knew it was not only a legal arrangement for transferring a title from one person to another; just as important, it was an informational arrangement for transferring the relevant facts and history about a real place. What any prospective buyer from Chicago might see and hear in the Kickapoo Valley could start or stop a sale. Hence Woodland Farms made it their first priority to control that information every step along the way to a transaction, beginning with their newspaper advertisements in Chicago or Milwaukee or Minneapolis: "Once privately held wilderness lands in S. WI are now being made available," claimed an ad in the *Chicago Tribune*.[1] "Divorced Owners Must Sell," began another in the *Minneapolis Star Tribune*.[2] "Bank Sale $7,500. This rolling woodland in a secluded river valley of S.W. WI is being offered by a local farmer to avoid foreclosure."[3] And the whopper, "Wilderness Church Camp . . . Father White sacrificing for $10,000."[4] Yes, Father White was actually realtor White. None of these advertisements was true.[5] In writing such ads at all, we might say that Woodland Farms was not selling land, property, or nature; it was selling a fraudulent emotional connection between a city-dweller sprawled out on the couch reading the Sunday paper and some pitiful rural landowner.

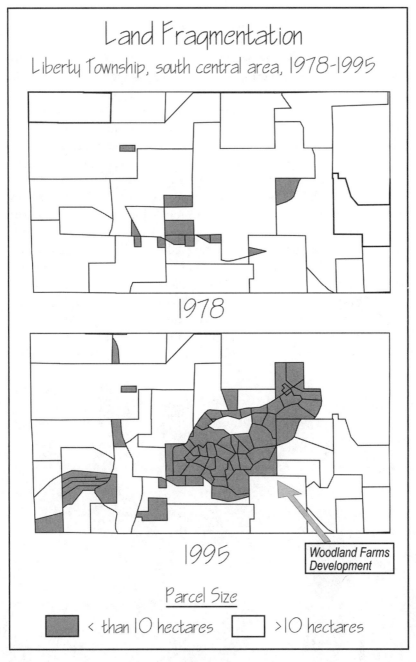

Figure 6. Land fragmentation in Liberty arose in large part from Woodland Farms. Note the large parcels surrounding the Woodland Farms development. This bifurcated pattern of land concentration and fragmentation became common in many rural places during the late twentieth century.

Visual images quickly followed the mental images. Like painters, White and Smith composed landscapes for their clients. Ideally a video would do. They produced films so captivating that many people went no further before deciding to buy, not even bothering to visit the property in question. Nor did Woodland Farms neglect those who wanted to walk on their prospective property first. White and Smith's advertisements and videos suggested a sympathetic bond between the urban reader and a down-on-his-luck rural landowner. Once on the scene, the agents acted like the village matchmaker, fanning an infatuation between their urban clients and the Driftless landscape. The firm provided lavish tours that might include round-trip transportation, food, drink, lodging, and a quick visit to the land in question. There was little need for a client to venture out on her own, to explore the Kickapoo Valley, or to talk with future neighbors. Smith, White, or their employees were right there, able to answer any query: *Of course you don't want to live in the country year-round. But you can escape to paradise; you can build on it, vacation in it, someday retire to it; and you can own it.* The relationship seemed promising indeed; however, it was based on surface appearances rather than shared history or compatibility.

Kickapoo Valley panorama: A scene that drew recreational real estate buyers from Chicago, Minneapolis, and Milwaukee. The Kickapoo River glistens in the bottom right. (Courtesy of Wolfgang Hoffmann)

While wooing their clients, White and Smith sold them beauty. They sold them a hypothetical way of life. They sold them abstract relationships with an abstract group of rural people, not one of whom the average buyer had likely met. Ultimately though, Woodland Farms was selling real estate, a commodity for which their ability—their genius really—to manipulate information put them in the ranks of the great scammers. Most property transactions include a number of semi-independent parties—real estate agents, appraisers, assessors, surveyors, lawyers, title companies, and most important of all, bankers. Any one of these officials should help ensure that the balance of information is not weighted too wholly toward the seller. For instance, an independent appraisal can give you a sense of what a property is worth. A bank will not loan you money if the appraisal falls too far below the purchase price. And so the information flows from seller to buyer and back again. Woodland Farms created a closed financial loop that kept these other parties away from the buyer.

The way that White and Smith closed the loop was simple. Woodland Farms provided the loans to its clients. Or it sold them property on land contract, often under the trade names American Investment Company or Univest. By availing themselves of this service, there was no need for Chicagoans to approach a bank in their own city. They could avoid the tedious process of pulling together years of personal financial information. The company then sold all its mortgages and land contracts to its partner, the First National Bank of Bangor, Wisconsin. If a borrower defaulted, American Investment or Univest bought back the loan, no questions asked. The First National Bank of Bangor maintained close ties with Woodland Farms (and its pseudonyms) for twenty-five years. At one point it held close to five hundred notes for the company.[6]

Though Smith and White's clients were not the richest of the rich, they were not poor either. They appear to have been a middle-class lot, some more prosperous than others but all able to make an initial down payment to Woodland Farms (or American Investment or Univest). Yet Woodland Farms clients defaulted in droves. In its Vernon County developments, which included Liberty, more than half of them walked away from their property and their loans.[7] In several cases two consecutive owners abandoned the same piece of land. Avoiding for the moment the obvious question (Why did they default?), anyone might reasonably ask how the agency and the bank fared when loans went bad. How could they maintain a happy union for decades under what outsiders might consider financial crisis?

The bottom line was that bad loans posed no emergency for Woodland Farms or the First National Bank of Bangor. To the contrary, it seems the higher the default rate the stronger the marriage between the agency and the bank. Defaults made up a critical, cyclical part of their financial loop. "We've never lost a nickel," said First National's vice president in 1992.[8] When a client stopped paying for his land, Woodland Farms insisted that he sign a quit-claim deed, thus returning the land to the agency. Of course, in walking away from the property an owner forfeited his down payment. Otherwise American Investment would foreclose. This it did with vigor. Woodland Farms sued clients so frequently that a simple search in the Vernon County Circuit Court will produce dozens of cases.[9] Most of the people involved lived in Chicago. The firm became a vertically integrated, highly efficient foreclosure factory. In the end, White and Smith got the land and the down payment. Then they sold the landscape all over again.

To understand why such a large number of clients defaulted brings us back to the informational nature of property as Woodland Farms practiced it. Smith and White specialized in theoretical space: they recycled paradise. Whether it was the Kickapoo Valley, the lake country of Wisconsin's north woods, or the beachscapes of the Lake Michigan shore, Woodland Farms marketed an aesthetic complement to the city home. Concerning the land itself, Woodland Farms provided very little information.

Real land has particular topographic and hydrologic features, patterns of soil, and biotic communities. Real land has legal boundaries. Real landowners have neighbors. All land has a history and no landowner can avoid that history. Woodland Farms guarded its clients from the real history until after the real estate sale. The great irony is how, in selling a landscape, Smith and White rendered land so completely invisible. Insofar as they never went exploring for information on their own, some landowners were complicit in their own blindness, for what they did not know about their "new" property often became much more important than what they did know.

Phillip Risser thought he had purchased twenty acres in the Kickapoo Valley from Woodland Farms. To his dismay, the property lines actually encompassed eleven acres. Woodland Farms settled Risser's subsequent lawsuit on the Vernon County courthouse steps, moments before their trial was to start (three years after the purchase). "I'm used to dealing with reputable people," Risser explained to a reporter afterward. "I thought if they owned the land themselves, I wouldn't need a survey."[10] In relinquishing their "dream land" Risser and his wife also gave up their idea of retiring in Wisconsin. "Wisconsin has always had that certain something that's really attractive to us," he said, "but we're going to think twice before looking north again."

Illinois lawyer Barbara Hayes contended that Woodland Farms had grossly overvalued her property. Whereas she had paid $27,000, the company had bought it for $8,000 only four months earlier. Worse still, she had contracted with Woodland Farms to build a home on the land. The result, according to her lawsuit, was shoddy construction and an uninhabitable dwelling.[11]

It seems Woodland Farms had some swampland to sell as well. A Milwaukee couple intending to buy lakefront property for a vacation cottage bought a wetland instead. A prior zoning change meant they could not even put up a tent.[12]

A younger couple did not realize that a railroad ran alongside their new land. They agreed to Smith and White's suggestion that, rather than sue, they "trade up" for a better property with a cute old farmhouse on it. Right before closing on *that* deal, they discovered through the lucky fluke of a flooded basement that the building had serious structural problems.[13] More than a decade later and now a lawyer herself, Andrea Baker, one member of the couple, looked back to that time. "We were truck drivers then [by profession], no kids, and had money coming out the wazoo," she laughed. "But we were too young and stupid to know better."[14]

When confronted by a reporter, President William Bosshard of the First National Bank of Bangor was untroubled. "I don't lose any sleep over it," he told her.[15] Nor was Bosshard surprised, for he was in the loop. Like White and Smith, Bosshard understood the ramifications of not knowing a place. Many buyers, he explained, were not familiar with rural property: "I go out on a beautiful day and I see this property and there's a deer on it. Now I come out again and there's two feet of snow and I don't want it anymore." The bank was bound to deal with some buyer remorse, Bosshard said.

Woodland Farms created a furor wherever it went. For a long time, though, consumer complaints came to naught. Because Smith and White were information specialists, information or its lack thereof tended to work in their favor. Federal bank examiners from the U.S. Office of the Comptroller of the Currency found the First National Bank of Bangor's involvement with Woodland Farms to be risky but legal. By 1992 the state Real Estate Board had investigated seven claims against Woodland Farms, but exonerated the company in all of them. "It's like a lot of things in life," the head of the board stated frankly. "You can say that it doesn't look right, but you have to be able to prove it."[16]

In a few cases, White and Smith had reason to think Woodland Farms would lose in court. These suits they settled, although they kept a grip on information. Haggling with tired former clients, White and Smith's lawyer would insist upon and receive strict confidentiality agreements.[17] The result was that everything these people learned about the land they once owned went with them when they left the Kickapoo Valley. The unique and cautionary perspective they now had (so different from that first look around) settled into bad memories. Their visits had been brief, whereas Smith and White remained, triumphant in proclaiming Woodland Farms "the Midwest's largest land company."[18]

Firsthand knowledge of Woodland Farms scattered like leaves on the breeze among anonymous enclaves in the urban Midwest. With no state action against Woodland Farms, each individual case became little more than a bureaucratic footnote. From that point, the information went home with the former owners. Smith and White were therefore free to dazzle new clients with images of spectacular landscapes, tranquil country living, and canny financial investments. Still, one person did manage to paint the more disturbing picture.

Investigative journalist Susan Lampert Smith wrote her first article on Woodland Farms in 1992. One day she got a tip from an unhappy client who had tried to alert the *Chicago Tribune,* the *St. Paul Pioneer Press,* and other big regional papers (all of whom published Woodland Farms advertisements) to no avail.[19] Only Lampert Smith and her paper, the *Wisconsin State Journal,* thought the hook strong enough to try and reel in a slippery fish. White was so confident during Lampert Smith's initial inquiry that he personally gave her a tour. Lampert Smith dutifully admired White's beautiful rural developments, "from rustic log cabins built in the pine woods around a sandy lake . . . to fantastic, double-decked executive retreats on the soaring bluffs overlooking the Mississippi River." She heard the romance in his voice as he "spoke eloquently of the need Chicagoans (his company's main customers) have to escape from the crime and violence of city life and to own a place where their children can safely play in the sand."[20] But White had miscalculated. Lampert Smith was no client, and she was not buying his land. More importantly she was an information specialist at least his equal.

Lampert Smith's first two exposés on the company began with the lovely rural scenery and ended with an enormous "but": "But if you are buying rural property and want to protect yourself . . ."[21] Thereafter she dogged White's steps, developing an extraordinary series of newspaper articles spanning five years. Lampert Smith became Woodland Farms's unauthorized biographer. She documented the questionable sales. She talked to bank examiners. She learned that Bank of Bangor's William Bosshard took the biggest profits while incurring none of the risks. She gave names and faces to anonymous landowners: "They had this disabled Vietnam veteran," she recalled, describing a man White and Smith had met at one of the sportsmen shows where they solicited clients. "They got him just loaded and drove him to the bank." It turned out that he was not physically capable of getting to the land he bought. This was a difficult time, Lampert Smith said, "really lonely."[22] Piece by piece, property by property, she pried loose the information Woodland Farms had heretofore held tightly.

The reaction to Lampert Smith's first articles was loud. Two of Wisconsin's Republican legislators demanded that regulators look more closely at Woodland Farms. Representative DuWayne Johnsrud was especially upset. His district covered southwestern Wisconsin, including the Kickapoo Valley and the Woodland Farms headquarters. Johnsrud became one of Lampert Smith's only allies. He accumulated "a huge moldy file" of complaints about Woodland Farms.[23] Such reports "are going to leave a bad taste in the mouths of potential newcomers to the area," Johnsrud fumed. "My fear is that people will begin to feel that they will get ripped off if they come to our beautiful part of the state."[24] "I'm a big supporter of real estate development," another legislator prefaced. "But when you have a company that misrepresents sales, it gives a black mark to everybody who helps people buy property and helps people sell property."[25] The *Wisconsin State Journal* ran an editorial entitled "Smudge on Reputation." "Those of us lucky enough to live in Wisconsin know what a great state this is," the paper boasted, "blessed with extraordinary scenic beauty; hard-working, honest people and a squeaky-clean state government that labors (sometimes to extremes) to protect its citizens." Then it waved a warning finger: "State regulators . . . need to remember that 'business as usual' in Wisconsin has to be conducted on a pretty high plane if the state is to retain its reputation for government as good as its land is beautiful."[26]

Woodland Farms exposed as myth the kind of idyllic city-country connections that brief landowners like Phillip Risser and Barbara Hayes had once hoped for. Wisconsin politicians and newspapers wanted to break the actual connection—city folks scammed by shyster middlemen. In *Nature's Metropolis,* a classic study of urban-rural relationships, historian William Cronon showed how nineteenth-century Chicago acted like a funnel, pulling in raw resources from the upper midwestern countryside, transforming both city and hinterland landscapes in the process.[27] A reverse pull occurred in the twentieth-century Kickapoo Valley: the countryside attracted urbanites like Risser and Hayes. In a sense, of course, Chicagoans were still consuming these rural places by buying increasing amounts of land. What is striking about the reaction against Woodland Farms, though, is how closely it mirrored the company's own concerns by adopting an urban point of view. Just like White and Smith, their critics saw the Kickapoo Valley through the eyes of a visitor, albeit a disgruntled one. "It was kind of a hard story," Lampert Smith said of the coverage, "because the locals . . . [would] never spend $40,000 on a piece of property. The people who did need to know didn't get the paper." Each new round of publicity sent the narrative farther away from the land and communities involved. The other side of the story, the one few people talked about, was the profound effect White and Smith had locally.

Plat maps are limited documents, but when you flip through them year by year, watching the moving lines the same way you would watch the running man on the page margins of an old children's book, you feel that something more powerful is at work. At the urging of prominent farmers, Sterling township enacted an ordinance prohibiting land divisions into parcels of fewer than forty acres—hoping to keep Woodland Farms out. By establishing zoning at all, Sterling stood out in the region as an exception. Liberty was the norm. As absentee ownership gained ground, Liberty's population dwindled.[28] Community cohesion in the township weakened. As land ownership became more fragmented, it became, in a sense, even more individual. A landowner who had never been legally bound to talk with her neighbors about selling her land now had less of a social reason (or opportunity) to talk with them either. And what of the cycle of new landowners who bought four or five acres of land on a Woodland Farms development? How did they come to fit into the community fabric?

"It changes every seven years," answered Liberty town chair Danny Deaver. "They build their chicken coops, then they get bored. What do they do when it gets like this, blazing hot? Or after three good winters and then the fourth one is bad? They want our life, but they won't stay long."

Longtime Liberty residents were generous and willing to make time for a newcomer. (I know, because they let a complete stranger and her team walk their land and poke about their histories.) But occasionally a new landowner tested local goodwill. "I can remember this one guy," said Liberty town clerk Judy Daily, "a major physicist—atomic type. He borrowed a haybine and brought it back broke. His reputation as an atomic scientist didn't go far."

Most of the newcomers were reclusive. "You just got the sense that they're afraid to meet the locals," said Susan Lampert Smith. "They're so isolated. Their only friend is the real estate agent." One of the first things new people do, continued Deaver, is put up a mercury vapor lamp. With the roguish grin of an Irish poet he finished, "They're afraid of the dark, they're afraid of the neighbors, and they're afraid to go into the bar."

Woodland Farms had environmental as well as social repercussions in Liberty. One of these involved the interplay between the geography of the parcels White and Smith created on the plat map and the geography of the land they sold. Because Woodland Farms kept its clients ignorant of geography to the greatest extent possible, a few owners discovered too late that their land could not support septic systems.[29] By 1995 much of the development had not developed at all. On those parcels, one-time agricultural land began returning to forest, a trend ecologists call "old field succession." When landowners could build, they generated a second kind of impact. Almost always people selected the top of steep hills as prime second home sites, for the lovely vistas. Much to the consternation of local officials, new owners laid their driveways straight uphill. To this day township residents comment on the severe erosion washing downslope from vacation homes in high rainfall years.

The relationship between parcels and geography manifested itself in a third way. In the company's Liberty project, as well as one in adjacent Webster, a few parcels turned out to be nearly landlocked. These owners had no convenient way to get from a main road to their property without crossing someone else's land. As with many spoken or unspoken negotiations among neighbors, this one so far as I know did not end up in the courts.[30] Semistranded owners solved the dilemma more informally, establishing odd dirt paths that veered off from new dirt and gravel roads through the development, all of which seemed to go nowhere in particular—until you looked at the plat map. One route led down a steep slope to a stream, across the streambed, and up the bank on the side. "The erosion was awful," said Liberty resident Eddi Blakley.[31] "It's a tragedy," agreed Joel Swanson, Blakley's neighbor up the road. "We used to own a farm there, so we feel strongly about what happened when Woodland Farms came in."[32] Local residents complained to police and DNR agents, who confirmed that crossing a streambed in a vehicle was illegal. The problem was, an officer or agent had to catch a driver in the act. Slowly but surely Woodland Farms reconfigured its own small part of the landscape. The process that White and Smith had begun of bisecting and fragmenting the landscape continued through each new generation of landowners.

The company influenced local landscapes in still more personal ways. Moving throughout the Kickapoo Valley, Woodland Farms became known as a company that followed the obituaries. Old widows at home alone might sell their farms to a charming, aggressive agent with a contract in his hand. White and Smith also engaged other real estate agents. Some worked openly on their behalf, while others kept the connection quiet. "It was a fraud," said Blakley of the secret arrangements. "They knew that people in the area wouldn't sell to them otherwise." More than one agent lost some community standing when their connection to Woodland Farms became public. One Valley resident recounted how a man had knocked on her door asking about her eighty-acre forest. He enjoyed hunting with his son, he claimed, and wanted to buy her woods for their outings. After some thought she agreed to the proposal, only to discover afterward that the man worked for Woodland Farms. Almost immediately the company logged the forest and divided the property into second home sites. "I felt I had done something awful," she said, embarrassed about the lasting consequences of her naïveté.

Underlying the deception was an environmental story that was not exceptional or illegal at all. The story of the woman who inadvertently sold her land to Woodland Farms had a climactic moment: After she sold the property but before the company resold it, Woodland Farms logged off the forest. Logging was the likely outcome of many land sales in the Kickapoo Valley. Some owners sold timber just before selling their land. Some buyers bought property primarily for the timber on it. Others— developers and speculators like Thomas White—profited from the timber when they could. Here is how a resident described a common encounter in the Valley: A real estate agent might approach a far-flung group of heirs who have little time to investigate their options and say, "Your 120 acres are worth $60,000." The agent says nothing at all about timber or its value. If the owners agree, the agent will arrange a sale to a business partner or close relative. Once the sale is complete, the partners will log the land and sell the property at a much higher price. Eddi Blakley put the matter differently. "What they [Woodland Farms] did was rape of the land. They logged the land and deprived these elderly people of the only other way they might have profited."

Despite any perceived injustice, the important point about timber harvests is that they were part of the system, not part of the scandal. Most developers and real estate agencies were shrewd enough to find out what timber was worth, whereas the people selling to them were not always so savvy in seeking the same information. Developers also knew that the market price of a small parcel of recreational land—say five or ten acres—would not change much whether the forest had a closed canopy of eighty-year-old trees or an open canopy of twenty-year-old trees. They had no financial incentive to leave a forest intact and every reason to harvest it. Woodland Farms highlights this pivotal period in the life of real estate. It gives us insight into far-reaching environmental changes across rural America. In Liberty, most farmland included at least a small woodlot and often many acres of forest. With farmers selling land, with absentee owners buying it and then selling again, with land turnover accelerating and property values going up, logging boomed in the region. In 1996, Liberty landowner Richard Langer noted that he might have one of the best (and only) unlogged stands left.[33] The loggers are constantly coming around, confirmed area resident Philip Groves.[34] "The incentive to log is pretty high under these circumstances," according to Joel Swanson. "Almost everyone who lives out here has to make money in many different ways—it's very diversified."

It is entirely possible, then, that land use practices of individual owners matter little for forests over the long run in places like the Kickapoo Valley. Few people hold onto land for long, and owning land longer than a decade is an unusually extended tenure. Liberty's experience of dynamic—or unstable—ownership is typical.[35] There are times when a forest is more likely to be logged no matter who a landowner might be—farmer or rancher, wealthy absentee landowner or poorer local one, young adult or retiree. A study in neighboring La Crosse County showed that "24 percent of the properties with a filing of intent to harvest timber also had a real estate transfer within two years of the filing date."[36] The more frequent the turnover the greater the likelihood of a harvest, perhaps because the seller has no future on the land, while the buyer has no attachment to its past.

Woodland Farms was important in this system of logging-then-selling the way any major landholder would have been. Because it accumulated large, contiguous areas of land, it had more forestland to harvest. Concentrated ownership was also very appealing to logging firms and sawmills, which sought work on larger tracts.[37] But what did this actually mean in ecological terms? Public foresters in the region had their own ideas on the matter. County and state foresters were advocates for timber harvesting on private land. If there was enough standing volume, and if the markets were good, they encouraged landowners to harvest.[38] They also believed that timber harvesting done properly would produce a healthy forest. Yet timber sales of the type Woodland Farms might contract for frustrated them. These were the harvests least likely to have a public forester involved; these were the harvests in which an owner might consent to removing every large tree in the tract, leaving only the young trees and those deemed worthless, a bad environmental practice in any forester's book; these were the harvests in which loggers had tacit permission to get the cut out as fast as possible without regard for erosion, soil

With logging just another part of an accelerating cycle of real estate turnover, foresters worried about destructive harvesting methods, especially on steep slopes. (Courtesy of the Department of Forest Ecology and Management, University of Wisconsin–Madison)

compaction, damage to the remaining trees, or even cleaning up the mess afterward; these were the harvests most at risk for timber theft by loggers tempted to take out more trees than a contract specified. Others in the Valley shared the concern. "Logging's gotten worse in the area," asserted lifelong resident Brian Turner. "We call it stump-jumping—they just let the trees fall wherever and then haul in the skidder."[39] The dilemma foresters faced was that forest health by any definition becomes irrelevant in a property system that makes timber just one component of the larger cycle of real estate turnover.

Forest ecologists in the region were also interested in timber harvesting. Logging is what ecologists call an anthropogenic disturbance, which means it is human caused, whereas a windstorm or lightning-set wildfire is a natural disturbance. Because logging has been a continuous part of the Valley's landscape history since settlement, scientists want to understand its connection to changes in the area's forests. I was part of a team of researchers that documented ecological changes in Liberty and two neighboring townships. The maps in figure 7 highlight changes in Liberty's forests since the 1930s. Forests are not a single mass in these maps; they look like pieces of a shifting mosaic. Yet it is clear that forests now occupy a greater share of Liberty's landscape than in 1939. The two most common hardwood forest types in the Kickapoo Valley are oak-hickory and maple-basswood.[40] The same data that generated the maps show that oak-hickory forests have declined in Liberty from a high of 4,695 acres in 1954 to around 3,707 acres in 1995. Maple-basswood has become dominant on many sites where oak-hickory once reigned, increasing by 950 acres since 1939. Ecologists have noted the decline of oak-hickory in many regions of the country.[41] What you see in the maps are ecological processes of forest succession extending beyond Liberty and throughout the eastern United States.

The possible causes of oak to maple succession range from postsettlement fire suppression to poor acorn masts and deer or rodent browsing.[42] A big piece of the puzzle is the tolerance of sugar maple (*Acer saccharum*) for shade: it can thrive for decades in the forest understory. If maple gains a foothold, the conditions are good, though not certain, for maple to eventually dominate a stand.[43] In the absence of a catastrophic disturbance the process would be slow, perhaps centuries long. As Liberty shows, forest succession has occurred remarkably quickly. This is why ecologists believe that logging is also an important piece of the puzzle.[44] A single harvest can change a forest from oak to maple overnight. Many harvests can

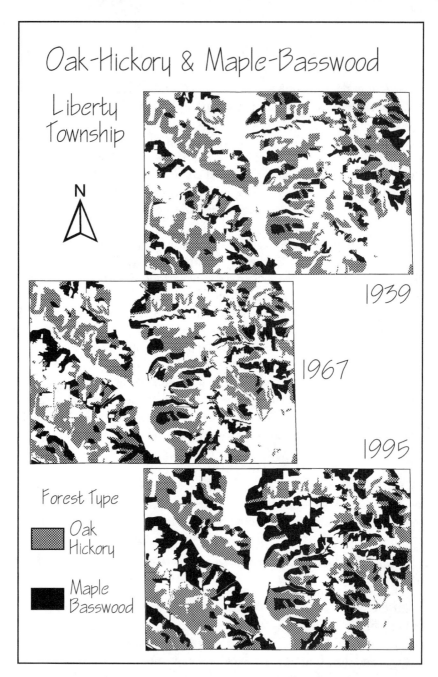

Figure 7. Forest succession from oak-hickory to maple-basswood in Liberty, 1939–95. Oak-hickory forests have declined throughout the eastern United States. Liberty (as well as Clinton and Stark) is a microcosm of the larger trend, which allows us to examine the complicated cultural and ecological drivers of both local and regional ecological change.

change an entire forest landscape over a few decades. Timber harvests that should theoretically result in vigorous oak regeneration often have the opposite result. Forests where oaks are a significant component of the seedling and sapling layers should benefit from the increased sunlight. Other vegetation, however, often grows more quickly, crowding out the young oaks. Woodland Farms opens a window to the larger ecological history of forest succession. Yet it is worth remembering that ecological patterns and processes are never clear-cut: some ecologists believe that old field succession on recreational land of the kind Woodland Farms specialized in offers the best hope for preserving oak-hickory forests (a topic we will return to in later chapters).[45] Like many landowners before and after, Woodland Farms played a part in these changes.

While the influence Woodland Farms had on the landscape would continue through a succession of new owners, White and Smith had the more immediate problem of Susan Lampert Smith. In 1993, seeking shelter from all the bad publicity she had showered on them, they reincorporated

A recreational vehicle in an old field on Woodland Farms Road, for sale or rent. (Courtesy of Michael Barrett)

their firm in different parts of Wisconsin as Four Rivers Realty, Thousand Lakes Realty, Country Lake Realty, Wisconsin Lakes Realty and Lighthouse Land Company.[46] These companies continue to operate; but Woodland Farms was first, and despite its reincarnation, the company had unfinished affairs. Implicit in Lampert Smith's straight news prose was a sense of frustration with public officials who, on seeing a pattern of dubious dealings, should have dug deeper. Privately Lampert Smith was shocked because "the state really didn't want to do anything about it." With her prodding they finally acted. In 1995, state investigators announced that Woodland Farms had violated a number of state laws, including faking independent appraisals and using unlicensed real estate agents. By 1996, four years after Lampert Smith's first article, the state reduced the charges to two counts, the first of which read: "That at diverse times and on diverse occasions between August 1, 1990, and September 1, 1991, the respondent [White and Smith] failed to supervise Woodland Farm employees who caused to be published various advertisements using descriptive phrases such as 'Divorced Owners Must Sell,' 'Lenders Repo,' 'Lake Lot Repo,' '6 Acre Sand Beach,' 'Last Lake Lot Left,' and 'Owner Leaving State.'"[47]

To these counts White and Smith submitted, via their lawyer, that "respondent neither admits nor denies the allegations . . . but for the purposes of resolving this matter, agrees to the discipline."[48] Discipline in the Wisconsin case started with suspended real estate licenses—eighteen months for Thomas White and ninety days for James Smith. Together with their company, they paid a total of $37,500 in fines. That was what three or four of their advertised sales might have garnered, "a stiff penalty," according to a *Wisconsin State Journal* editorial at the time.[49] The state also dissolved Woodland Farms, although nothing in the sanctions prohibited White and Smith from owning the spinoff baby Woodland Farms they had created.

A fairly dry and bureaucratic finish to Woodland Farms was at hand, but the same was not true for Thomas White. Where the state of Wisconsin left off, the federal government continued with a grand jury investigation of his actions. During the Wisconsin investigation, White and his lawyer had responded in writing to a number of queries about specific employees, focusing on whether any of them had improperly acted as a broker. An October 13, 1993, letter to White's attorney questioned one real estate sale. "Who was the selling broker in this transaction?" the investigator asked. "You did not mention or indicate anything concerning Jean Krolick's involvement in this matter," he continued. "What was her involvement in the transaction?"[50] The letter went on to demand wage statements, asking if Ms. Krolick received commissions prior to getting her license, to which Attorney Ebben replied, "Ms. Krolick was retained by Woodland Farms as a contract landscape designer." As for the wage statements, "My clients have indicated that these records were not immediately available; however, they will forward them directly to you under separate cover as soon as possible."[51] The gist of the queries was that White had hidden the commissions he had paid to unlicensed sales staff, including Jean Krolick. By responding so in writing, through the mail, White was found to have committed fraud—not a real estate swindle, but federal mail fraud.[52] To this crime he pleaded guilty in federal court. On May 6, 1997, a U.S. District Judge sentenced Thomas White to fourteen months in prison and fined him $62,000. The judge also recommended against any furloughs or work release privileges during his time, saying of White: "He was the leader of the band. He was the organizer. He was the innovator."[53]

A formidable vision marks this saga from beginning to end, as far as anyone can write it. Thomas White wielded power in everything he had done, using his personal charisma and his constant control over information to build a real estate empire. On that earlier day in 1992, when reporter Susan Lampert Smith first met with Thomas White, one of his employees had also gone along on the tour. In 1994, that same employee alleged that White had raped her in his car on their way home from the 1992 trip. "I remember that day because it was my birthday," said Lampert Smith. "Later I found out [about the rape]." A jury did not convict White because he had alibis from his wife and two men who worked for him.[54] But the headlines changed abruptly in 1997. "Real-Estate Empire Founder Indicted for Perjury in Sex Trial," announced the *Wisconsin State Journal* in an article describing new charges against Thomas White and his wife.[55] According to Lampert Smith's report, "Steve Eggen [one of White's alibis] lied about seeing the Whites together at the restaurant, while Raymond Powers lied about working at White's home the day of the alleged assault and not seeing the employee's car there." For White, power—and power over information—knew few bounds.

There was no belated justice for this one of his victims. There was no resolution at all. In 1997, while serving his prison sentence, White made his last real estate transaction in Wisconsin. He and his wife sold their home on the bluffs of southwestern Wisconsin, turning their backs once and for all on the exquisite landscape that had helped shape their lives. To speed the deal along they had offered a $10,000 bonus to their buyer for closing quickly. The Whites then fled the country. "I bought the house from them Oct. 15, and the next day he broke out of prison," said buyer Robert McMahon Jr.[56]

White escaped from federal prison in Colorado one week before his formal indictment for perjury. Lampert Smith was rueful later when she talked with the federal prosecutor who had tried White. "In my career as a journalist I sent one person to prison, and you let him go," she joked. Federal marshals believed that the Whites fled with their two daughters to Cuba, and were perhaps cruising the Caribbean in a yacht. There they might still be for all we know, a long way from the Kickapoo Valley, where Thomas White's legacy still shows on the land.

In Liberty, Thomas White was the disturbing face of change. Yet for long-time residents, it was the less sensational story of farmers going out of business, absentee beef ranchers moving in, and a cycle of recreational landowners coming and going that made the lasting mark on the place. It is tempting to explain these changes as the work of an invisible hand of market forces. Thousands of individual decision makers, so the story goes, responded to the logic of the market as it applied to them alone. Collectively but not with collective consciousness, all of these people wrought far-reaching changes. This interpretation of the history of Liberty and thousands of other places like it is convenient. It explains land fragmentation, accelerating rates of land turnover, and the volatility of land use. The invisible hand makes social and ecological changes in Liberty mere by-products of a nearly unstoppable process, with or without Thomas White. This is one narrative trajectory.

But when a person like Thomas White comes on the scene, the invisible hand becomes less persuasive. Practically speaking, the narrative overlooks a systemic condition of rural real estate—unequal access to information among participants in the market. This is an important symptom of larger problems. The narrative excludes any possibility of choice and self-determination—a say in its own future—on the part of a community. It renders actual landscapes invisible and the future of those landscapes irrelevant. Ultimately the narrative disconnects morality from decision making, whereas Thomas White and Woodland Farms make it impossible to separate the two. In Liberty's history, property has undeniable moral dimensions.

On the surface (in the market), property appears to be an object—a rectangle on a plat map that individuals buy, use as they see fit, then sell.

Below the surface, however, as Thomas White taught his unwilling pupils, property is a vast social system that governs how we live with each other on the land. Quite literally, property governs the patterns of our everyday lives.

Also below the surface, property is a primary, even sacred, idea in our culture. Historian Ted Steinberg says that property "may be the only ecumenical passion left."[57] This makes property the terrain on which we express deep values. Here we have the lesson of Liberty and the key to understanding Liberty's equally complex neighbors in subsequent chapters: competing notions of property are really expressions of different values.

Liberty experienced firsthand what can happen when the common interests of residents—their shared values—become submerged beneath the individual interests of an unpredictable line of landowners. And so, not surprisingly, refined ideas about land ownership began to emerge. "Land ownership is one of the most basic forms of power," wrote local editorialist Lonnie Muller. "As the ownership flows out of the valley and away from the farms, so does the power to control our own lives." Community-centered values rose to the surface of local discourse on private property:

Woodland Farms had many successors to continue a process of land fragmentation and recreational development. (Courtesy of Michael Barrett)

"Instead of seeing dollar signs all over the landscape," said Muller, "sellers should examine more closely who they are selling to and how the buyer proposes to take care of the land."[58] These values, community and environmental well-being, did not replace values of individual and economic autonomy, but they gained enough local legitimacy to coexist alongside them. In a recent survey assessing support for local zoning under Wisconsin's Smart Growth law, 70 percent of Liberty's residents wanted zoning, but only at the township level, not at county or state levels. "They're people who really love the area, and have respect for it," said Eddi Blakley of community discussions over Liberty's future.[59] "In our plan for zoning," said town clerk Judy Daily, "we're exploring values first—true values of the people who live here."[60]

PART 2

A Community
on the Land

4

Outsiders

In 1965, when ranchers began buying land in the township of Liberty, another group of people had its eyes on the Kickapoo Valley. On first arriving in the Vernon County seat of Viroqua, Gideon Miller remembered making quite a stir as he and his colleagues descended the steps of their Greyhound bus. Two ladies saw them, he recalled. "They asked the driver to inquire where we were to perform that evening." One of the men with Miller said, "Tell her we are not the Beatles."[1]

Forty years ago an assembly of good-humored Amish men might have stopped traffic anywhere, with their wide-brimmed black felt hats, their untrimmed beards and clean-shaved lips, their black trousers held up by suspenders, their black vests and black jackets fastened with metal hooks and eyes rather than buttons.[2]

Miller's group was Old Order Amish, one of the Anabaptist religious sects that also included the Mennonites, Hutterites, and Brethren.[3] They had decided to leave the urban congestion around their settlements in Geauga County, near Cleveland, Ohio.[4] Farmland in Ohio had become scarce and expensive, making it hard for new generations to obtain enough land to farm. Conflicts over land use and zoning were on the rise. Their ability to control contact with what they considered an intrusive modern society had also become a challenge. For those Amish who wanted to limit the temptations that a secular world offered their children, and to ensure that farming remained their core occupation, the rural isolation of the Kickapoo Valley made migration out of Ohio a hopeful prospect.

Their reconnaissance began in the township of Clinton, where they toured a few farms on the market. They also assessed real estate trends, looking for signs that more land would come up for sale. The group returned

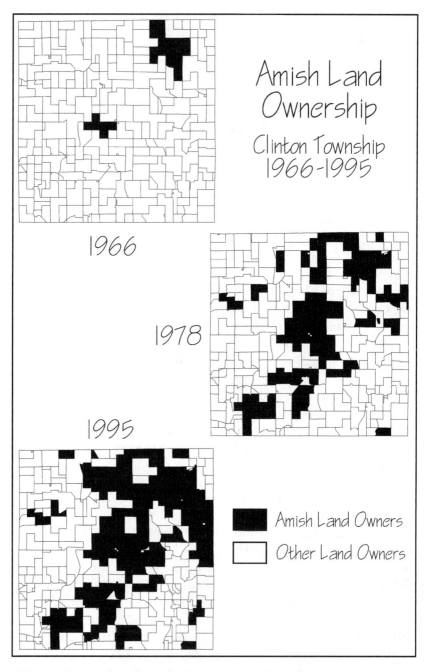

Figure 8. Amish land ownership in the township of Clinton, 1966–95. Today the Amish own more than half the land in the township, and their settlements have spread throughout the Kickapoo Valley.

to Clinton a month later with a few Amish women, seeking "their consent of making the move," as Gideon Miller recounted it.[5] Though a novelty then, the Amish would soon become a familiar sight throughout the Kickapoo Valley. No one in the area would ever again mistake them for traveling performers.

Clinton's settlement by the Amish leads off the second in this series of reflections on property. This chapter will explore what happened when an entire community of outsiders acquired a great deal of land in a short time. What were the reactions of the people who already lived there? How did they relate to this new community? Today, Amish farmers in Clinton are undeniably local residents and they are undeniably in place for the long haul. This fact alone sets Clinton apart from Liberty, whose history became dominated by absentee land ownership. Clinton, however, offers more than a local counterpoint to that trend. An altogether different story of property unfolds in the history of this township. The Amish illuminate what is not obvious on a plat map, that control of land involves deep cultural conflict and accommodation. It transcends individual owners who imagine themselves separated by property lines. Thus the Amish compel us to move our scale of analysis from individual parcels to ethnic or cultural territories. In scaling up, the Amish also allow us to reconsider how community prerogatives and environmental stewardship can fit in a system of private property. In their separateness, the Amish shine a light on non-Amish culture and cultural landscapes. At a time when we are struggling none too successfully over how to achieve sustainable agricultural communities, the Amish raise fascinating—and uncomfortable—questions.

Starting with the first farm in January of 1966, the Cashton settlement—as the Amish still call it, after the nearby village of Cashton—expanded rapidly in the township of Clinton. Today the Amish own more than half the land in Clinton. Amish land ownership meant a lot of things for the township. Far more land stayed in local hands than was the case for its neighbor, Liberty. More land also stayed in agriculture. As a measure of the continuity, think about the basic Valley landscape mosaic of fields, forests, and pasture. From 1939 to 1995 forest cover increased considerably in Liberty, whereas forests expanded very little in Clinton over the same period, from 31 percent to 39 percent of the township. Likewise Liberty developed large areas of "old fields," while old fields remained an insignificant part of Clinton's landscape. The Amish maintained the general landscape features and boundaries they inherited from their predecessors early in the twentieth century. Also like their predecessors, they managed medium- or small-scale mixed dairy and crop farm systems. The Amish would appear to represent stability, yet stability was not what the Amish symbolized to the communities where they settled. In fact, the Amish represented exactly the opposite. They focused attention on the instability gripping the Kickapoo Valley and much of the rural Midwest.

During the period in which many Amish first moved to Clinton, Wisconsin was experiencing a 6.6 percent decline in dairy farms, its steepest rate of loss up to the mid-1990s.[6] The structure of agriculture was changing, beginning with a cost-price squeeze in the 1960s. The prices farmers paid for agricultural inputs such as fertilizer and pesticides rose more quickly than the prices they received for their products, a trend that has not let up.[7] The Kickapoo Valley was also facing rural depopulation as more of its young people left the area. "What does it take to keep you people here?" a local realtor was quoted asking area youth.[8] Of those who stayed in the Valley, fewer entered farming.[9] Those who did faced the new paradigm and paradox of scale. While farm numbers declined, the average farm size was on the rise in Wisconsin. The larger farms were accounting for a larger share of gross sales until, by 1992, slightly more than one-fourth of all farms accounted for three-fourths of all agricultural sales.[10] Unfortunately for Valley farmers, their steep and stony land did not lend itself to the capital-intensive concentration of dairy cattle and cropland possible on the expansive landscapes and fertile prairie soils of other agricultural regions in the Midwest. Try though they might to compete with their colleagues elsewhere by buying the same new machinery, expanding and modernizing their buildings, and intensifying their use of new crop varieties, fertilizers, herbicides, and pesticides, hardship and uncertainty remained a fact of life for most farmers in the Kickapoo Valley.

Contrast this grim scenario with the scene the Amish presented in Clinton. The township was bustling with their activity. Clinton became one of the few townships in the Valley whose population was not stagnant or in decline.[11] The Amish community was growing due to the large families they raised and migration of other Amish into the area.[12] Beginning with a population of 70 during their first year in Clinton, Amish numbers increased to around 770 by 1994.[13] Consequently, their internal real estate market was in constant motion. An Amish couple might aggregate land and then subdivide it. They might buy land from a father or an uncle or a non-Amish neighbor, or they might sell land to a son, a son-in-law, or another Amish family migrating to the Valley. From 1978 to 1995 over 55 percent of all Amish land in Clinton changed hands yet remained within the Amish community. Over the same period, the township as a whole experienced its highest turnover since 1930, with nearly 75 percent of the land going to new owners.

Amish settlements did not stay confined to Clinton. The influx became regional, expanding outward from Clinton throughout the Kickapoo Valley. By the 1990s, their population in the Valley came to number around three thousand.[14] Wisconsin became one of the most popular states for Amish relocation during the 1980s and '90s. (As of 2004 only Pennsylvania had a larger number of settlements.) "I heard say every time it rains, a new settlement springs up in Wisconsin," said a writer to *Die Botschaft,* an Amish weekly.[15] Rural communities throughout the state were becoming acquainted with their new Amish neighbors.

Amish farms were as dynamic on the ground as their real estate was on paper. Families would gather by the dozens to raise houses and barns. Their large white homes, a windmill standing sentry and a black buggy in the driveway, became the defining feature of Clinton's vernacular landscape. Amish women tended enormous home gardens, while the men

A prosperous Amish farm in the Kickapoo Valley. (Courtesy of Wolfgang Hoffmann)

guided draft horses to plow fields of corn, oats, and hay. Children fed the chickens and helped milk the black-and-white Holsteins that dotted pastureland throughout Clinton. With an energetic clip-clop, buggy horses moved people between fields and home, or farther down the road for bi-weekly religious services or any other errands and visiting that needed doing. All these became common sights and sounds.

While the Amish spread across parts of the Wisconsin landscape, non-Amish farmers were having a hard time passing a whole farm on to family members, or on to any young farmer. Amish farmers only exaggerated the comparison by continuing to farm much as non-Amish families had earlier in the century (a topic for the next chapter). It was impossible to ignore how well they did at a time when others were facing outright loss. This was the rub: when it comes to land ownership, for someone to acquire a lot of land someone else has to relinquish it. Since the Amish made up a community apart from the mainstream of society, there was no way for other residents to avoid thinking of them as a group rather than as individual landowners. Eighty Amish families buying land in Clinton over the course of a few decades felt like a more drastic change than eighty absentee though non-Amish families might have in their stead. Land ownership became a symbol separating the haves from the have-nots, the Amish from their land-poor neighbors. In this setting, an issue not normally in the foreground of property disputes brought out deeper resentments. Residents in Clinton began an emotional argument over the pitfalls and merits of different kinds of horseshoes.[16]

Township officials had become convinced that they were seeing enormous cost increases in road repairs from the particular type of horseshoe that Amish farriers put on buggy horses. Carbide cleats welded to the surface of the horseshoes for traction cut and chipped away at the pavement. The town board wanted the Amish to use rubber or plastic horseshoes or to pay for the damage they caused. Otherwise road repairs would exceed $160,000 into the foreseeable future, and the township budget only provided $83,000. "What will we tell the people of the town?" asked Clinton's town chairman Robert Kelbel (for a moment overlooking Amish residents). "We worked hard to get out of debt and now we have to borrow."[17]

Amish buggy drivers were sure that the studded horseshoe was the safest, most durable, and inexpensive shoe for traveling the Valley's hilly roads. According to them, the other varieties cost more and wore out quickly. Besides, the Amish doubted whether their horses caused all the damage that officials and residents attributed to them. Townships without large

Amish communities had likewise exceeded their road repair budgets, perhaps because of bad weather. What's more, the Amish community noted, large trucks tore up the pavement when they applied their breaks on steep hills, especially in hot weather. "We need these shoes," said an Amish farmer. "We've tried plastic and rubber and they don't last. Even in summer, during wet times or in the cool of the morning or evening, horses slip on the pavement. Women drive the buggies and we don't want accidents."[18]

Although the details being argued were clear, the larger implications of the debate were buried beneath the technical fine points. One right in land that American society takes almost entirely for granted is access to the country's roadways. Whether we are on mental cruise control driving home from work, or keeping both hands tightly on the wheel while negotiating a treacherous two-lane county highway, or speeding along a straight freeway to visit the in-laws for Thanksgiving, we all feel confident in our right to the road. This seems as central a tenet of daily life as one could imagine in the twenty-first-century United States. One of the reasons for our nearly unconscious faith in a guaranteed place on the pavement is that we pay a variety of taxes to build and maintain roads, and we therefore expect to use them at will.

For local units of government like Clinton, the connection of roads to property was almost as obvious as the sober citizen's right to use them. Property tax revenue paid to fill potholes, repave surfaces, and build new roads. Township officials also relied on smaller amounts of road aid from the state, which in turn came out of a tax on all gasoline sales. One of the most burning questions that local officials faced anywhere was whether they had met their constituents' demand for handy, well-kept roads. Much less burning in the world of local and state transportation politics was whether each user had paid her fair share of the costs associated with those roads.

In Clinton, township officials asked the Amish a version of this second question. In its most candid form the query can be expressed as: Why should the township have to pay for the damage you cause with a mode of transportation that virtually no one else uses? The question was not a sign of hostility so much as financial distress. But leveled at the Amish, the question reinforced their separateness. The Amish were not constituents; they were outsiders. "If they voted," a woman remarked at one public meeting on horseshoes, "you'd have a township run by the Amish and then what would you have?"[19] Because car and truck drivers in Clinton need never submit to a cost-benefit analysis of their travel patterns, the township was suggesting a hierarchy of road rights between two large groups of landowners, Amish and non-Amish. It was also setting the stage for other cultural grievances to creep into the discussion.

Most of the public comment on Amish horseshoes took place during two meetings in June and July 1983.[20] These came about after town officials had approached Amish leaders in private, without success. Feeling rebuffed because the Amish had not agreed to switch horseshoes, town chairman Kelbel sought help from the county district attorney. The DA told him that there was no basis for a legal complaint, although he might ask the area's state legislator for advice. State Representative Brian Rude in his turn offered little hope for legislative intervention.[21] But he did offer to coordinate meetings where area residents, township and county officials, and experts from the state Department of Transportation could hash out the issues. At the time, Clinton officials must have felt incredibly frustrated. They had no clear way to force a change and no indication that the Amish might relent. All they had was the public forum their representative had provided. It should therefore not be surprising that some resentment would come through in the proceedings.

For a while, those who attended the first meeting stayed focused on studded horseshoes, looking closely at the damage they caused and alternative shoe technology. The aim was getting the Amish "to cooperate in solving the problem." Later the conversation shifted as people started giving voice to the cultural subtext of the conflict. Just how much right did the Amish have to the road in the first place? "They pay their share in taxes, don't they?" responded a representative from the Department of Transportation. "We pay gas tax toward roadwork and they don't," countered Robert Kelbel. "They pay school tax and don't make use of the schools," a resident from a neighboring township shot back. "I'm not picking on them," the town chairman said at another point. "They've paid their taxes and been good. But look at the bakeries they have all over. My wife made cakes and she got a telephone call saying it was illegal." This was followed by complaints about how the Amish violated sewer and milk house regulations. Concluded one woman, "I don't think it's religious. They've got economics they use as religious."

Amish residents were not present to respond because they had not been invited to the meeting. Their absence seemed to create some edginess. "I've heard through the grapevine they know what we're talking about," fretted Kelbel. "They've heard about the meeting, then you'd better get to them . . . before they get disturbed about no input," replied a transportation official. "You need to work this out locally; you all live here day by day."

Amish leaders did attend the next meeting on horseshoes, where the tax theme continued unabated. "There are hard feelings among some non-Amish about the Amish not paying registration, gas and sales taxes," said one participant. Amish resident John Schmucker responded that the Amish paid taxes on gas for the engines in some of their farm equipment, and also for their hired transportation. They paid property taxes on their land, he added. Another Amish resident felt that the Amish community added to the township's property tax base. As for sales tax, they paid that on their buggies. In the debate over horseshoes-cum-taxes no one mentioned that state aid from the gas tax made up only 5 percent of Clinton's annual budget for road repairs. Nor did anyone attempt to estimate the sales taxes that any single resident might pay in a year, Amish or non-Amish. It was unnecessary to establish hard numbers because the precision of each tax point and counterpoint was (and still is) beside the point. What was more telling was the basis on which the Amish defended themselves to the larger community.

By citing their property taxes, the Amish justified their place in the fabric of Clinton, including the roads that ran through it. Many non-Amish in the Kickapoo Valley were strong property rights advocates so this would seem to be a persuasive argument, and to some it surely was. After all, *I paid my property taxes, therefore* . . . is a declaration that has acquired real meaning in our culture. Ideologically, property taxes may bolster your right to be in a place doing what you are doing. Financially, they bind you to the community where you live because you are helping to pay for its infrastructure and services no matter how great or little your actual use. John Schmucker summarized the Amish version of the sentiment, saying, "We humbly ask we each bear our burdens, in a kind and neighborly way and that people live in peace with respect for each other."

Nevertheless, in a region where the Amish were becoming major landholders, this argument did not convince everyone. It did not weigh in the Amish community's favor that its members paid a growing share of property taxes in Clinton. A few people wanted to move away from the fact altogether. They interrogated the Amish on their rights and duties within the larger community by citing the consumer taxes a hypothetical average citizen might pay. In this context frugality was suspect, and the privilege of land ownership was not so privileged.

Such debates were not confined to Clinton or the Kickapoo Valley. Different versions were occurring everywhere that the Old Order Amish had recently settled. Across the state border in Fillmore County, Minnesota, non-Amish residents worried that their rapidly expanding Amish community intended to buy out one of the county's large villages. They thought that the local economy was suffering from Amish thriftiness, and that local schools were losing state aid because the Amish would not enroll their children.[22] Fillmore County, too, had its conflicts over the road. The question there was whether local officials could compel the Amish to use neon orange slow-moving-vehicle signs on their buggies.[23]

Nearly twenty years after the emotional meetings in Clinton, the state of Illinois confronted an identical debate over horseshoes, roads, and taxes. "Are you going to tell me those trucks roaring up and down our roads aren't causing more damage?" asked Amish farrier Reuben Schrock in response to a new Illinois law that allowed townships to levy an annual buggy fee for road repairs. "I can't deny the horses are gouging the roads, but I pay taxes just like everyone else."[24]

Questions surrounding Amish land ownership always became more complex than a transfer of deeds would typically suggest. The idea of community—often in the background of individual lives and individual rights—came to the fore and became the focal point. It was community boundaries and cultural boundaries that people were debating. When vastly different cultures come together on a common landscape, the rights, obligations, and relative power of each will be negotiated. In more benign terms, they all had to get used to each other.

The great risk, of course, is that people might not get used to each other. Disputes can lead to the resolution and peace John Schmucker appealed for or they can lead to something worse. The overwhelming presence of the Amish in both their numbers and the amount of land they controlled always carried the danger of worse conflict. No matter how well intentioned the public discussion in Clinton and places like it, language used in the heat of the moment could create an opening for outright bigotry.

In many places where the Amish were expanding, what began as private gripes became verbal slurs, and what began as verbal slurs turned violent. East of the Kickapoo Valley on the border of Marquette and Columbia counties, the Amish endured a frightening year of vandalism. Among the crimes, four men burned an Amish buggy worth three thousand dollars; they opened barn doors and chicken coops to release the animals; they threw bricks, bottles, and beer cans at buggies; they yanked out mailbox posts to build a bonfire; and they painted slashes through warning signs on the road about slow-moving buggies. The harassment persisted in part because the Amish remained silent about it, refusing to report the crimes until they had escalated to a dangerous level.[25] Thomas Jerome, one of the people eventually arrested, lived next door to the family whose buggy he burned. According to the police, Jerome called the Amish "coons" who did not pay taxes. He said he was "sick of driving through horse manure, that the buggies ruin the roads."[26] Afterward, Jerome's aunt commented on how much their whole community had changed since the Amish came. "There's only four of us left who aren't Amish," she said. "We keep to ourselves and they keep to themselves."[27]

Elsewhere in the country during the 1990s, both Amish and Hutterite settlements faced vandalism, arson, and personal threats.[28] In Big Valley, Pennsylvania, an arsonist struck the Amish, torching seven barns and killing 139 cattle and 38 horses. Also destroyed were the families' plows, wagons, threshing machines, milking sheds, and seed for spring planting.[29] Near Ledger, Montana, a Hutterite community lost $100,000 worth of lumber to arson.[30] Rather than denounce whoever set the fire, residents around Ledger complained to a reporter that the Hutterites did not pay their share of taxes. One farmer in the area claimed that the Hutterites had forced him into retirement because of what he called their free labor and a religious exemption from Social Security taxes. "I couldn't keep up, so we gave up," he said.[31] Added a rancher, "They don't do anything illegal, but they're tough for an ordinary family to compete against."[32] Still another farmer said, "I think they use their religion as a front to hide their grand plan, which is to control a good share of agriculture." As to how the community could remain unsympathetic to the Hutterites in the face of actual criminal destruction, Ledger's undersheriff explained, "they're making a go of property and land that others aren't able to."[33]

Back in the Kickapoo Valley, the language of property, property taxes, and roads had also created a convoluted moral space for criminal behavior. Simmering resentment in some quarters reached a sudden ferocity when a man named Michael Vieth fired his .22-caliber rifle six times at a buggy with three young Amish boys and their older brother inside it. The children were not hurt, although the bullets did injure their horse. Vieth then kidnapped a fifteen-year-old Amish girl, attacking and raping her. He claimed an Amish buggy had provoked his behavior by somehow forcing his car off the road.

United in horror, Kickapoo Valley communities recoiled from Vieth. There was no defense of him, no justification for what he did. Michael Vieth was obviously a person with deep emotional problems, and in one day he became a vicious criminal as well. Anyone might reasonably ask what Michael Vieth's crime had to do with Amish land ownership in the Kickapoo Valley. Perhaps the answer is that the repulsive actions of this individual had nothing to do with it. But Michael Vieth said a few things after his arrest, and those statements were highly suggestive. The attack was "a way to get one-up on the Amish," Vieth told police. "I wanted them to know they don't own this world. I wanted to let them know there are other people in the world."[34] Here, then, was a man who articulated his own actions in a language that had everything to do with territory and ownership, and more implicitly, a sense of displacement.

This is not to say that people encouraged Vieth to do what he did, or that he might not have found other ways to vent his rage apart from the Amish. Certainly no one condoned the violence afterward. But, significantly, the crime was not a random one either. He not only targeted a group of Amish, he singled out for particular brutality an Amish girl. One of the profound yet little mentioned transformations that the Amish brought about was a visible female presence on the land. With their great vegetable gardens, their large families (seven children on average), their laundry billowing from the clothesline, even their bare feet and demure blue or black or dark purple dresses, Amish women and girls claimed a conspicuous place in the Kickapoo Valley. The land was *hers* too. What more effective revenge than to steal her personal security of place? (And what more common tactic in the history of ethnic fights over territory?)

Amish women were not at all naïve about the possibility of crime in the Valley. Nor did they necessarily see themselves as helpless, although they were religious pacifists. The contours of their outlook become clearer in this account from Sally Kempf. A robust, dynamic Amish woman with a slow country voice, not to mention a keen appreciation for a leisurely tale, Sally narrated the story of a friend of hers who had moved from a city to a rural area in order to get away from urban crime. Almost immediately after moving to the country "a couple of crazy criminals" robbed, then kidnapped, this friend and members of her family, taking them as hostages on a long ride. Sally's friend used her wits to outwit them and everyone escaped unhurt. The moral of Sally's story was that you can't escape crime.[35] Pragmatic and adaptable, Amish women have a broad perspective on owning land, because for them the community is more central than the individual. The community will support and guide its families; it will care for all its members, the strong and the vulnerable—and also the wounded. The community is where a person's real security lies.

Michael Vieth's words—*they don't own this world*—suggest that the control of land is never a tame issue. To the contrary, it is quite a dangerous one. When control moves from one cultural group to another, a backlash may follow, no matter what the laws on owning property. When someone like Vieth comes along, creating the cultural equivalent of a seismic tremor, he reveals hidden fault lines in our patterns and systems of land ownership. These fault lines are places where surveyed boundaries and legal titles will not always keep the peace. Though cultural violence can fall along a wide continuum—from seemingly random explosions to more systemic persecution—it arises out of a historical context. Often therefore, it is the larger community, rather than law enforcement, which must ultimately decide what to do with that history.

Throughout the Valley, people grieved with the Amish at the assault. In Clinton, too, residents felt strongly that Michael Vieth's crime should not reflect on their community. To be sure, complaints against the Amish were part of the story, but they were only part of the story. To many, the Kickapoo Valley was an accommodating place, even during hard times. Sometimes conservative and parochial, sometimes funky and eclectic, this was a place where people of dizzyingly varied viewpoints had made their homes over the years and become neighbors. There were longtime residents and new ones, conventional farmers and organic farmers, back-to-the-land hippies, artists, aging retirees, and well-to-do young parents who moved to the area for the sole purpose of sending their kids to one of the country's few rural Waldorf schools. If Vieth accomplished anything of worth, it was that this other history of property and community—made up of the daily interactions among neighbors rather than the harsh words of public conflict—was summoned from the background of everyday life and put forth as the regional identity many people embraced most of all.

A pitfall faces anyone interested in the history of Amish/non-Amish relationships. With two different groups it becomes easy to imagine a sameness, or homogeneity, within each. Truth be told, cultural diversity would not be the first term that springs to mind for describing the rural Upper Midwest. The more likely image would be Garrison Keillor's portrait of an austere community of Norwegian American farmers who do battle with the wintry elements of their lives in Lake Wobegon.[36] Before the Amish arrived, Clinton and its surroundings might have appeared awfully close to Keillor's caricature. Its dominant European ancestry was Norwegian, with some Irish, English, and Czech mixed in. Maybe the Bohemian influence added a touch of local diversity by nineteenth-century European standards. But that would hardly be the case today, with our awareness of the complicated racial, ethnic, and regional mosaics that have shaped U.S. history. Less than ten miles east of Clinton, however, lay Cheyenne Valley. Before the Civil War, Cheyenne Valley became one of Wisconsin's first communities of black farmers. The Cheyenne Valley settlement makes a striking aside for the more sweeping light it sheds on land ownership in the Kickapoo Valley. Cheyenne Valley shows how far astray one might go by making assumptions about intolerance without looking closely at the history of a place.

In 1855 Walden Stewart, a free black born in North Carolina, bought land and became the first settler in the township of Forest and what would later be called Cheyenne Valley (within the Kickapoo River watershed).[37] Five other families followed Stewart. Like the Amish over a hundred years later, this group prospered from their move. By 1860 two of them had accumulated enough land and livestock to place them among the wealthiest families in the township. By 1870 the settlement had expanded to eleven families and sixty-two people.

What makes Cheyenne Valley such an interesting supplement to Clinton is the way in which Euro-American farmers absorbed African American farmers into their community.[38] Integration became a spatial fact of life as African American farms came to alternate with Euro-American farms. It became an economic fact when the farmers began sharing horses and chores and working together to cut timber throughout the region. Ultimately integration became a social fact as, one by one, African American families began intermarrying with Euro-American families.[39] The 1880 census of Forest Township is an impressive document for its racial diversity. Very few households did not list a black or mulatto father and white mother, or conversely, a black or mulatto mother and white father.[40] Descendents of the Cheyenne Valley settlers still live in the area.[41] Cheyenne Valley shows better than any other example that different groups of farmers getting to know each other via the land was not a new process in the Kickapoo Valley.

Though the likelihood was small that Amish and non-Amish families would intermarry in Clinton, a sympathetic understanding had been developing between them not unlike that in Cheyenne Valley over a century before. The Amish were defining all sorts of new boundaries, while Valley communities were redefining their own sense of boundedness vis-à-vis the Amish. Rancor was not an inevitable outcome. Almost on first

acquaintance the Amish and their neighbors began forging informal relationships grounded in the land. Many of them worked out mutual access
to their property for hunting, fishing, gathering mushrooms, tapping
maple trees, and grazing livestock. "The past week a young man stopped in
to ask for permission to hunt ginseng, which we gave him," wrote Amish
scribe Clarence Yoder in his submission to *The Budget,* a national weekly
paper for Amish and Mennonite communities. "He was very respectful
and conscientious, and came by with about ⅓ lb. of the valuable roots, my
first glimpse of it. Although not a big money-making deal because of its
scarcity, he had turned to this to help get by in supporting his family during this time when the economy was lagging and he was laid off."[42]

Young Amish boys asked their English neighbors, as they referred to the
non-Amish, to go fishing. Their fathers occasionally helped an English
farmer bale hay. One old farmer in Clinton, eventually surrounded by
Amish, counted himself a holdout. He remained reticent toward them for
years, but after his wife died, Amish neighbors pitched in with chores on
his farm. Afterward, he allowed them to keep horses in his forest, telling
his family that his ideas about the Amish had changed a lot.

Being neighborly about their land helped forge connections between
Amish and non-Amish landowners. But it was an outside threat to the
Kickapoo Valley that pulled everyone together into a visibly united community. In January of 1995, the Air National Guard announced plans
to expand its hardwood bombing range in west-central Wisconsin. The
plans included adding two low-level air training corridors stretching from
Madison, Wisconsin, to Iowa and South Dakota.[43] Pilots in F-16 fighter
planes, along with B-1 and B-2 stealth bombers, would practice their
maneuvers during twenty-one hundred training flights a year along the
corridors. The two paths would converge directly above the Kickapoo
Valley at three hundred to five hundred feet overhead. For a few months
the Amish knew nothing of the plan. Meanwhile, residents throughout
the Valley had joined with three western Wisconsin counties to prevent
the flights. Eventually they warned the Amish community, asking for their
help in opposing the Air National Guard.

The Amish rarely intervene in the affairs of "Caesar," their generic term
for the state.[44] This has held true over three centuries, even when their
material interests, and sometimes their lives, were at stake. Ordinarily the
Amish will not vote in public elections or engage in civil protests. Only
reluctantly will they report crimes to their property. What is not so easy
for people outside their culture to see, however, is that the Amish, whose

clothes and transportation create a façade of timelessness, have always adapted to the time and place in which they live. "The common impression that the Amish do not change is false," said Amish scholar Donald Kraybill. "While some of their cultural compromises appear odd, they are, in many cases, ingenious arrangements that permit the Amish to retain their distinctive identity and also to survive economically."[45] The Amish have cultural bargaining sessions, according to Kraybill, some that continue for decades.[46] Their internal negotiations have spanned the use of telephones and automobiles to their participation in scientific research on genetic defects unique to their group.

Despite their tradition of nonintervention in society at large, the Amish are not passive bystanders to events that could threaten the viability of their communities. They make exceptions to their own cultural guidelines. In Intercourse, Pennsylvania, Amish attended a public hearing to show concern over a proposed four-lane highway going through their farms.[47] In Ohio they asked officials to stop a $25 million dollar incinerator in their community. "We plead with meakness to please accept our protests with an open mind and sincere concern," said the Amish spokesmen.[48] In Lancaster County, Pennsylvania, Amish residents turned out to vote for township supervisor candidates who had pledged to protect farms from subdivision.[49] In these cases it was a threat to their place on the land that moved them to respond. The Amish followed a similar process of decision making in the Kickapoo Valley. They decided to join forces with a new community group opposed to the Air National Guard, Citizens United Against Low-Level Flights.

Amish religious leaders in Clinton became central actors in the events that followed by making themselves accessible to the press. "We try to live peacefully," Gideon Miller told a reporter from the *Houston Chronicle*. "The planes would knock the peace right out of it."[50] Menno Hershberger, an influential Amish bishop whose family, like Miller's, had been among the first to settle Clinton, also questioned the Guard's plan. The Kickapoo Valley is peaceful, Hershberger explained to a Minneapolis reporter. That was why he and his people moved there thirty years earlier, because "this area was better suited to our lifestyle." Lurking on the horizon and menacing their lifestyle were the jets. "One comes, then another comes, then one comes again," he illustrated. "So much noise. It would be better to have it stop before it starts."[51]

An amazing letter to the Air National Guard added weight to the bishop's words. In fifteen pages of graceful calligraphy, Amish church leaders laid out their fears that the jets would put their lives and livelihoods in jeopardy by frightening farm animals. "We plead with you to stop this plan because it would be alien and disastrous to our entire, simple, way of life including our religious beliefs, physical safety and livelihood," they wrote. "Our religious beliefs are derived from the Old and New Testaments—the Word of God—and are rooted in a deep reverence for pacifism which would be shattered by the continued presence of military bombers in the skies."[52] With words such as these newspaper readers around the country saw the Kickapoo Valley through Amish eyes, and they heard the war planes through Amish ears.[53]

For more than a year the Air National Guard held out against a barrage of anticorridor petitions, citizen letters, and phone calls from anxious politicians. "How can we believe that noise will not be a problem . . . if one-low-level airplane flying directly overhead will make noise that exceeds 100 decibels?" asked Clinton landowner Amos Miller. "We will not accept these noise events, or their 'unavoidable adverse impacts,' as mentioned in section 2-27 [of the Draft Environmental Impact Statement]."[54]

Editorial cartoon by artist Ken Stark criticizing the Air National Guard's proposed low-level flights over the Kickapoo Valley. "All who understand the plan, oppose it," wrote Stark in a letter to the editor. "We are young and old; passivists, and veterans; Limbaugh Republicans and Kennedy Democrats. We are united only in our desire to preserve the peacefulness, integrity, value, and safety of our home, hills and valleys." (Used with permission of Ken Stark)

"Our own military is trying to force American citizens against our will to suffer a long-term war-time experience; to endure life in a simulated war zone," protested Valley resident Stephen O'Donnell.[55]

"Are we to be attacked by the very force whose mission it is to protect us?" wrote Chris Stark. "Bombarding us, at will, with deafening, polluting jet engines at 300 feet . . . as our children try to play outside . . . as our livestock graze contentedly . . . as our precious endangered and threatened species struggle to survive . . . as we scrape to earn a living in an economically depressed area . . . would only destroy our lives. What a price to pay!"[56]

"If you can't dazzle us with brilliance," wrote Leo Engel of the Air National Guard's Environmental Impact Statement, "then baffle them with Bull Shit."[57]

Images of small Amish children fleeing frightened horses and cattle as adrenaline-filled Top Gun pilots buzzed the Valley were particularly hard to withstand. Harder still was the bishops' suggestion that thousands

Editorial cartoon by artist Ken Stark criticizing the Air National Guard's proposed low-level flights over the Kickapoo Valley. (Used with permission of Ken Stark)

of peaceful Amish farmers might flee the Kickapoo Valley to escape the onslaught. The Guard surrendered in 1996, dropping its plans for the low-level flights.[58]

No one in the Valley doubted that the Amish were instrumental in the military retreat. The case had gained national coverage because of the Amish way of life. A Guard spokesman confirmed the consensus, saying, "We consider [the Amish] to be a very valuable cultural resource that we needed to be aware of."[59] In thinking back on the protest, Valley resident Ken Stark did not find this rare intervention by the Amish all that surprising.[60] Everyone had a stake in this special rural place they were shaping, said Stark, an artist who had done his part in the protest by creating biting editorial cartoons about the flights. In a way, he explained, the Guard would have been taking away everyone's land because it would have obliterated the best part—the Kickapoo Valley's air of peace and solitude.

Afterward, Amish and non-Amish residents remained separate. In their separateness conflict was one side of the story, accommodation the other side. Yet they had also become united by their shared devotion to the place where they lived. Friendly bonds were as simple and grounded as one person letting a neighbor harvest ginseng. But they could also reach high to fight a threat from the sky. Rooted in neighborliness and a sense of place, such relationships have immense consequences. Through them property boundaries—like cultural boundaries and community boundaries—can be transcended, or at least crossed from time to time. As we will soon see, through these relationships nature can also be transformed. Amish farmer and Clinton resident Gideon Miller said it best when he extended Amish loyalty to the whole of the township and the Kickapoo Valley: "But do say we love the community. Its gentle rolling hills and valleys, to the more steep hills, and fertile soil, the friendly people, the winding Kickapoo river and many more God Given gifts."[61]

5

An Amish Environment

Cultural conflict and accommodation were two dimensions of Amish land ownership, yet culture was by no means the whole story. The land itself had an intimate place in the history of twentieth-century Amish settlements. The Amish never settled a new area by chance. They called themselves plain people, but before making a move they would perform spatial analyses so sophisticated that any geographer would be impressed. When deciding where to go, the Amish compared local land prices and assessed the potential for expansion. Expansion was crucial for Amish communities struggling to establish male children on their own farms. There was a lot at stake, for research showed that when families succeeded in finding land for the next generation, young Amish were much more likely to remain Amish than leave the community.[1] In places like Lancaster County, Pennsylvania, or in Geauga County, Ohio, real estate prices were higher than many Amish families could afford. Thus they began migrating to the Midwest. The Amish also examined regional transportation networks, calculating distance to markets for their goods.[2] "A rural area with considerable farm land available and not near large cities was their goal," said Bishop Menno Hershberger, one of the first settlers in Clinton. "Also, they wanted good bus and train service within reasonable distance."[3]

Spiritual considerations rested on top of practical analyses. The Amish sought out locations that would allow them to maintain some separation from what they called the world. Cashton, said Bishop Hershberger of the village nearest their first settlement in the Valley, "is not the most desirable atmosphere due to the large number of saloons; but, the grocery stores, lumber mill, implement, feed, and hardware centers are well-stocked and

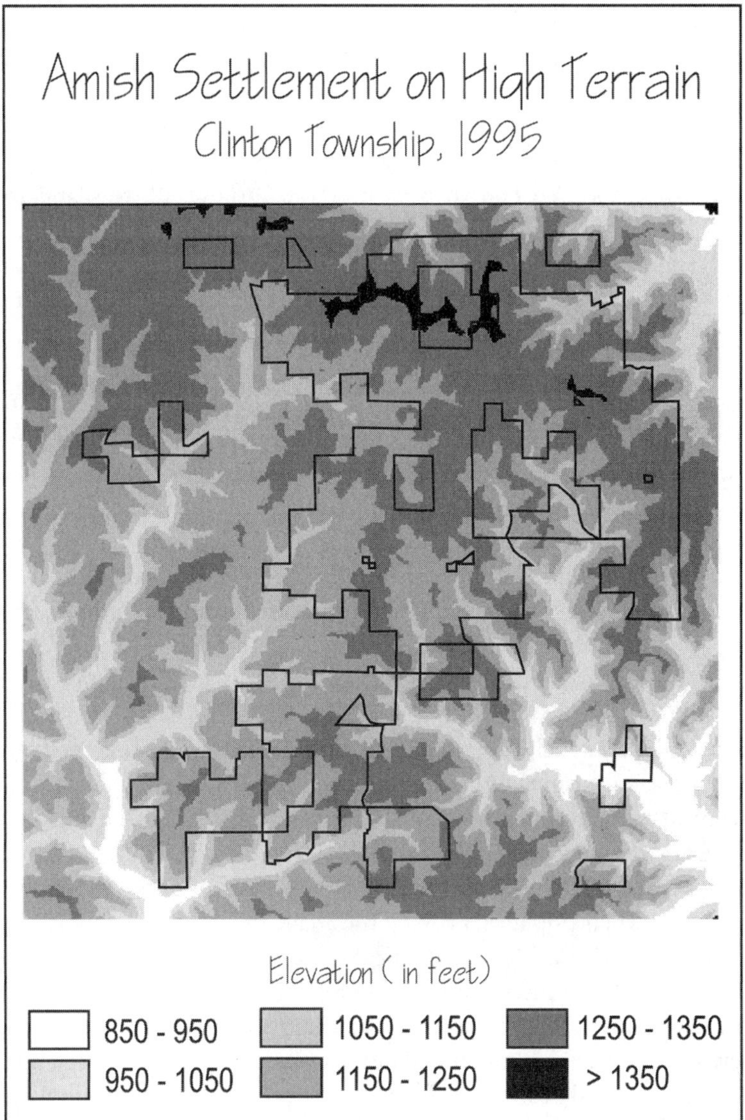

Amish Settlement on High Terrain
Clinton Township, 1995

Elevation (in feet)

850 - 950	1050 - 1150	1250 - 1350
950 - 1050	1150 - 1250	> 1350

Figure 9. Township of Clinton topography and Amish settlement by 1995. The black lines delineate Amish land. The Amish used sophisticated geographical considerations when deciding where to settle and what land to buy. Here you see that they initially chose land on higher terrain, which was the most productive agricultural land.

adequate."[4] The task of Amish groups seeking to relocate was to find a place that permitted social isolation but was not so remote that it created economic isolation.[5] Using these measures, the Amish weighed the pros and cons of moving to Clinton in the 1960s. But still they did not have enough information.

The landscape also had to be acceptable.[6] Above all, the land must sustain their agrarian way of life. The Amish sought what ecologists call a heterogeneous landscape. Heterogeneous simply describes a complex landscape where diverse land cover types coexist in some recognizable pattern. In deciding whether to move from Ohio, the Amish were not looking for a single expanse of cropland to plow; they wanted fields, pasture, and forest, along with ample water from springs and streams.[7] "The area near and centered around where the first Amish settled has many hard maple trees," said Bishop Hershberger, who also noted that "There is an abundance of wildlife here especially deer, fox, coyote, turkey, grouse, coon, beaver, etc."[8] Out of such a landscape came crops, pasture, maple syrup, fuel, timber, and wild game. This was their preferred environmental niche, and it was the reason many Amish communities spread into the Midwest and parts of Canada but not the Great Plains or the American Southwest.[9] Landscape, in effect, provided an environmental rationale to veto any place for settlement.

The Amish had decided that Clinton's landscape would meet their needs for a long time. As figure 9 shows, they chose land strategically, concentrating on fertile ridge tops. Less clear than their choice of land was what Amish ownership might mean for their new landscape. Would it change because an Amish community was there? Would the environment benefit from their presence, proving the adage that Amish are light on the land? These were not idle or rhetorical questions. To the contrary, people concerned with the sustainability of family farming had an intense interest in the answers. The same questions came to preoccupy county-based government agencies whose mandates encompassed land use, agriculture, and environmental protection. This chapter explores both the moral economy and the ecological economy of Amish land use in the Kickapoo Valley. In so doing I hope to tackle what seems to me a still more interesting matter. Like other farmers and ranchers, the Amish worked within and even embraced a system of private property. The question is whether we can discern an overlay of community values and community-level decision making on top of the more eye-catching movement of individual parcels and landowners.

By acquiring a great deal of land very quickly, the Cashton settlement drew scrutiny to its land use practices in Clinton. Admirers saw Amish agriculture as fitting in well with a vibrant organic farm movement in the Kickapoo Valley. The Valley was home to the Coulee Region Organic Produce Pool, or CROPP, the first organic dairy cooperative in the United States and today one of the largest and best known for its Organic Valley line of milk and cheese.[10] Although some Amish farmers used pesticides and herbicides, as well as antibiotics for their sick livestock, many others farmed organically.[11] CROPP had a number of Amish members. One settlement in the southern part of the Valley formed its own organic cooperative, Sweet Earth Produce. There was enough overlap between Amish and organic approaches that the Amish became important role models in the region. They represented what one group of researchers called "ecological agriculture." Ecological agriculture, according to Katherine Blake and her colleagues, is farming through "which the ecosystem on the farm can reach a sort of permanence, accomplished when nutrient inputs and eventual outputs are balanced and do not exhaust the natural resources of the farm."[12] The Amish helped relegitimize farming on rural landscapes where many people had become concerned about environmental degradation via agriculture.[13] The Amish also helped frame a theoretical critique of conventional American agriculture by establishing a real-life alternative to it.

The modest size of Amish farms was among the attributes that local people most admired. For Amish families in Clinton, a 120-acre farm was large. Eighty to 100 acres was the norm. By farming only land for which they had enough human labor and horsepower, the Amish reduced their reliance on modern technology.[14] This put a strict limit on the scale of their agriculture. Clinton followed patterns set in northern New York, Pennsylvania, and Ohio, where a single team of horses could work the typical Amish farm. One virtue of smaller farms was that they accommodated a larger number of farm families spread throughout the township. Clinton's relatively uniform distribution of medium-sized parcels stood in conspicuous contrast to the concentration and fragmentation of property in Liberty. Scholars in this country and other areas of the world have shown strong links between concentration of land and concentration of political power.[15] In places as far apart as the Appalachian Mountains and the Brazilian Amazon, the twin results of land concentration have been environmental degradation and disenfranchisement of rural people from the political decisions most affecting their lives. Amish farming produced

a more equitable distribution of land, labor, and capital than highly concentrated systems of agriculture. This was an outcome, the scholarship suggested, that boded well for decentralized decision making as new Amish
settlements spread across the Kickapoo Valley.

In concert with the scale of Amish farming was its diversity. Dairying
and field crops were central, but also important were fruits, vegetables,
chickens, maple syrup, and the occasional specialty plant.[16] Here again
was a parallel with organic farming. Underlying both was the idea that a
mixed farm system allowed the maximum use of a landscape without its
wholesale reengineering into a more homogeneous place. Diversification
reduced a farmer's need for agricultural inputs. When one group of scientists compared the energy budgets of Amish farms in the Cashton settlement (mostly in Clinton) with non-Amish farms of the same size and
number of cows, they found that the Amish used a fraction of the fertilizers, pesticides, fuel, feed, and equipment: 31,379 Mcal in comparison
to 362,990 Mcal on small non-Amish farms and 518,890 Mcal on large
non-Amish farms.[17] Amish yields were also 22 percent lower than small
non-Amish farms. This work is especially interesting because of the way it

Small scale and diverse, Amish agriculture in the Valley was reminiscent of farming
in the nineteenth and early twentieth centuries. (Courtesy of Wolfgang Hoffmann)

identified differences in efficiency among Amish farms in Pennsylvania, southwestern Wisconsin, and eastern Illinois. In Pennsylvania, on a landscape comparable to the Kickapoo Valley, the more progressive Old Order Amish farmers came closest to matching the yields of their non-Amish neighbors while using a quarter of the inputs. In eastern Illinois, by contrast, Amish farms could not come close to the yields of highly mechanized non-Amish farms because that region's fertile prairie soils gave the land an extremely high productive capacity. Apparently the Illinois Amish were aware of the lost potential. "I've heard Amish farmers say this land is just too rich for us," said one of the study's authors. Home gardens and small animals also provided more of a family's subsistence needs. The Amish gained once more by forgoing large machinery, not to mention the staple Chevy or Ford truck. Amish families in some communities had as much disposable income as neighboring non-Amish families who farmed conventionally on more land.[18]

One case highlights how important the ability to diversify was for the Amish in Clinton. In the 1980s, large dairy processing plants in the region decided to stop accepting raw milk from the Amish if they continued to

Sugar maple tapping is common in Amish woodlots. (Courtesy of the Department of Forest Ecology and Management, University of Wisconsin–Madison)

use water-cooled milk cans. The processing plants scorned this earlier technology in favor of highly mechanized bulk tanks. The Amish community did not complain about the turn of events, nor did it acquiesce to the new requirements for milk processing. Instead, the Amish built their own cheese factory and hired their own cheese maker, thereby creating a more dependable outlet for their milk.[19]

It is important to understand that not all Amish communities made the same choices. Whereas the Amish in Clinton rejected bulk milk tanks, Amish scholar Donald Kraybill traced a very different decision in Lancaster County, Pennsylvania, where Amish communities faced the same "riddle of technology."[20] For the survival of dairying in that region, Amish bishops in Lancaster County made a complex bargain with milk companies to use milk tanks. The important point is that the Amish were highly decentralized, with local settlements making their own doctrinal decisions on whether to adopt new technologies. In the case of the Kickapoo Valley, geographer John Cross found a quantitative relationship between Amish settlement and stability of dairy production. Cross cited Clinton as one of the most stable dairying areas in Wisconsin from 1989 to 1999, a period when the township lost only 5 percent of its dairy herds.[21] By building stability into their dairy enterprise, the Amish retained the power of choice over their way of life.

What many people might take as a sign of self-sufficiency was actually a conscious effort by Kickapoo Valley Amish to foster regional interdependence. They were always looking for new outlets for their milk. In an update to the national Amish weekly, *The Budget,* scribe Melvin Miller wrote, "Milk vending machines are becoming more popular in schools, which should work in farmers favor with chocolate, strawberry and root beer flavored milk being the best sellers."[22] In another example, they initiated a produce auction available to "anyone who grows produce within a 100-mile radius."[23] The auction, according to their brochure, "is the fairest way to sell, as it creates a true supply and demand environment." Amish organizers hoped that the auction would attract large as well as small buyers. "Encouragement was given to raise more produce this year to support some of the larger chain stores, including our local Wal-Mart store," wrote Melvin Miller after a growers meeting.[24]

Organic farmers in the Kickapoo Valley admired the Amish community's resilience in the face of modern structural and technological demands on agriculture.[25] The Amish, in turn, bore witness to the struggles of organic growers. "Two organic farmers here in the valley lost their farms recently," observed Melvin Miller, "which makes it uncertain for other farmers to decide whether organic farming is the proper route to take, although we also hear of successful organic farmers, of which their products appear to be a good demand for."[26] The Amish became *prima facie* evidence of at least one long-term alternative to industrial agriculture. Sociologist Marc Olshan has argued that decisions of the kind that led to the cheese factory near Clinton belie representations of the Amish as a simple folk society. Amish society is quintessentially modern, he said, because of the self-conscious way it directs its own evolution.[27] Following Olshan's line of reasoning, making intentional choices about technology was a more convincing sign of modernity than uncritically accepting a high level of technology as the only possible way to live.

Scale and diversity were two of the most visible outcomes of the defining characteristic of Amish agriculture—its moral framework. The Amish viewed their mode of production as a moral economy tied irrevocably to the Bible.[28] More than any other livelihood, they believed that farming facilitated the clear separation from the world called for by Romans 12:2 in the Bible, beginning with, "Do not conform any longer to the pattern of this world," and also by 2 Corinthians, which says, "Do not be yoked together with unbelievers. For what do righteousness and wickedness have in common? Or what fellowship can light have with darkness?"[29] Within this belief system the farm nourished the biblical cornerstones of life: family and community. Through their farms, the Amish could fulfill biblical injunctions to work hard and live plainly.

Some readers will see patriarchy in the Amish worldview and will be uncomfortable with it. An ideology in which large families, hard physical labor, and a strict interpretation of the Bible hold sway raises important questions about women's production, reproduction, and self-determination. Laura Kusnetzky and colleagues challenged those who promoted the morality and sustainability (and also the implicit transportability to non-Amish) of Amish farming without considering potential social costs. The authors were wary of overlooking how gender, class, religion, and ideology led to the group's differentiation from the rest of society. If discourse on sustainability and the Amish did not encompass their actual social history down to the household, they cautioned, then "our arguments will become indistinguishable—as is evident in much of the literature on sustainable agriculture—from those prevalent among New Right commentators. For the Right and many in the agricultural movement, family is not only God-given, but may be based on essential differences between men, women, and children. Biologically, from this standpoint women must be mothers and can be fulfilled only through motherhood and mothering."[30]

The most explicit response to this concern (and one that predates Kusnetzky) was from Ericksen and Klein, who examined the roles and status of Amish women in farm production. Their research suggested a fairly egalitarian mode of decision making in Amish farm families, mainly because the women had high-status roles in both production and reproduction. "Amish society is patriarchal, especially in its ideology," the authors acknowledged, "but the division of labor is more equal than might at first be supposed. This provides a contrast to the rest of American society where there has been an egalitarian ideology, but where at least until recently, women's economic dependence on their husbands leads to considerably less equality in practice."[31]

The same worldview shaped Amish ideas about the land. According to Genesis, God gave man dominion over nature, including the fish, the birds, and "every seed-bearing plant on the face of the whole earth and every tree that has fruit with seed in it."[32] But nature was also God's creation and hence a sacred trust. Amish farmer David Kline made this point when he referred to a common Amish prayer book, which translated reads, "and help us not to harm your creatures and creation but that we may be brought to eternal salvation and may abide therein."[33] Many Amish farmers believed that their earthly survival depended on the health of their land.[34] Theologian Thomas Finger traced this conviction to their early history in Europe, where "skillful care of the land enabled Anabaptists to survive and win toleration, and they developed a reverence for the land."[35] Four centuries later, on another continent, a farm's plants, animals, soils, and water were still necessary for sustaining the Anabaptist family, and they still entailed the earthly responsibilities of nurture and respect.[36] "We don't make the vegetables," said an Amish (and organic) farmer in the Kickapoo Valley. "A higher power works through us. You see, we consider ourselves as only stewards of the land."[37] "We should conduct our lives as if Jesus would return today but take care of the land as if He would not be coming for a thousand years," said an Amish bishop.[38]

That the Amish valued nature on their farms as more than a collection of economic assets to be bought, sold, and used up was no small virtue for back-to-the-landers and organic farmers in the Valley who did not otherwise hold the same religious outlook. The Amish put their belief system to work on small, diverse farms, which they plowed for the development of a moral economy rather than a purely market economy. For many, the

Amish embodied the idea that land stewardship and community stewardship can walk hand in hand.[39] They evoked what some consider the
twentieth century's most profound treatise on how to live well on the
land, Aldo Leopold's land ethic in *A Sand County Almanac*. Like Leopold,
the Amish had developed a firsthand appreciation of wild things.[40] "Son
Tobie saw his first bobcat while in [Missouri]," wrote coulee region scribe
Clarence Yoder, who wanted to share with readers of *The Budget* his son's
wonder. "After spending the night with us at Perry T. Millers', he walked
across the section to visit some at Wm. Yoders'. Crossing an old abandoned railroad bed, he came across the stub-tailed hunter, pouncing and
catching crickets in the open field beyond the grown over roadbed. Breaking through on the run, he was able to come within 50 feet before the cat
saw him, after which it was gone in a flash."[41]

In another *Budget* posting Yoder (again like Leopold) took a keen interest in the wildness of his own land. "On the last day of harvest, there was
a sudden disruption of the finches' happy day, when a kestrel dropped
from the sky, pursuing and catching one of their number. The tiny bird
tried his best in dodging back and forth, but the larger hawk was even
more agile and snatched him in mid-air for a tasty meal."[42]

The Amish also shared Leopold's tenet in *A Sand County Almanac* that
"Perhaps the most serious obstacle impeding the evolution of a land ethic
is the fact that our educational and economic system is headed away from,
rather than toward, an intense consciousness of land."[43] It is easy to imagine an Amish farmer nodding sympathetically at the point when Leopold
says, "Your true modern is separated from the land by many middlemen,
and by innumerable physical gadgets. He has no vital relation to it; to
him it is the space between cities on which crops grow."[44] It seems plausible that an Amish farm might have approached Leopold's ideal farm
where "there is a harmonious balance between plants, animals, and people; between the domestic and the wild; between utility and beauty."[45]
Certainly Valley Amish saw this in themselves, just as they saw a long
distance between themselves and Leopold's "true modern." "Cash cropping with corn and soybeans seems to be taking over in this area with
bigger machinery being used every year," wrote scribe Melvin Miller for
Budget readers. "I met my neighbor while planting corn at the end of
the field, and across the line fence he was planting with his new 12-row,
no-till $120,000 John Deer [sic] planter, so I felt pretty small with my old
McCormick 2-row planter, but the joy of it is that we can still peacefully
live among these farmers and farm our land the way our ancestors did."[46]

Leopold wanted to touch other people with his ideas, while the Amish in Clinton harbored no such ambitions. Their aim was to touch God, not modern society. Yet their view of the natural world, like Leopold's environmental philosophy, did reach people outside of their immediate sphere. In the Kickapoo Valley, many of these were organic farmers who believed as the Amish did that nature was worthy of care and restraint in its management. "Our individual well-being," began a label on one of CROPP's products, "is dependent on the health of the world around us: the land, water and air as well as our families, neighbors and the larger community. Recognizing our interdependence on one another, we are practicing food production which mirrors the natural laws of living organisms and emphasizes respect for all life." For both Amish and non-Amish organic farmers, agriculture was a commitment to a better way of living in the world. In this they understood each other very well.

Embedded in the tripartite argument about scale, diversity, and moral economy is the notion that Amish farming is more sustainable and thus more environmentally stable than other conventional systems of production. The underlying assumption is that agricultural landscapes and ecosystems fare better under Amish land tenure. The specific measures by which you gauge well-being may support or challenge this assumption. A few people looked more closely at Amish land use in Clinton and were not entirely satisfied with the results. In principle the Amish were good land stewards, they agreed, but how about in practice? Asking the question were agricultural and natural resource extension agents whose jobs entailed persuading Valley landowners to improve their land use practices. Some of what these agents saw in Clinton worried them.

Their concerns centered on three issues present in both Liberty and Clinton before the arrival of the Amish: water quality, livestock grazing in forests, and soil conservation. Amish farmers, it turned out, were just as willing as non-Amish farmers and ranchers to let their cattle into streams. In the 1990s, when Trout Unlimited began a program of stream rehabilitation in the Kickapoo Valley, their field surveys showed that many of the most degraded riparian stretches were those running through Amish farms.[47] Again, however, it is important not to overgeneralize beyond the boundaries of the Kickapoo Valley. In their study of Amish and non-Amish landowners in Ohio, Sommers and Napier found that Amish farmers were more concerned about ground water pollution than non-Amish and "were more willing to act to prevent degradation of the resource."[48] Clinton's

Amish also let horses and cattle pasture large areas of the township's forests. They not only used their own forestland for grazing, they rented or borrowed forestland from their neighbors. Most troubling of all was a practice that agents never expected. When the Amish bought farmland, they removed contour strips from their new fields.

Since the 1930s, contour strip cropping had been a pillar of soil conservation in the Kickapoo Valley. It was possible that anecdotal observations involved isolated cases rather than a pattern, though backsliding by even a few farmers would have caused chagrin within the conservation community. Data from this study, however, confirmed the trend up to 1995. There was a shift away from contour strip cropping on land that went into Amish ownership. Cropland in contour strips declined from approximately 2,666 acres in 1967 to 1,410 acres in 1995, a drop of 47 percent. The extent of the change across the landscape might have surprised even the people who watched it up close. By comparison, contour strip cropping on non-Amish land in Clinton increased by approximately 339 acres, or 10 percent. The conservation practices of Amish and non-Amish farmers diverged, but not in a way that people would have wanted.

Whether the farm was non-Amish or Amish, it was not uncommon to see cattle pastured right up to stream banks. Notice the eroded areas on this Amish farm. (Courtesy of the Department of Forest Ecology and Management, University of Wisconsin–Madison)

Resource agencies and policy makers faced two dilemmas with respect to the Amish. First, the language of degradation risked inflaming cultural conflict. Suggestions that the Amish wrecked the land and lowered property values were common. So were comments that county officials gave the Amish preferential treatment in the enforcement of zoning rules. Amish outhouses, for instance, posed thorny zoning and water quality issues for Vernon and Monroe Counties (whose shared county line the Cashton settlement straddled).[49] Invoking their religious injunction to remain separate from the state, Amish landowners refused to get permits for their outhouses. Here was the contradiction: the counties tried to avoid conflict by overlooking Amish violations of the pit privy law, but they continued to enforce the law with non-Amish landowners. This was a sore point. Government agents, moreover, had to be extremely careful that they did not exacerbate local tensions with their own disapproval of a few Amish practices. Second was the reality that public agencies had much less influence over Amish landowners than they did over other farmers. The Amish did not enroll their land in agricultural and forestry programs, such as the Conservation Reserve Program, or CRP. Keeping separate from the state, or Caesar, when Amish farmers bought enrolled land they removed it from the program.[50] Policies enticing landowners to fence livestock from forests or use contour strips on fields were as irrelevant to the day-to-day farm operations of the Amish as they were for ranchers like Bob Djerdingen a few miles down the road in Liberty.

Conservation agents wondered how they could convince Amish farmers to modify some of their methods. They tried to understand the Amish. If they could get at the root of Amish ideas, whether cultural, economic, or something else altogether, they might find a way to work with them, even if it was outside the parameters of formal programs. The district conservationist and the DNR county forester had alternative hypotheses about contour strips.[51] Forester Jim Dalton took what might be thought of as a "cultural constructionist" position. The Amish, he surmised, practiced old-fashioned farming based on their religious beliefs and antitechnology ideology. Because their culture did not readily embrace change, persuading them could be difficult, especially the older farmers who were set in their ways. Conservationist Jim Radke took an "environmental determinist" stance. He noted that the Amish in Clinton had developed their farming methods in Ohio, where farmland was flat and soils rich in comparison to the Kickapoo Valley. Though they were experienced farmers, they were inexperienced in this particular place. Over time, he thought, the Amish would adapt to the Valley's steep, erosion-prone slopes by using contour strips, as had many farmers before them. The Amish themselves gave agents varying, rather unclear answers. The discussion was reminiscent of debates that soil conservation agents in the Valley had had during the 1930s and 1940s (and which we followed in the township of Liberty). Time eventually revealed a measure of truth in both ideas.

For Clinton, the verdict on these hypotheses will not be in for some time. Still, there was no evidence that Amish communities had any kind of cultural injunction against contour strip cropping. Quite the opposite; Amish elsewhere had long histories of plowing along the contour. More telling yet, one comparison of soils in Holmes County, Ohio, showed an Amish farm to have a deeper layer of humus—the rich, organic part of the soil—as well as better water infiltration and less compaction than a conventional farm.[52] In Iowa, a county extension agent was sure that Amish soil conservation practices helped Amish farmers weather the drought of the late 1980s better than their non-Amish neighbors.[53] The most encouraging sign in Clinton was that contour strips did not disappear from the Amish landscape. Perhaps a third, more individualistic hypothesis also fits what the data show so far: Amish farmers were like all farmers, and there will always be differences among them in their attitudes and practices.

Just as Clinton's landscape consisted of more than cropland, Amish land use involved more than crops. Forests were always on the scene alongside fields, not as a backdrop to Amish production but as its vital other half. Despite the importance of forests, information is sparse on how the Amish have actually managed them in different places.[54] Soil conservation and soil fertility have tended to get all the attention. The same one-sided focus frequently holds true for research on the land use practices of farmers who are not Amish. Those who study agricultural landscapes may need to correct such oversights, for changes in Clinton's forests turn out to be one of the most provocative pieces of its environmental history. With forests we return to the importance of diversification in the culture, economy, and ecology of Amish communities.

In Clinton, many Amish farmers were accomplished foresters. Using draft horses they selectively logged their own land for fuelwood and lumber. They often left mature sugar maples. Maple syrup production, recalled one farmer, had gotten his family through some hard times. Their forests could change dramatically. "In his latter days, my dad saw the wood supply on the home 80 [acres] dwindle to a dozen trees in the woodlot behind the barn," Clarence Yoder said of his father's land in a nearby

Amish settlement.[55] Bill Kempf had once used wood from his own forest to make furniture, but his supply also declined and he began buying his lumber elsewhere.[56] Amish logging quickly extended beyond their own property boundaries. The group established a loose but extensive timber network throughout the area. By the 1990s, a person driving Clinton's winding roads would have encountered at least twenty-five sawmills.[57] The sawmills themselves became controversial. "It's very disconcerting to see where some buildings are located," said nearby landowner Rosanne Boyett, "an Amish sawmill built on a blind curve in the middle of the nicest cornfield."[58] The Amish built such an impressive capacity for processing logs using only small gasoline-powered saws that larger sawmills in the region started to subcontract work to them.

Becoming part of the region's timber industry allowed the Amish to further diversify.[59] Establishing workshops for making fine furniture and crafts, the Amish gained value-added income from their forests.[60] Small, hand-painted signs guided visitors along confusing valley roads to barns or sheds where they might buy rustic bent-wood hickory rockers or formal

A common scene around Clinton: logs by the side of the road. On average you will see an Amish sawmill every three miles or so on ridge top roads. (Courtesy of Wolfgang Hoffmann)

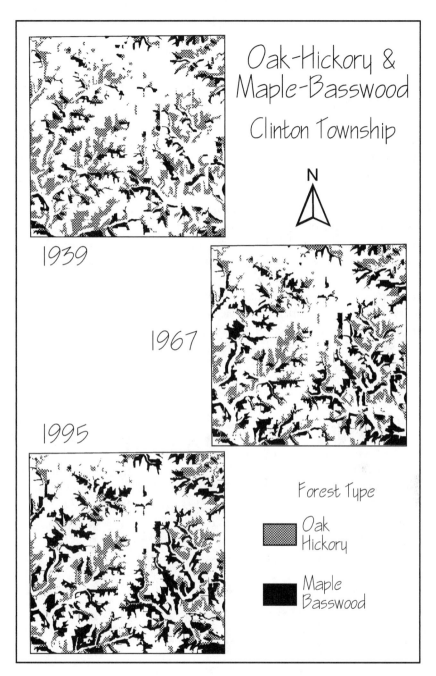

Figure 10. Forest succession from oak-hickory to maple-basswood in Clinton, 1939–95. Like Liberty, Clinton shows a pronounced trend in which maple-basswood forests have steadily replaced oak-hickory forests. As we will see, the spatial trend was somewhat different in the township of Stark.

dining room tables and chairs. More than a few oak trees became modern
entertainment centers for suburban families around the Upper Midwest.
The Amish also established a popular niche market in small, inexpensive
cabins for recreational landowners in the Kickapoo Valley. Now scattered throughout the region, these petite structures are so constant in their
design that they look prefabricated, like a sturdier and more charming
version of something you might buy at Home Depot or Menards.

The actual intensity and rate of timber harvesting on a landscape like
Clinton's is notoriously difficult information to collect. Forester Jim Dalton
thought it impossible to secure good estimates because logging took place
on private land, not public land.[61] By forestry standards, Kickapoo Valley
tracts were small and numerous, making them difficult to keep track of in
the absence of a formal requirement to report timber harvests. Neither
logging companies nor sawmills would provide disaggregated data on harvests because prices varied from sale to sale and place to place. (Such information is regarded as a trade secret to be kept from competitors and

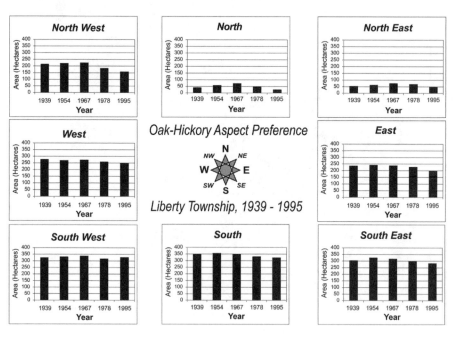

Figure 11. Spatial history of oak-hickory forests in Liberty, 1939–95, by landscape
aspect (using points on the compass). Compare this figure with that for Clinton.
(Heasley et al., "Claims on Paradise")

landowners alike.) Many landowners, including the Amish, were reluctant to talk about logging on their land. Logging by a previous landowner or at a neighbor's place was often a different matter, but that information will be imprecise. All this is to say that collecting reliable data on timber harvests is beyond the scope of this study.

What is possible though difficult to assess and compare is forest succession. Scientists generally agree that timber harvesting has contributed to

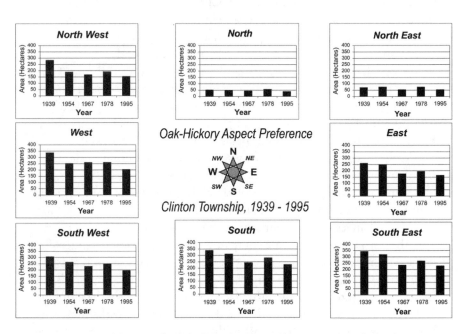

Figure 12. Spatial history of oak-hickory forests in Clinton, 1939–95, by landscape aspect (using points on the compass). Note the decline of oak-hickory in Clinton and Liberty on even south-facing slopes where oak is most competitive with maple. Although the socioecological reasons for the decline are complex, persistent logging in the area is part of the explanation. Chapter 7 will revisit the causes of forest succession.

Readers will notice a possible discrepancy in the Clinton data. Oak-hickory appears to increase between the years 1967 and 1978. A momentary reversal of the trend is possible though unlikely. It is more plausible that my research team's interpretation of air photos and archival sources on local land use produced the discrepancy. This is one of the challenges of re-creating historical landscapes for multiple dates, at a fine-grain resolution, and across several areas as large as a township. The richness of the dataset, however, gives us confidence that the overall trends and conclusions are sound. (Heasley et al., "Claims on Paradise") a shift from oak-hickory to maple-basswood forests in midwestern and northeastern parts of the country. But this does not mean that the trend has occurred uniformly in places like the Kickapoo Valley. Will two townships like Clinton and its neighbor Liberty show the same rate and extent of change? The answer could be yes—if site conditions are similar and if patterns of logging have not significantly differed across the two townships over time. The answer could also be no. Barring environmental variation, differences between Liberty and Clinton would provide an indirect indicator of the relative harvest pressure in each. By examining histories of forest succession, a picture of timber harvesting in the region emerges, even without specific board feet and sales receipts in hand.

We already know that Liberty's landscape mosaic diverged from Clinton's as Liberty landowners took fields out of production. The ecological question is whether the two townships diverged at the finer scale of the forests themselves. Like trends in the township of Liberty, figure 10 shows forest succession in Clinton from oak-hickory to maple-basswood.

Clearly a larger pattern of change transcended township boundaries. But there are intriguing subtleties in the data. What follows are two figures summarizing the spatial history of oak-hickory forests in Liberty and Clinton since the 1930s (figures 11 and 12).[62] The graphs do two things. First, they show changes in the extent of these forests in each township. And second, they make sure that we are comparing oak-hickory forests under similar environmental conditions, in this case landscape "aspect." Aspect means the direction in which a hill faces. This is what the compass display is for; it shows forests on slopes that face north (which receive less sunlight and retain more moisture), south (the driest sites receiving the most sunlight), and so on around the points of the compass.[63] Aspect is a key environmental variable because maples will almost always come to dominate cool, shady north-facing slopes, while oaks thrive when they face south, directly into the sun. The figures show that oak-hickory forests declined in both Liberty and Clinton, although there are differences in timing. But what is most striking is the comparative steepness of the declines on the south-facing slopes. Oak-hickory had a more severe decline in Clinton.

Though indirect, the evidence suggests that harvest pressure was heavier in Clinton than in Liberty. The graphs bolster local perceptions that logging intensified in Clinton during the 1960s and again in the 1980s and 1990s. Most people know the Amish as farmers, not as lumbermen. But the typical Amish scene in the Valley has always been complex. It includes hundreds of logs piled in high, neat stacks by the side of the road.

Many commentators have looked to the Amish for an alternative model of rural life. Wendell Berry, a leading critic of industrial agriculture, sees in Amish farming a corrective to the corporate rural landscape. In *The Gift of Good Land,* Berry contends that "while conventional agriculture, blindly following the tendency of any industry to exhaust its sources, has made soil erosion a national catastrophe, these Amish farms conserve the land and improve it in use."[64]

Amish farmer and writer David Kline reproaches American society for the loss of its agrarian traditions. "When that link to the land or the earth is severed, life revolves around plastic, asphalt, steel on rubber, false-security lights—human created things—and the weather becomes something to complain about or escape from. . . . Nature becomes an adversary, something to be subdued and altered to one's liking, a resource from which to profit, seldom loved for its own sake."[65] By contrast, Kline says of the Amish, "We farm the way we do because we believe in nurturing and supporting our community—that includes people as well as land and wildlife."[66]

Like Kline, Anabaptist scholar Heather Ann Ackley Bean sees in the community centeredness of the Amish and other Anabaptist groups a key to social and environmental sustainability for the rest of us. "Anabaptist community is expressed through mutual aid and the sharing of material resources," she says. "The tendency to put the good of the group before personal interests also acts as a check and balance to American individualism, a system that drives consumerism and other ecologically thoughtless behaviors."[67]

Of all farmers in the country, according to Wes Jackson, the Amish are the most ecologically correct.[68] For these authors, the Amish have demonstrated a community-centered ethic of land stewardship.

A few in the Kickapoo Valley came to believe something different, that Amish landowners degraded the land. This is not a case of the idealist pitted against a practical-minded opponent. Berry and Kline are farmers themselves. Jackson has been a pioneer in developing sustainable cropping systems that mimic prairie ecosystems. They have no illusions about agriculture. Instead, this is one of those deceptive contradictions that should be recast. When cast as a question of scale, comparison, and complexity, the two points of view are not entirely at odds. Human-induced ecological change is an obvious fact of agriculture. Any farmer, simply by farming, is aggressively intervening in and shaping the landscape. The issue is where to begin and end an environmental evaluation. There is a basic question about the nature of the changes, including their scale and rate. This involves an analysis in which sweeping ideas about balance, stability, and harmony must give way to the dynamic histories of particular landscapes. Some of the trends in Clinton were undesirable, including less contour strip cropping, greater soil erosion and stream degradation, and, to some people at least, the extent and intensity of logging. Active in agriculture and the regional timber industry, the Amish influenced landscapes beyond their property boundaries. Like any influential group, they should not be exempt from scrutiny.[69]

But there is the subsequent question of whether this mode of production—or that one—poses the greater risk of harm to people, plants, animals, soils, and so on, or offers the greater prospect of sustaining families, farms, communities, and local economies. The assessment is necessarily comparative. Officials in the township of Clinton, for example, need never worry about an Amish landowner building a slurry to hold ten million gallons of cattle manure because the Amish do not raise livestock in that manner. By this criterion Amish farming is safer than the confinement livestock operations that have started to gain a foothold in the Kickapoo Valley. Just as important, Amish farming provides a certain predictability of land use that people can work with and plan on in the future. Valley residents have begun making these kinds of comparisons for themselves. "Unfortunately this area is moving to that dichotomy of big farms and small horse-drawn or organic operations," said Rosanne Boyett. What happens when a business fails, or when a manure pit fails? she asked. "I would much rather see Amish anything than to see [land] subdivided." Fifth-generation Valley resident Brian Turner concurred: "I'd just as soon sell to the Amish, cause they'll take care of the land."[70]

What people actually want for their landscapes and communities is the lingering question. This is the query historian Donald Worster posed nearly twenty-five years ago to another community of farmers and to all of American society. "Will there be a community here not only forty years from now, but forty centuries?" he asked. "Or will it have become a graveyard of industrial farming?"[71] "The problem is," said Rosanne Boyett, "that they divide into two sides—those that want to plan for the future to maintain the present, and those that don't want any interference with landowner rights." She hoped eventually that "a majority of people [will] see it the other way, that we as a community are trying to protect all of us and what we have."

The Amish help us to envision the other way. What they have accomplished seems ordinary to them. They have realized to the best of their ability a community ideal for the kind of life they should lead on the land. Moreover, they have sustained what their community prizes in a landscape. All this they have done in a system of small privately owned parcels where individual owners work their land as they see fit—mostly. The Amish have flipped the broader prerogatives that go into land use decisions. The community comes first, setting broad parameters for what is acceptable. Within these parameters the individual landowner is autonomous. The parameters can change, too, and when they do, the Amish address questions of fairness differently than do non-Amish communities. When judging between harm to the community and restrictions on the individual, the Amish privilege the community. As a result, they have enacted their collective vision for the place where they hope to live for many generations. Through their encounters with a larger culture, and through the ecosystems they farmed and changed, the Amish point toward a community approach to private property. "That's the shared vision," avowed Rosanne Boyett, "what we have now—the wooded areas, the open spaces, the active farms, the small town." Yes, said Joel Swanson, "We're more alike than we often acknowledge."[72] Indeed, examining the Amish is to examine all of us.

PART 3

Negotiating the Past and Future Landscape

6

A Dam for New Times

Throughout the twentieth century, farmers along the Kickapoo River found their situation both a blessing and a curse. Catastrophic floods marked the years 1907, 1912, and 1917.[1] In 1935, after a respite of nearly twenty years, one of the most destructive floods on record raged the length of the Kickapoo Valley.[2] At that time, stretches of riparian forest ran sporadically along the river's edge, but for most of the way agricultural land—fields and pasture—spread outward on either side. The river passed by the village of La Farge in the township of Stark, just as it passed by half a dozen other villages. With 12½ inches of rain in a single night, the river swelled its banks. It swept away crops and animals and rushed through La Farge, damaging homes and businesses and submerging roads and bridges. "Waters of the Kickapoo . . . cut off La Farge, Vernon County, both by highway and railroad, from the outside world," announced the caption to an aerial photo published in the *Milwaukee Journal*.[3] "The residue left by the receeding [*sic*] water was slime and mud," described Grace Hocking. "Tracks of the railroad bed were left suspended in mid air."[4] For a time the economic fabric of the area unraveled and families had to make do however they could until roads reopened, buildings were fixed, livestock and equipment replaced, and the next year's crops safely harvested. A dreadful sense of anticipation seized Valley communities afterward. Everyone knew that the floods would return, but the maddening question became "when?" Soon after the 1935 flood, the Valley sent representatives to Washington, D.C., to secure federal help for flood control.[5] The delegation arrived at a propitious moment, for they were not the only people clamoring for action.

The nation was on the brink of a new era in flood control planning. As of 1935, Congress had not formed comprehensive plans for the Mississippi River basin, the upper portion of which included the Kickapoo Valley.[6] But Congress was enduring a flood of its own, inundated with proposals large and small for flood control projects throughout the Mississippi Valley.[7] At the same time, the U.S. Army Corps of Engineers was completing a study of all two hundred of the country's major river basins. When the Kickapoo Valley delegation arrived, Congress was awaiting the last few reports from the Corps.[8] In 1936, Congress pulled together all the studies and requests into one enormous national policy, the Flood Control Act of 1936.[9] Under this act Congress agreed to finance flood control projects in most American communities. It also gave the U.S. Army Corps of Engineers responsibility for the majority of federal projects. The Corps had not been a passive bystander to the legislation. Corps supporters had in fact initiated it, to the intense frustration of the U.S. Department of Agriculture.[10] As the nation's primary flood control agency, the Corps would now decide how local communities should carry out flood control, or more precisely, the Corps would now carry out flood control for them. The Flood Control Act of 1936 had extended the Corps's reach into almost

Tombstone on the terrace of the Rockton Bar: "In Memory of Those Who Sold Us down the Kickapoo River." (Courtesy of Michael Barrett)

every nook and cranny of the country. The Kickapoo Valley became one of those nooks when, in 1937, Congress authorized the Corps to make a preliminary survey of its river.[11]

In retrospect, the trip Valley residents made to Washington, D.C., marked a psychological turning point. It would give rise to a cultural origin story about private property (lost) and public property, about the federal government and local places, about land ownership and environmental protection. Stark takes us in a completely different historical and environmental direction from its companions on the landscape, Liberty and Clinton. In this chapter, Stark brings us closest to modern perceptions of property debates. In no small part its history is the history of grievances in the making—grievances that always shout out for attention in any discussion on public land policy. Later chapters will hush the din and listen for other voices, human and nonhuman, to challenge and enrich Stark's

Wednesday, August 7, 1935, *Milwaukee Journal* article on the Kickapoo River flood that submerged much of La Farge. "Bernard Woods, 4, of La Farge got out of his home safely by boat," reads the caption under the boy, "but it was discovered afterward that his pup had been left in the house. Bernard's father, Hubert, waded back to the rescue."

seemingly familiar narrative. In the 1930s, Kickapoo Valley communities had hoped to reshape their environment through a new relationship with the federal government. They never imagined how well they would succeed. What emerged along the Kickapoo River would be unbelievably different from their vision when they sought federal aid in the name of their crops, their livelihoods, and their communities.

Residents thought their continuance on the land was at stake when the Corps of Engineers took its first look at the Kickapoo River. The Corps seemed a godsend, and better yet, it did not insist on any of the uncomfortable trade-offs that the Soil Conservation Service had begun negotiating with area landowners at the same time (the evolution of which I traced in the first chapter). For the Corps, the central task was not to change how people in the Valley used their land. The task was to change the Kickapoo River and its tributaries to accommodate those land uses. After all, the Corps was an organization of engineers. It prided itself on a tradition that united engineering and construction with physical science, and it regarded itself as the nation's premier expert on river dynamics. According to one historian of the Corps, "Army waterway science was order and classification. Rational and precise, it spelled out the theory or natural laws that reduced river construction to a regimen of standardized steps."[12] Flooding along the Kickapoo River presented the Corps with what it considered a standard engineering problem, one it was fully equipped to solve.

Not everyone agreed that the Corps's approach to water projects was appropriate in places like the Kickapoo Valley. Gilbert White, now considered one of the nation's foremost geographers, became renowned for his scholarship on floodplains. In the 1940s he was a participant in national debates over water policy, and he served alongside officers of the Corps on a number of prominent presidential and congressional committees.[13] Unanticipated problems from flood control had come to the fore of their deliberations. This "was a time when many of the technical people in federal agencies and many state people were gravely concerned about the way in which small reservoir projects were being built around the country," White said. "The files were full of horror stories of reservoirs that leaked, dams that failed, dams that didn't serve their purpose, drainage projects that destroyed large areas of wildlife habitat without proportionate gains in economic production."[14]

White proposed beginning any potential project with a different set of questions than those the Corps usually asked. Rather than asking how a project might prevent flood damage, the alternative question White posed had to do with the best use of the floodplain. White suggested that, rather than establishing the dollar value of single crops, planners should examine larger patterns of land use throughout an entire community. White, the Corps, and many others at the time were arguing the merits of competing paradigms of flood management. The Corps's paradigm emphasized social liabilities, while White's emphasized social and environmental values. The former assumed a linear form during the planning process, while the latter laid out an array of alternatives for any one project, then a still wider array of environmental and social consequences for each alternative.[15] For years to come the Corps would continue along a linear path to flood control. But White's ideas would eventually prove prescient, and in the Kickapoo Valley circumstances would compel a new generation of officers to return to White's basic questions about land use.

Valley communities suffered a quick letdown in their hopes for flood control. Although the Corps was a public works agency, it was also a military organization whose overriding mission was to support the nation's defense systems.[16] The Corps's work in the Kickapoo Valley had barely started before World War II and the Korean War interrupted it. The Kickapoo Valley endured two more catastrophic floods in the interim, one in 1951 and another in 1956.[17] In 1962, the Corps at last unveiled a proposal to build a modest earthen dam above the village of La Farge, filling an 800-acre reservoir, and to make channel improvements farther downstream.[18] Had the Corps implemented this proposal, it would have fulfilled its initial objectives for the Kickapoo River. But within a few years agency engineers had changed their plans. They formulated new blueprints for a massive dam 103 feet high.[19] A more impressive La Farge Lake would sprawl twelve miles behind the dam.

At first glance such a radical change might not make sense. For decades Valley communities had clamored for flood control, not for a huge reservoir submerging more farmland than floods had ever inundated in a rainy season. Nor had any of the Corps's earlier reports discussed a project on this scale. The Corps's vision of water planning had evolved, though not in the way Gilbert White had once advocated. At the turn of the twentieth century, the Corps had strongly resisted multiple-purpose projects, and it had frowned on reservoirs.[20] It had resisted, for instance, multipurpose reservoirs for flood control and hydropower, or for hydropower and recreation. The Corps ultimately lost that debate in Congress. But in losing, its influence would be greatly enhanced in the future, reaching its peak in the 1960s, the time when plans for the Kickapoo Valley were finally coming to fruition. The Corps's shift of emphasis reflected a governmentwide response to a boom in recreation after World War II. By the mid-1960s, Corps priorities no longer centered on flood control. Public recreation now dominated its agenda. In the Kickapoo Valley, flood control became a secondary aim.

The ways in which the Corps made recreation its priority depended on the region of the country. The Army Corps of Engineers had a hierarchical chain of command, but where individual projects were concerned the Corps was one of the nation's most decentralized bureaucracies.[21] Its smallest regional units, called districts, often wielded the greatest amount of influence because they were the ones that studied a place, formulated a plan, and implemented a project. The St. Paul District, based in St. Paul, Minnesota, was the office that analyzed the Kickapoo River in 1938.[22] It was this office that developed flood control plans for the river; it was this office that changed plans to accommodate a large dam; and it was this office that would acquire land, contract for work, communicate with Valley communities, deal with politicians and the press, and carry out any additional task needed to build the La Farge dam and every other Corps project falling within its regional boundaries—a six-state area. Rather than responding to a chain of command that impressed on subordinates the importance of recreation, the districts were helping to shape and direct the goal.

The La Farge dam had presented the St. Paul District with an ideal opportunity to bolster its new master plan for recreation.[23] Justifying a bigger project was easy. The Valley's spectacular scenery would undoubtedly attract tourists. The whole region was impoverished, so it could use the economic stimulus from tourism. Valley communities had once talked of taming the Kickapoo River. Now the Corps convinced them that a dam could solve much larger economic problems.[24] Local boosters consented to the Corps's high price for economic development: 8,500 acres of land, over half of that from the township of Stark.

Many public controversies involving the La Farge dam were about to come to the fore. Notably, the condemnation and purchase of thousands of acres of private property was not one of them. A no-nonsense brochure, *Questions and Answers Concerning the Acquisition of Your Real Estate by the Government,* created little stir in the Kickapoo Valley when the Corps distributed it in 1968.[25] "It is recognized that various, and often conflicting rumors may come to your attention regarding the acquisition of your property," the Corps said. "You may be sure, however, that you will be

U.S. Army Corps Land
Stark Township, 1995

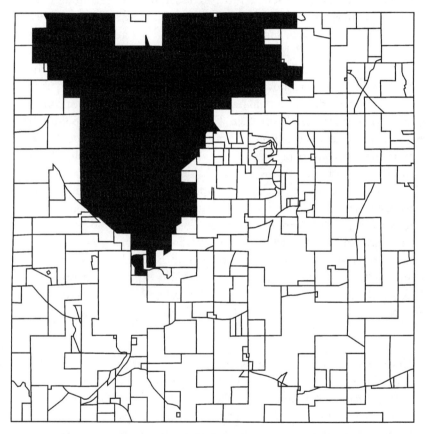

Figure 13. U.S. Army Corps of Engineers land in the township of Stark. These new boundaries would become contested in ways neither local people nor the Corps nor national politicians could have imagined when the land first changed hands in the late 1960s.

officially notified at the earliest possible date when action is to be taken on your particular ownership."[26]

In 1969, the Corps started acquiring land in Stark. Proceeding upstream, the federal government soon became the township's, and the Kickapoo Valley's, largest landowner. "When the Corps of Engineers came in here they literally treated us as a bunch of dumb hillbillies who didn't know what we had," said Brian Turner, whose father Clifford lost his farm to the dam and was one of the few to protest condemnation. "Dad fought to the last straw. He wasn't against it (condemnation) because of the dam, he was against it because it put him out of business."[27] But any anger or grief individual landowners felt at their loss was apparently their own affair.

That the Corps could attract so little negative comment about this— perhaps its most overt show of bureaucratic authority and power—is a testimony to the influence it held nationally and locally. But lack of comment does not mean lack of significance. The Corps has said little in public about the powers of condemnation and purchase it has wielded since the 1930s. It has preferred to focus on its technical expertise, with which it has performed feats of engineering. Yet the Corps became highly proficient in real estate, so much so that by the 1960s it had become the military's chief real estate agent.[28] Contemporary debates over federal control of land have rarely featured the Corps of Engineers. The Bureau of Land Management, the National Park Service, and the U.S. Forest Service have always been more prominent. Nonetheless, you would be hard-pressed to identify another agency that has asserted its authority to condemn private land as widely and as regularly as has the Corps.[29] To provide some measure of what the incremental accumulation of land can accomplish, by 1991 the Corps owned 24 million acres.[30]

Until 1970 the La Farge dam seemed to be perpetually in the works. At this moment, when construction of the La Farge dam was finally about to begin, three pivotal events took place. First, the National Environmental Policy Act of 1969 went into effect. Second, Brigadier General Ernest Graves arrived in Chicago as the new division chief for the Corps's North Central Division. And third, diverse groups joined forces to fight the La Farge dam. Together these events would shift the slow trajectory of the La Farge dam.

When Congress passed the National Environmental Policy Act of 1969, it immersed itself in the political tidal wave of the times.[31] NEPA, as most people called it, became the apex of like-minded legislation establishing new safeguards for the country's air, water, land, and wildlife.[32] Its scope was grand: "To declare a national policy which will encourage productive and enjoyable harmony between man and his environment; to promote efforts which will prevent or eliminate damage to the environment and biosphere and stimulate the health and welfare of man; to enrich the understanding of ecological systems and natural resources important to the Nation; and to establish a Council on Environmental Quality."[33] The legislation had an almost instantaneous effect on the Corps of Engineers. Hereinafter, the law said, all federal agencies must include a "detailed statement" on any action "significantly affecting the quality of the human environment."[34] Congress had instituted the environmental impact statement. For any Corps activity that might alter the environment (presumably all of them), the law now required a statement specifying not only the environmental impacts and adverse effects the project would have, but also alternatives to the proposal.[35] This brought the Corps full circle back to the paradigm that Gilbert White had proposed almost thirty years earlier. In Washington the Corps adjusted its organizational procedures to conform to NEPA, while in Minnesota the St. Paul District made hasty plans to put together an environmental impact statement for the La Farge dam.[36]

Coincident with NEPA was Brigadier General Graves's new appointment as division engineer of the North Central Division. His job description made him responsible for all Corps activities in the division's twelve-state region and—very importantly here—he oversaw the work of the St. Paul District. Historian Todd Shallat noted that the Corps of Engineers had always been rooted in national power structures and local communities.[37] If so, Brigadier General Graves balanced on the axis between these poles, one being the corridors of Washington, D.C., the other small-town communities like Stark, Wisconsin. With a foot in both worlds, Graves had the authority to mediate between them or to intervene outright as the circumstances demanded. He stood in a unique place from which to survey both NEPA and the La Farge dam.

Graves had entered what he called a "post-NEPA" world, which meant above all else "coming to terms with the environmental requirements."[38] Completing a draft environmental impact statement for the La Farge dam presented the North Central Division (and the St. Paul District) with one of its first opportunities to apply NEPA, to test the law's limits, and to adapt to a new environmental era. This last was especially important to Graves because, as he recalled, "The Corps was probably under heavier attack in the North Central Division than in any other at that particular time." By way of explanation he noted that "the environmental movement was more active up in that part of the world. . . . Minnesota, Wisconsin—Michigan, also."[39] For Graves the draft environmental impact statement (EIS) carried good and bad news.

The draft EIS conveyed the inexperience of its authors. These were people steeped in engineering methods trying, perhaps for the first time, to carry out the work of social scientists, biologists, and ecologists. From this vulnerable position they attracted some polite derision from fellow agencies. "The data on fish and wildlife biology is qualitatively weak," said the Fish and Wildlife Service in its comment on the draft, and furthermore, "we seriously question the implications that conifers give off 'noxious emissions into the air.'"[40] The Bureau of Outdoor Recreation found fault with a section of the draft that began: "Most of the flood plain and bluffs are non-productive except for some timber."[41] "This statement," scolded the bureau, "does not acknowledge the value of these and associated resources as wildlife habitats, recreational areas, and complementing features of the valley landscape." More troubling was the bureau's sense that "the draft statement could be interpreted as an attempt to justify the project, rather than objectively discuss the environmental effect."[42] Significantly, none of these federal agencies opposed the La Farge dam project. The tenor of their letters suggested that, like the Corps, they, too, were not entirely sure of their role. Did the law permit them to interrogate a whole project, in effect giving them a veto over Corps's projects, or only to comment on particulars? With the La Farge dam they appeared to decide on the latter, becoming strict editors who scrutinized every line of the statement but accepted the overall premise and inevitability of the project.

Though these agencies offered no real opposition to the La Farge dam, their comments on the draft EIS did not bode entirely well for the Corps. From Brigadier General Graves's perspective, they were likely the first sign of a fundamental problem the Corps would have with NEPA. Complexity is the key concept here, and for Graves, finding any kind of social or environmental order in a tangled web of alternatives and outcomes could easily paralyze the planning process. "If you had a simpler idea," he explained, "for instance, if it was a flood, you went out and built a flood wall or channelized the river or built a dam—you could do it. But when you had to consider everything that happened as a result of this construction, the environment was just too complex."[43] To many who served in the Corps during those first years post-NEPA, complexity seemed awfully close to chaos. "[Y]ou could study for a thousand years and you wouldn't get it right," Graves concluded. "It's beyond man to divine."[44]

A growing group of people opposed to the La Farge dam could not have disagreed more. The John Muir Chapter of the Sierra Club had recently pulled together environmentalists, university scientists, a few Valley residents, and people from around the state who simply enjoyed canoeing the Kickapoo River, all united by their opposition to the La Farge dam. With little time to spare, the coalition moved into action. Sierra Club chapters were fighting Corps projects around the country, and for this reason the Sierra Club eventually came to symbolize an omnipresent adversary, "the environmentalists." "What groups caused you the most trouble?" an interviewer asked Graves. "The Sierra Club was the most aggressive group," he replied. "They had a good organization, and they were everywhere, helping to organize the people that were opposed to these projects."[45]

Where Graves saw murky waters and confusion emerging out of NEPA, the environmental coalition saw clearly what would be lost under the waters of La Farge Lake. The area held unique biological features, including rare

By the 1970s, the Kickapoo River had become a prime destination for canoeing. Along with the Sierra Club and some university scientists, recreationalists were vociferous in their opposition to the La Farge dam. (Courtesy of Wolfgang Hoffmann)

plants endemic to the Driftless Area—the arctic primrose, the northern monkshood, and sullivantia. Although these plants would be flooded, the draft EIS said nothing about them. A number of priceless archeological sites lay within the property's boundaries—prehistoric campsites, burial mounds, rock shelters, and petroglyphs. The Corps had done no research on water quality, a seemingly important consideration for a large man-made lake. What's more, critics asserted, the Corps had not seriously considered alternatives to the dam, a reservation echoed in a few of the agency comments as well. To dam opponents, the Corps's problem was not the complex analyses that NEPA required of it (complexity was a virtue, not a fault). The problem was that the Corps did not have the institutional capacity to prepare adequate environmental impact statements, or the institutional will to deviate from a linear path of planning.[46]

Marshalling its arguments, the Sierra Club filed two consecutive lawsuits to halt the dam in 1971 and 1972. The Corps's draft environmental impact statement was inadequate, the group claimed. District Court Judge James E. Doyle (father of Governor Jim Doyle) dismissed both suits. The Sierra Club lost again on appeal.[47] As far as the federal courts were concerned, the Corps had complied with NEPA.

The courtroom was not the only public arena available to the Sierra Club. Using the Corps's own lack of data against it, the group convinced Governor Patrick Lucey to request a halt to the dam. In response, Brigadier General Graves as well as St. Paul District Engineer Major General Charles McGinnis traveled to Madison to meet with Governor Lucey. Reminding the governor of the project's popular support, they suggested a short public review of the issues. Governor Lucey, "who had sort of gotten his neck out a little bit on this," according to Graves, agreed to the idea.[48] The governor appointed a committee of local Valley residents and environmentalists, thereby setting up a local-environmentalist dichotomy that has persisted in the Valley to the present, even when the environmentalists are local too. Both sides of the committee made their case at the public meeting. Graves and Valley residents persuaded Governor Lucey of the project's merits. Saying he would "give somewhat more weight to those directly involved than those with peripheral interests," the governor gave his blessing to the project.[49] Graves later recalled that Governor Lucey "had been tremendously impressed with the responsiveness of the Corps and McGinnis and myself and with the way we had come in and done the review."[50] Graves seemed pleased that the governor thought they had shown great "responsiveness and integrity."[51]

On August 13, 1971, a beautiful day by all accounts, the Corps of Engineers broke ground for the La Farge dam. The St. Paul District had planned a big event and was not disappointed in the turnout. Five hundred people came to celebrate. Wisconsin's lieutenant governor made a speech, as did the region's U.S. congressman and also new District Engineer Colonel Rodney Cox, who had just replaced McGinnis in the St. Paul District. Afterward bulldozers began stripping dirt and moving rocks. Very soon bedrock would stand exposed on what was to be the dam's left abutment.[52]

Work in Stark had begun, but the Corps had not yet completed its environmental impact statement. The Corps had won congressional authorization for the dam years before, in 1962, so it was violating no law. Yet this was an odd parallel track—work advancing side by side with research potentially critical of that work. In a pre-NEPA world, the Corps would have completed the dam with no further ado. Post-NEPA, however, the Corps could continue construction, but it also had to complete the EIS.

Before submitting the final EIS to the Council on Environment Quality, which Congress had established to oversee compliance with NEPA, the Corps was required to hold public hearings and respond to public comment. This comment period formed the basis of new relationships between the Corps and other agencies and also between the Corps and its critics. When, a few months after construction had started, the St. Paul District asked the Sierra Club for review and comment on the next iteration of its environmental impact statement, board member Robert W. Smith replied as follows: "If there was the slightest indication that the Corps was attempting in good faith to comply with NEPA, we would respond. . . . Obviously the Corps' 'mind' has been made up and it certainly isn't going to be changed by the 'facts' or by whatever is thrown together under the title of 'Environmental Statement.'"[53] The Sierra Club had questioned the Corps's professionalism in the strongest possible language.

Colonel Rodney Cox immediately wrote back to Smith. "I am most disturbed," he said, "that you feel that your reply to our requested comments would only be 'an exercise in futility' and for this reason I feel a straightforward response on my part might solicit your most needed, and I am sure, most helpful comments." The aims of the environmental impact statement, Cox explained, "are to introduce our thoughts to our new partners and to help us get to know them." (The Sierra Club would have disagreed that this was the aim of an environmental impact statement, and so, most likely, would the Council on Environmental Quality.) The Corps had entered a learning process, Cox continued, the reasons being "both because of the recent enactment of NEPA and also because traditionally in the United States, development of the Nation's resources has been left to the professionals." Perhaps unaware that his tone had become condescending, Cox nonetheless acknowledged a new day. "We recognize that in recent years there has been a marked change in public attitude. The people of the United States have taken an increased interest in project planning and now the man in the street wants to take part in the determination of how his resources are being used, and in many cases his attitude has been militant." Getting to the crux of the matter: "You say that our mind has been made up and is certainly not going to be changed by the facts. I can only say sir, that you have read our mind incorrectly."[54] Despite Colonel Cox's lengthy attempt to reach out to the Sierra Club, the group had reason to be cynical about the St. Paul District's open-mindedness.

Together, NEPA and opponents of the dam revealed a dissonance within the Corps. On the one hand, the Corps viewed itself as a dispassionate group of experts whose purpose was to serve the country. "We are not advocates," Brigadier General Graves told a reporter in 1971.[55] "The civil works program was the Corps of Engineers out there doing for the citizens of the United States what they wanted to be done," Graves continued to insist more than twenty-five years later. To be at odds with the public was "the antithesis of the philosophy of the civil works program."[56] On the other hand, Corps personnel were not neutral toward their projects; they were as zealous as any of their opponents. As Graves's intercession with Governor Lucey made clear, the Corps aggressively shaped and adapted to its political milieu. "Here they had been," he explained, referring to the St. Paul District, "working away on these things three, four, five, six, seven, even ten years, and they came up with their report as to what was to be done and the citizens all got up and said, 'We don't want it done.'"[57] NEPA and the La Farge dam made it almost impossible for the Corps to assert even to itself that it stood outside the fray—that planning and project implementation were neutral exercises in decision making.[58]

In Washington, D.C., Chief of Engineers Lieutenant General Frederick Clarke was coping with the same dissonance. In Washington as in Stark, NEPA was prodding the Corps toward new relationships with its environmental opponents. In Washington as in Stark, the Corps continued to vet and promote controversial projects. Clarke debated how to approach

NEPA. As head of the organization, his choices would set an important tone for Corps divisions and districts. He decided to appoint an Environmental Advisory Board. The board would try but fail to influence the La Farge dam project. Conversely, the La Farge dam would intrude on the relationship General Clarke hoped to establish with his new board. So, then, have local events reconfigured the national context in which they occurred, in this case national-level policy debates over flood control, river development, and environmental protection.

In appointing an Environmental Advisory Board, Lieutenant General Clarke aspired to make the Corps the most forward-looking of all federal institutions. He selected renowned leaders in the environmental movement to serve on the board, among others Roland Clement, ecologist and vice president of the National Audubon Society, and Harold Gilliam, a well-known environmental reporter. Charles Stoddard, former director of the Bureau of Land Management, became the board's first chairman. "There were many people in our organization who thought I was completely crazy—sort of inviting the enemy into the camp," Clarke remembered. Board members were equally leery of their new role on the inside. The Corps's first internal environmental policy, its *Environmental Guidelines,* confirmed doubts all round.[59] The guidelines did make environmental preservation, conservation, and enhancement part of the Corps's mission.[60] They also included public participation and environmental analysis in the planning process. Even so, the Environmental Advisory Board thought they were vague rather than explicit, reactive to controversy rather than proactive during planning, and tending toward project advocacy rather than objectivity. Overall, wrote Stoddard, "It is no wonder that many of these conservationists have felt forced to resort to political activism or even litigation."[61]

Chairman Stoddard became highly critical of the La Farge dam when Governor Lucey's public review came to his attention. In Stoddard's words, Brigadier General Graves had put the governor "on the political spot by encouraging further pressure for construction from the local people with the most to gain."[62] He saw a clear conflict of interest in the St. Paul District's actions. Over time he became ever more frustrated with the decentralized way the Corps made decisions about projects like the La Farge dam. Early in his tenure, Stoddard had proposed that the Environmental Advisory Board have a role in the planning process by reviewing documents and making recommendations on controversial projects. The La Farge dam was one project that Stoddard wanted the board to review.

But General Clarke never intended the board to participate in actual Corps decisions. According to General Graves's recollections, Corps leaders from Clarke onward became "very skillful" in steering the board away from specific projects and toward general policy.[63]

Stoddard took away a larger lesson from the exchange over the La Farge dam. "The time has come," he declared, "for a transfer of this civilian function from a para-military one and for separating planning from construction in the same agency."[64] Decades later Stoddard would be vindicated. In 2000, a federal investigation would conclude that the Corps had an "institutional bias" toward large construction projects, to the point that it put heavy pressure on its own staff to justify projects, to get to "Yes," even by manipulating economic and environmental data.[65]

To be fair to Clarke and Graves (who were not implicated in the future scandal), they had accepted environmental opponents as part of the new political landscape. Clarke had created the Environmental Advisory Board in the first place. Likewise, Graves never denied the Sierra Club, Charles Stoddard, or other like-minded critics their point of view, even conceding later that, "Whether the projects were good or bad is a difficult judgment to make because it depends on what your goals are for a particular area."[66] All the same, the St. Paul District, the North Central Division, and Brigadier General Graves himself made up a quietly passionate group of advocates, though all would have denied the very idea of advocacy. They might have entered a new era, but the earlier era still held sway. The Corps at every level remained unambiguously in favor of the La Farge dam whatever the environmental questions their environmental impact statements might raise along the way.

The St. Paul District was preparing to build the dam's intake tower, outlet works, and spillways while also preparing its final environmental impact statement for the Council on Environmental Quality. How the council responded to the report would help decide NEPA's larger impact on the Corps. With a favorable review, the Corps would have successfully assimilated NEPA into its mode of planning and implementing projects. A negative review might do more than call the La Farge dam into question; it could force the Corps to reconsider myriad other projects. Rather than assimilating a new environmental culture into its own professional culture of civil works, the Corps would face fundamental changes. One sign that the St. Paul District felt some anxiety is that it waited three months after completing the EIS to submit it to the Council on Environmental Quality.[67]

Reading the report, one can see the fine line the St. Paul District walked: on the one side carrying out a respectable EIS, on the other doing as little harm as possible to its project. With each new draft, the Corps's analysis had become more sophisticated. By the final version, the St. Paul District had examined an array of alternatives to the dam, including the option of no action. The report bluntly stated the dam's impact on ecosystems, fisheries, and wildlife. It anticipated, for example, "severe adverse impacts, even possible extermination, of unique cliff vegetation."[68] (The Endangered Species Act was one year in the future, so the loss of rare plants would not in itself have been a barrier to the dam.) The district adopted its lightest touch on the topic of the future reservoir. Here is what the St. Paul District said about La Farge Lake: "Present levels of nitrogen and phosphorus in the Kickapoo River are sufficient to permit algal blooms in a standing water body such as the proposed impoundment." Moving farther down the same section: "Chemical fertilizers which are used on farms in the basin also result in some nitrogen and phosphorus pollution." A few sentences later: "At current rates of erosion and sedimentation, La Farge Lake would also trap an estimated 100 acre-feet of silt."[69] Finally, fifteen pages later in a different chapter: "Siltation is expected to be a concern in the upper end of the reservoir due to the high silt load carried by the Kickapoo River."[70] Buried in the report as they were, these sentences brushed over what some people might have considered important questions: What will the recreational lake look like in the future? (Clear? Swimmable? Like pea soup from algae blooms? Like a mud pit in places from sediment loading?) What will the lake be in the future, biologically speaking? (Decent habitat for game fish? A new stop on the migration routes of water fowl? A eutrophic lake so loaded with nitrogen and phosphorus that weeds will choke out many other living organisms?) With four scattered sentences, the final environmental impact statement raised a bright red flag over the La Farge dam—water quality.

The statement's short summary preceding the report did not mention water quality as one of the dam's "environmental impacts" or "adverse environmental effects." Nor did the longer document list water quality as one of the "adverse environmental effects which cannot be avoided should the project be implemented." The final EIS only hinted that water quality in La Farge Lake might deteriorate over some unstated period. The report asked no questions beforehand and provided no answers afterward. The EIS did aver that "improved sewage treatment . . . would contribute to improving the water quality in the reservoir" and also that "the

The U.S. Army Corps of Engineers eventually documented the ecological impacts of the La Farge dam, which would have flooded rare and endemic cliff-dwelling plants. (Courtesy of Wolfgang Hoffmann)

acquisition of project lands is expected to remove approximately 5,000 acres from agricultural production and Soil Conservation Service personnel are continually promoting improved land management in the area."[71] These, however, did not make up an analysis so much as an insinuation that the dam's effects might possibly be mitigated, although not by the Corps. The Corps had made little of the dam's greatest weakness, and what an Achilles heel it was.

The Council on Environmental Quality and the Environmental Protection Agency castigated the Corps's environmental impact statement.[72] Both recommended that the Corps halt work on the dam altogether pending further study of water quality in the reservoir. Roland Clement, Stoddard's successor as chairman of the Environmental Advisory Board, prodded the Corps to improve its environmental impact statements.[73] Governor Lucey demanded another intensive review of the dam with an explicit focus on water quality. "Lucey was a very charming guy, but he wasn't resolute," said Graves of the turnaround, though plainly there was more substance behind the governor's call than fickleness.[74] Still testing the limits of NEPA, the Corps did not halt construction, but neither could it ignore the governor. Governor Lucey ensured that the uncomfortable parallel tracks of construction and study would continue.

Almost two years earlier, Brigadier General Graves had suggested that the governor form a committee to review the La Farge dam. Now the St. Paul District engineer tried a similar tack, proposing a "partnership team" of local Valley residents, environmentalists, state agencies, and the governor's office. Once more Governor Lucey agreed, but this time he asked for an independent scientific study of the project. Backed into a corner, the St. Paul District acquiesced. It commissioned a study from a group of scientists in the Institute for Environmental Studies at the University of Wisconsin–Madison.[75] Their research confirmed dam opponents' worst fears: sediment would fast fill many areas of the new lake, while nitrogen and phosphorus would make it highly eutrophic. The Institute's report left no hope for a technological solution either, showing that even under the strictest land-use controls and with the most advanced sewage treatment technology, the lake would become polluted in a short time. The economic ramifications of the report were equally severe. Given the high cost of limiting nutrient flows, along with the low economic return from a polluted lake, alternatives to the dam were more feasible. At length the project fell short in the Corps's own economic cost-benefit analyses.[76] While the scientists involved in the water quality study stated clearly in their report that, "We were not charged with making recommendations about whether or not the dam should be built," they had little need to take a stand. Their findings suggested such serious shortcomings with the La Farge dam that almost everyone concerned recognized the implications.[77]

During this time, Valley communities had watched with satisfaction as the dam advanced foot by foot in Stark. The Corps had relocated Wisconsin state highways 131 and 33 out of the project area, a costly endeavor at nearly $11 million. It had nearly finished the outlet works, which consisted of a 110-foot-high intake tower, an energy dissipator, and a stilling basin.[78] Lawsuits, environmental impact studies, correspondence between the Corps and the Council on Environmental Quality, all were moving in tandem with the physical work of the project, but a finished dam was a finished dam. Then, ominously, the Corps canceled an important contract for one of the next phases of construction.[79] The Corps appeared to be awaiting the fallout from the university study on water quality before going any further. The report had cast a shadow over the future lake.

Valley people did not sit still for this sudden turn of events. Opposition to the La Farge dam came from outsiders, residents fumed. "It took the grit of the early pioneers to come to this vast wilderness and make the Kickapoo valley what it is today and their descendents have enough of the fighting blood in their veins to not let it go back to the wilderness again," said local author Grace Hocking.[80] They demanded support from politicians. They wrote letters to the editor in local and regional newspapers. They packed every meeting on the dam's status. They even created a folk tradition around the project, thus continuing a long local literary history of lamenting hard times with poetry. The high stakes here warranted homage, so poet Virgil Munns rose to the occasion with "The Ballad of the Kickapoo."[81]

It seems they've wrote a song,
about every thing on earth.
The joys and sorrows of time,
Ever since it's birth.

Now comes a song so sad,
it touches me and you.
How some folks are a fuden,
over damming the Kickapoo.

Well son, I lived downstream
from that famous place.
I wish you'd seen my crops
wash away in disgrace.

I've buried your dead cattle,
I've burned your pretty trees,
I scrubbed your mud and refuse
on cold and aching knees.

And I ain't done no fuden,
My wishes are so few
I wish they would just finish
Daming the Kickapoo.

We took your waste and water,
the hard times that they spew
Just wanting for a dam
across the Kickapoo.

You've wash my sock en shoes
away from me too.
I think I'll join the fuden
for daming the Kick-a-poo.

It would be such a joy,
known by very few,
to fish behind the dam,
across the Kick-a-poo.

Valley residents took particular exception to what they considered academic interference in their lives. Robert P. Vosen hammered the point in a letter to the Corps: "We believe it boils down to a matter of prodection of life, limb, and property from flooding," he began. "This is what our forefathers went to Washington in 1938 to secure. Since that time we have been studied and muddied, assessed and recessed, charted and graphed, reviewed, halled into court by by-law and in-law, held trial by court and newspapers, delayed and relayed by wars, and during all of this time our crops are being flooded, our fences washed out, our cattle drown, our tobacco wash away. While someone says 'lets study the solution some more.' Amen."[82]

With palpable anger on all sides, powerful Wisconsin politicians were caught in a vice. First there was Governor Lucey, who had questioned the dam, then approved it, and then questioned it again. The environmental community was one of his strongest allies, and he was not alone. There was also Wisconsin Senator Gaylord Nelson, a prominent environmentalist best known as one of the founders of Earth Day in 1970.[83] Senator Nelson had been the governor of Wisconsin from 1959 to 1963, a time when he had personally reviewed and approved the Corps's plans for flood control along the Kickapoo River.[84] Finally, there was Wisconsin Senator William Proxmire, who was fast acquiring a national reputation for scrutinizing the financial logic of congressional appropriations. Proxmire had made himself a foe to many federal "pork-barrel" projects, which he would soon mock with annual "Golden Fleece Awards."[85] Like Lucey and Nelson, Senator Proxmire had once been in favor of the La Farge dam, even writing a supportive letter to Governor Nelson many years before.[86] That a single civil works project in an obscure part of the Upper Midwest could drag on so long with so many twists and turns along the way must have amazed even these savvy politicians. In the early 1960s, the La Farge dam had suggested little more than a good-faith effort by the Corps to control floods. In the late 1960s, it had appeared to be a popular and innocuous regional development scheme. By the mid-1970s, the La Farge dam had become one of the Corps's most controversial projects nationally—and one of Wisconsin's most popular projects locally.

The three could not escape the project's history, but that history tugged in opposite directions. For Governor Lucey and Senator Nelson, a hard decision became easier when the Council on Environmental Quality and the Environmental Protection Agency each officially demanded that the Corps halt work on the dam.[87] The environmental evidence against the project was now overwhelming. Senator Proxmire's misgivings did not involve the environment per se, so he took a little longer to make up his mind. For him two facts came to dwarf the others: the project's costs had tripled, while the estimated economic benefits to Valley communities had plummeted. In 1975, Governor Lucey and Senators Nelson and Proxmire formally withdrew their support for the La Farge dam.[88]

Being no coward, Senator Proxmire traveled to La Farge to announce his decision. Commiserating with the audience, he said to them, "in spite of the overwhelming support of the people who have lived with this project and dreamed of this project for years and count on this project for their salvation, I must oppose the project."[89] Offering less compassion in return, local residents burned Senator Proxmire in effigy, then drove the corpse to its burial via a manure spreader. A sign on the manure spreader read, "Our dam was locked in limbo, our bridge ain't safe to walk, cause Foxy Proxy took our dough and gave it to New Yawk."[90] The Corps's response was drier in tone but just as dogged in intent. It recommended in yet another report that "the United States undertake the completion of the partially constructed La Farge Dam as presently designed in the interest of flood damage reduction."[91]

Though the Corps had long refused to halt the La Farge dam project, environmental, political, and economic pressures became irresistible. At Senator Proxmire's behest in November of 1975, the Senate Subcommittee on Public Works eliminated funding for the project.[92] Three-fourths of the way along and only a thousand feet left to go, the Corps left the dam unfinished—midstream in the Kickapoo River. This was a significant moment in the history of the Corps, which had never before stopped construction of a dam on environmental grounds. "I trust that the Activists

La Farge dam intake tower. Observe the nearly completed dam to the left of the tower. (Courtesy of Wolfgang Hoffmann)

and the DNR and the Institute for Propaganda are proud of their work of destruction," wrote one Valley resident bitterly. "There it stands, a monument to negativism. . . . Ten-thousand acres of nothing stand as a monument to the negatives."[93] And so it still stands today. The dam's concrete intake tower rises tall like a sentinel on the Kickapoo River, a tomb that marks the passing of a community, or a monument to an environmental nightmare averted.[94]

Ten years later and by then retired, Lieutenant General Graves mused on the dam. "It's hard to say about a project like La Farge," he said. "I think it was neither as good as some people claimed, nor was it as bad as others said."[95] In Stark the sentiment was not so cool or pensive. The dam's demise provoked a local fury that remained hot through the 1990s. Over time anger coalesced around specific histories. First were the property histories some residents held dear as former owners of the now-public land that was supposed to have been a nice lake. Second was the township's recent history with the federal government. Local residents were always ready with the facts: after the Corps had acquired land for the dam, Stark had lost 60 percent of its population. The Corps had moved, torn down, or burned all the buildings on the site, obliterating the little village of Seeleysburg. (It razed the community's heritage too.) In a fiscal blow, the federal government paid no property taxes on the Corps land. (Once their land.) A spate of new academic studies proposing economic development could not compensate or placate them for their losses.[96] As they saw it, academics continued to benefit professionally from their plight, just like the ones who did the water quality study had benefited. (By the way, they still remember their names.) There were clear winners in all this—environmentalists, canoeists, politicians, university researchers, the state of Wisconsin, and the federal government. And there were unmistakable losers—themselves.

In 1978, the Kickapoo Valley experienced the worst flood in its recorded history. While water surged through village streets, "people in the valley were cursing the politicians who have long fought in stopping the La Farge dam project," reported the *La Farge Epitaph*.[97] "In memory of those who sold us down the Kickapoo River," recapitulated the tombstone standing on the patio of the Rockton Bar.

Each spillover from the dam reinforced a mood of decline. Regret for the past and fears for the future; the mood made some Valley residents promising recruits to the property rights and militia movements new to

Wisconsin in the early 1980s. The sequence of events and rhetoric that make up the story of the La Farge dam is reminiscent of many rural places. The federal government (or just as often, environmentalists) against local people has become a shorthand description for rural conflicts and changes of many sorts. It has also become a default narrative for the way people have come to understand their relationship to private and public land. But in Stark, what exactly is the narrative about? In a strange way, a prominent part of Stark's history is the tale of what did not happen. The La Farge dam did not get built, although artifacts of the project remain. A large lake did not submerge fields or pastures or rare plants that cling tenaciously to sandstone cliffs. The La Farge dam, however, did mark a place and a moment when two eras collided: the period following the Flood Control Act of 1936, when water planning by the Army Corps of Engineers became national policy, and the period following the National Environmental Policy Act of 1969, when environmental protection became national policy. What did not happen in Stark turned out to be a vitally important event.

Ruins of an old springhouse on the U.S. Army Corps of Engineers land. The Corps tore down buildings on the site in anticipation of the La Farge dam. (Lynne Heasley)

7

Deer Unlimited

In 1979, an editor for the *La Farge Epitaph* made verbal war on deer hunters. "The deer season has come and gone," he stated flatly. "The red shirts, the four wheel drives, the vans, no longer creep by my farm with rifles ready and eyeballs staring at the hillsides. Strangers, people from God knows where, keeping me pinned down beneath my rock as the boom-boom-boom of high powered rifles blast all around for nine tedious days." The annual deer hunt was a fact of rural life, yet remarkably here was a local farmer questioning the ritual. "Why must I wear a blaze orange jacket and shiver in abject fear as I journey out to spread a load of cow poop on my rocky acres?" he asked. "Where in the hell were those trespassers and hillside scanners when it was tax paying time?"[1]

Property boundaries are essential but not sufficient for answering this editorial. They are essential because part of the answer lay in the complicated relationship of the new Corps land to the land surrounding it. From the beginning this involved private and public property whose boundaries were at once geographical, legal, and as the *La Farge Epitaph* made crystal clear, psychological. Property boundaries were also natural in that they manifested themselves on the landscape. But property boundaries cannot fully explain a property dynamic in which people wear blaze orange every fall to signal their presence on the land. Nor are they sufficient for understanding property dynamics as inherently ecological.

This chapter will explore another form of land tenure—common property. Though not a household word, common property is nonetheless an essential part of the answer to "why?" and "where in the hell?" Initially the chapter sets a broad context for change on and off the Corps land. But its central focus will be on fusions: of the human-influenced landscape to the wildlife-influenced landscape, and of common property regimes to wild game regulation.

Almost immediately after the Corps of Engineers had acquired land for the La Farge dam, fields and woodlots on the property began reverting to a wilder condition. The herbaceous layer of the forest floor rebounded from a history of cattle grazing.[2] Jack in the Pulpit, a spring ephemeral, enjoyed a comeback, as did bloodroot, wild ginger, dutchman's breeches, and large trillium. Wild geranium became a common sight under stands of oak in early summer, while hog peanut showed itself in August and September. In the bottomlands, pasture and cropland regenerated to wet meadow and riparian forests, whose silvery soft maples, cottonwoods, and droopy willows created a new buffer along the river. An aggressive mix of goldenrod and quackgrass colonized old agricultural fields in the drier uplands. Competing with forbs and grasses were woody plants—aspen, elm, box elder, and staghorn sumac on the sunny edges between fields and roads. Led by these hardy pioneers, a process of old field succession

Riparian regeneration on the U.S. Army Corps of Engineers property along the Kickapoo River. Much of the Corps land reverted to a wilder condition. (Courtesy of Wolfgang Hoffmann)

began. A few relics remained of old private property boundaries. The occasional gnarled apple tree stood its ground. A Norway spruce looked out of place without a house and yard to shade. These were touchstones for another era.

While the forest grew wilder, it was not left alone. The Corps land had a real presence in the region. "The Fed" some people started to call it, but nickname aside, no authority enforced rules there. The Corps of Engineers had jurisdiction, but without a dam to build the agency largely withdrew from the scene. Many people started to blaze paths across the land. During winter months snowmobilers roared through, and cross-country skiers whooshed up and down hills, across old fields, and into the woods. Come early spring, hikers and horseback riders tested how passable the paths were. By summer they could fully enjoy the shade of the forest. Bow hunters opened deer season in the fall, followed by rifle hunters. Then the place reverberated with gunshots. Gutted deer hung by vehicles parked at the forest's edge.

Among the first people to make a place for themselves in the forest were thrill seekers in pickup trucks and all-terrain vehicles. For twenty years after the demise of the dam, they were the designated forest outlaws. Carousing in the "wilderness," as they called it, they bumped into trees with their vehicles, ripped up the soil with their fat tires, and created a muddy mess.[3] That state-owned forests can be sanctuaries for wild, antisocial behavior is old news. The writer Robert Pogue Harrison has argued that forests have a long history of standing outside the ordinary domesticated world. Asserting that "Forests lie 'beyond' the law, or better, they figure as places of outlaw," Harrison invoked the great legends of the Middle Ages.[4] Arthurian knights Lancelot and Yvain were examples in his analysis, as was the most famous forest outlaw, Robin Hood.[5] Forests can still harbor society's fugitives. Bomber and self-proclaimed white supremacist Eric Rudolph became a forest outlaw and local legend when he disappeared into North Carolina's Nantahala National Forest in 1997.[6] Before Rudolph there was Theodore Kaczinsky, the Unabomber, in Montana, as well as the Viper Militia, a property rights group hidden in an Arizona forest. The humble Corps land never hosted a standoff between government agents and social critics turned criminals. But one Corps employee got an eerie feeling when he came across an old trailer on an illegal campsite, a line of animal skins strung up nearby. "I thought I had entered 'Deliverance country,'" he said, referring to the backwoods movie.[7] Even this midwestern forest could "turn social logic upside down," as Harrison put it.[8]

Muddy, rutted tracks through the U.S. Army Corps of Engineers land, for twenty years a "wilderness" haven for pickup trucks and all-terrain vehicles. (Lynne Heasley)

Horseback riders competed with trucks and ATVs for access to the U.S. Army Corps of Engineers land. (Courtesy of Wolfgang Hoffmann)

Harrison offers one way of looking at the Corps land—by the kind of landscape it was. Another way is to look at the kind of property it was. Legally the place was federal property. By default, however, it was unmanaged, undefined land. Yet even without a viable state presence, the community sought ways to control behavior in the reserve (herein a convenient shorthand for the Corps land). Certainly many people wanted to rein in the pickup drivers. One local legend told of horseback riders who laid spikes on the trails to cause tire blowouts. Other people wanted to deal with the household trash that occasionally materialized on the land. Perhaps, then, the reserve more closely resembled common property— land held by or for the community.

What notions most people have about common property probably trace their roots to Garrett Hardin's famous 1968 essay, "The Tragedy of the Commons." With the words "Picture a pasture open to all," Hardin created an indelible image of nature used up by individuals, Hardin's fictional herders, whose own private gains motivated each to act in ways that would inexorably destroy the land for all. Maybe the reserve was an analogue to Hardin's pasture and the pickup drivers akin to his herders. Yet several generations of scholars have criticized "The Tragedy of the Commons" for the sloppy way it defined common property.[9] In practice, common property has rules, customs, and social norms for its use, as have public and private property. Such rules will differ from place to place; they will evolve over time; they might not protect the environment; but they do regulate access to the commons. Hardin's pasture was not common property; it was what property theorists call an open access regime. Nor was the reserve common property. People did what they did because the reserve was a certain kind of property, public yet neglected, and also because it was a certain kind of landscape, an extensive forest. Like Hardin's pasture, the reserve risked becoming an open-access free-for-all. Such freedom—from management, from regulation, from organized community oversight—made for a raucous beginning in the history of this particular piece of public land.

Besides changes on the reserve, the La Farge dam created spillover effects that rippled across private land. Up until the 1960s, no one had paid much attention to the regular turnover of land. When the dam seemed at hand, private land ownership changed to the point that the community took notice. Figure 14 shows that between 1965 and 1978 over 60 percent of the land around the future reserve changed hands, while from 1978 to 1995 land turnover reached 70 percent. In itself this might not have been noteworthy except that a wave of absentee owners had also appeared. The newcomers were not the corporate ranching types who had concentrated land in Liberty during the same period. Few corporations of any kind held land in Stark. Nor was the trend another version of fragmented recreational development schemes like Woodland Farms. Absentee recreational ownership in Stark was the historical prelude to Woodland Farms—its genesis really. Whether they lived north or south, in the East, the West or the Midwest, urban dwellers had begun spying out rural areas for hobby farms and vacation homes. With the La Farge dam, the Corps could respond to this growing tourist demand. The Corps's plan, in turn, attracted recreational buyers to the Kickapoo Valley. In the two-year period following the Corps's announcement of a large reservoir near La Farge, more than 80 percent of the land sold in the vicinity of the project went to nonresidents.[10] Over time, absentee owners accumulated 32 percent of all private land in Stark. When you add the reserve to the calculation, permanent residents held less than half the land in the township by 1995.

The first absentee owners in Stark bought parcels ranging from forty to one hundred acres. Early on they did not compete with local farmers for prime farmland. Rather, they favored steep rocky slopes with breathtaking panoramas.[11] The Kickapoo Valley had long been a landscape of cultivated ridges and valley bottoms separated by forests on steeper slopes. This was a happy fact for deer in the region, which thrived on edges between fields and forests. Deer stayed robust on corn, beans, and alfalfa, while nearby woodlots protected them from the weather and unhappy farmers. Eventually, though, the Corps of Engineers and absentee landowners changed this agriculture-forest mosaic by taking cropland out of production. Between 1939 and 1967, the township's acreage in crops declined by only 1 percent, whereas the period 1967 to 1995 saw agricultural acreage decline by 48 percent.

Figure 15 vividly illustrates how cropland gave way to forests and old fields (which is former cropland or pasture on its way to becoming forest). Forests were at their low ebb during the 1930s, occupying less than 40 percent of Stark's landscape. By 1995 forests covered nearly 60 percent of the township, while old fields covered 27 percent of the reserve and 12 percent of the private land around it. Private absentee and public land ownership were not solely responsible for latter-day forest boundaries, nevertheless their effects would overshadow earlier trends. Prior to the La Farge dam, for example, forests overtook pasture, not cropland. Many of these pastures

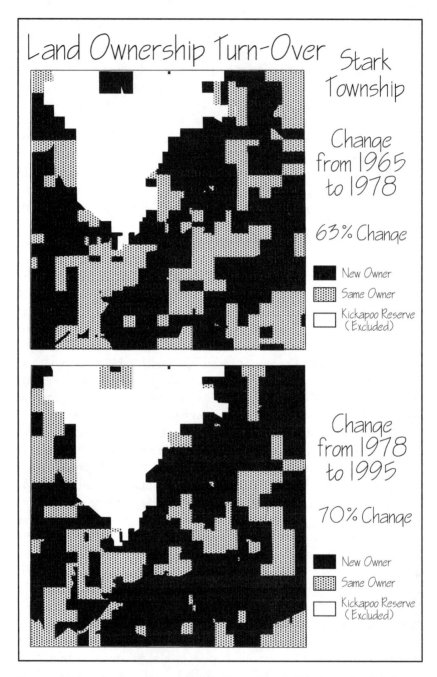

Figure 14. Private land turnover around the Army Corps of Engineers land in the township of Stark, 1965–78 and 1978–95. Land ownership had always been fluid in the Kickapoo Valley. But increased and accelerated land turnover meant more volatility in local land use and in community dynamics.

had been on steep, deforested hillsides. During the 1930s and '40s, farmers had allowed steeper land to regenerate to forest, in part because of the erosion crisis and in part because they were moving away from horses, which reduced the need for pasture, and toward tractors, which were dangerous to drive across steep slopes. In addition, the Forest Crop Law, the Woodland Tax Law, and the Agricultural Conservation Program provided cost sharing for reforestation projects on degraded land. Under these programs, Stark landowners planted 64,000 trees between 1958 and 1965—mainly red and white pine and white cedar, along with some Norway spruce, sugar maple, and walnut—on approximately fifteen hundred acres. From 1939 to 1967, forestland increased by 16 percent. Much more dramatic, however, was the 33 percent increase from 1967 to 1995. Whereas the earlier period had slightly modified Stark's landscape, public and recreational land ownership during the latter period completely transformed it.

How might a herd of deer respond to more forest cover at the expense of cropland? The white-tailed deer is a keystone herbivore in eastern deciduous forest ecosystems. This means that its presence has strongly influenced the numbers and distribution of other plants and animals and, by extension, the structure of the ecosystem.[12] So a discussion of deer should not simply describe their movements across a landscape when what is most important are their interactions with that landscape. This is more difficult than it sounds. It would be disingenuous to assert simple cause and effect between fluid phenomena like land ownership, landscape dynamics, deer populations, hunting behavior, and community attitudes. Even a basic task like estimating deer densities in an area the size of a township can cause debate among professional wildlife biologists.[13] People who are not wildlife biologists must therefore approach deer ecology with some restraint. That said, making sense of connections and changes in a cultural landscape shaped by property boundaries and ecosystems, by humans and nonhumans, is a fundamental undertaking. Otherwise we cannot assess ways in which people have owned and managed land. Neither can we understand shifting negotiations over individual prerogatives in owning, managing, or getting access to land and a community's prerogative to act for some larger common good. Federal and state governments have often become chief mediators in these negotiations. But because they have complex agendas and institutional relationships, the prerogatives they will support are rarely clear-cut. The question of deer—and deer hunting—makes a perfect case in point.

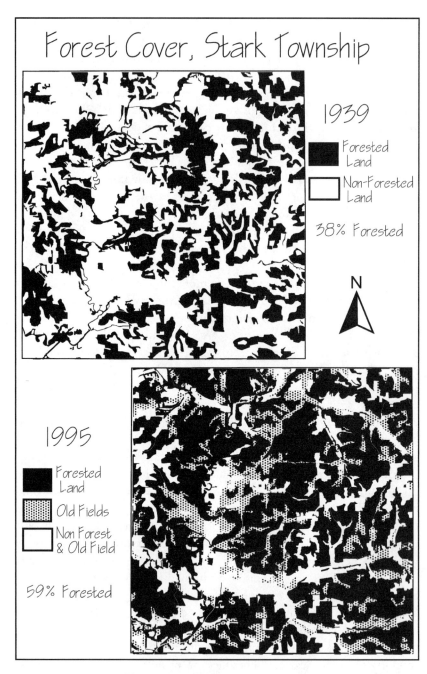

Figure 15. Expansion of forests in Stark, 1939–95.

White-tailed deer prefer edges between fields and forests, from where they can browse several hundred feet into a field and then dash back into the woods for cover. Hence any reduction in either edge habitat or the total area of cropland might be expected to lower their numbers in the long term. This would be especially true if the population had reached a size where the land could no longer provide enough food. Wildlife biologists call this limit the land's "maximum biological carrying capacity."[14] In places like Stark, the maximum biological carrying capacity could be as high as 100 deer per square mile of deer range, with deer range defined as everywhere in the township except the village of La Farge and the middle of the Kickapoo River. In the Kickapoo Valley actual deer density can range from 30 to 45 deer per square mile. Even though cropland had dwindled, deer had no problem subsisting on the fields that remained. One fall day Pam Munson counted 120 white-tailed deer in her cornfield.[15] The nearby reserve, she felt sure, had sent the whole herd her way.

As long as agriculture remained a part of the landscape mosaic, forest cover afforded important benefits. The denser forest canopy of the reserve

By 1995, old fields regenerating to forest occupied 12 percent of the private land and 27 percent of the U.S. Army Corps of Engineers land in the township of Stark. (Courtesy of Wolfgang Hoffmann)

provided deer with ideal shelter from wind and snow, and in winter, residents often came upon their telltale concave beds. Forests also supplied deer with forage. Because of this, the impact of Wisconsin's deer herd became an important ecological debate.[16] Some ecologists argued that deer did as much damage to forests as logging. They accumulated strong evidence that deer herbivory (browsing) had reduced the abundance and diversity of herbaceous plants in Wisconsin's northern forests. This occurred even though deer density in the north was considerably lower than in the southern part of the state. The issue of deer ecology was different in the Kickapoo Valley than it was in the north woods. Research suggested that in southern Wisconsin's mixed agricultural-forest landscape, deer did not put as much pressure on the herbaceous layer.[17] Deer would have certainly browsed forest herbs during the winter if they were available, but the plants had senesced until spring. The more pronounced impact involved the woody plants, or trees. In the Valley this meant mixed hardwoods, primarily oak-hickory and maple-basswood forests.

Oak-hickory forests have had a prominent place in the eastern U.S. landscape for at least six thousand years.[18] They have supported and been

White-tailed deer prefer edge habitat where fields and forests meet. (Courtesy of Wolfgang Hoffmann)

shaped by critical ecological processes like fire.[19] They have contributed to the biological diversity of the region. Important game species, such as deer, squirrels, and turkey, have depended on them for acorns and other nuts, berries, leaves, and shelter from the weather or airborne predators like hawks and owls. These forests have also played an important historical role in regional cultures and economies—supporting Indian subsistence patterns prior to European settlement, for instance, and then facilitating that settlement afterward.[20] But in recent decades ecologists have noted a sharp decline in oak-hickory forests.[21] Forest ecologist Craig Lorimer called the trend "one of the most serious silvicultural [forest management] problems in the eastern United States."[22] Readers first encountered forest succession in the townships of Liberty and Clinton. Now is the time to bring deer into the discussion and to examine them alongside logging.

When professional foresters talk about oak regeneration, they emphasize the growth of the tree. Mature trees must produce a sufficient acorn mast; these seeds must grow to saplings; and some saplings must survive until they are full-grown trees. For an oak to survive, foresters tell landowners, lots of sunlight must reach the forest floor. Otherwise it cannot compete with sugar maples, which are also present in the understory. In a shady understory, by contrast, sugar maple can survive for decades while oak saplings will die. A landowner who wants to maintain oak-hickory forests, according to foresters, must therefore create openings where lots of sunlight can penetrate to the forest floor. The solution, in other words, is to log mature forests. Versions of this argument abound in letters and conversations between foresters and landowners, in public meetings, and in other forums where oak regeneration is the theme.

The argument is true as far as it goes. Oaks do need sunlight. But will logging mature hardwood forests halt forest succession to maple? The ecological histories of Liberty, Clinton, and Stark say no. This study provides evidence that, far from slowing down succession, logging has accelerated the process.[23] Unlike Liberty and Clinton, the overall area in oak-hickory forests did not decline in Stark after the 1930s; it increased. Stark's township "average" is somewhat deceptive because it conceals succession from oak to maple on about twenty-four hundred acres over the sixty-year period. Two reasons, however, explain why the total acreage in oak rose. The first is that oak-hickory communities were part of one probable successional trajectory as old fields reverted to forests. Oak and other sun-loving species were able to colonize old fields. Second is that no timber harvests occurred on the reserve after the 1960s, where large tracts of oak-hickory forest persisted. Of the three adjacent townships, only the one with relatively low harvest pressure in the past forty years (Stark) has sustained oak-hickory forests.

It is important to reiterate the tangled strands of cause and effect. Researchers have examined a number of possible explanations for the loss of oak. Postsettlement fire suppression, tall understory vegetation, and poor seed masts are all likely candidates.[24] So, too, is the combination of timber harvesting and deer herbivory.[25] Logging has had the opposite effect that foresters claimed for it in part because a high whitetail population will suppress oak regeneration after harvests. Pawing for acorns is a major deer pastime after the last crops have come off the fields. Come spring a forester may poke around for new oak seedlings and find none. Even when seedlings and saplings become established, they must withstand a combination of deer browsing and competition from understory trees. This is the irony: white-tailed deer thrive in and around upland oak forests, but this habitat is vulnerable to deer in the long run. Perhaps this is why landowners hear little from foresters about deer predation. Barring a steep decline in white-tailed deer populations, there is only one way to protect trees. For approximately one dollar a landowner can purchase a narrow tube to place around a sapling: one tube, one tree; one acre of planted saplings, five hundred to a thousand dollars; one acre of standing forest, perhaps a few thousand of dollars. Though simple, the technology is too expensive to counter the one-two blow of intensive logging and deer browsing across rural landscapes.[26]

It is no fluke of nature that white-tailed deer have put pressure on North American forests. The high deer numbers that created this pressure arose from new public policies. Prior to 1800, the entire southern half of Wisconsin might have supported anywhere from twenty to fifty deer per square mile.[27] According to nineteenth-century pioneer accounts, the first settlers in the Kickapoo Valley found deer plentiful. Early loggers in the area that became Stark told their children stories of shoving curious deer away from oxen teams during winter months when the men were hauling logs.[28] But deer numbers rapidly declined. Vernon County farmer C. A. Neprud told Aldo Leopold that he "had 7 deer eating pumpkins and corn on his farm in the fall of 1888."[29] Hunters killed them all that winter. "He saw only one deer after that," wrote Leopold in his notes on the conversation, "a stray in about 1908." By the end of the nineteenth century, unchecked hunting had all but eliminated white-tailed deer from southern Wisconsin.

Then the U.S. Supreme Court issued a landmark decision on "common property," which set the stage for expanded wild game regulation in the states.[30] The setting was this: On October 19, 1889, Edward M. Geer was charged in New London, Connecticut, with violation of Connecticut game law. State statutes held that no person could kill a woodcock, ruffed grouse, or quail for the purposes of transporting it across state lines, while Geer had in his possession birds he had intended to take out of the state. He was convicted and fined, and he appealed his conviction until it reached the Supreme Court. Was it constitutional, the court asked in *Geer v. Connecticut,* for the state to confine the uses of wild game killed during an open season to within state borders? The court said yes, relying for its primary rationale on a theory of property derived from ancient Roman law and later English common law.

"The solution of the question," the court said in its decision, "involves a consideration of the nature of the property in game and the authority which the state had a right lawfully to exercise in relation thereto." Roman law had explicitly classified public and common property, the court pointed out. "The latter embraced animals ferae naturae, which, having no owner, were considered as belonging in common to all the citizens of the state." Following Roman law, an "unbroken line of law and precedent is summed up by the provisions of the Napoleon Code, which declares (articles 714, 715): 'There are things which belong to no one, and the use of which is common to all. Police regulations direct the manner in which they may be enjoyed.'" The court further decided that the Connecticut law had not violated the Commerce Clause of the constitution. "The power of a state to protect, by adequate police regulation, its people against the adulteration of articles of food (which was in that case maintained), although, in doing so, commerce might be remotely affected, necessarily carries with it the existence of a like power to preserve a food supply which belongs in common to all the people of the state, which can only become the subject of ownership in a qualified way, and which can never be the object of commerce except with the consent of the state, and subject to the conditions which it may deem best to impose for the public good."

Eighty-three years later the Supreme Court would overrule Geer in *Hughes v. Oklahoma* (1979).[31] The "application of the 19th century legal fiction of state ownership of wild animals" had been wrong, the court would say, because it permitted states to discriminate against interstate commerce. "States may promote the legitimate purpose of protecting and conserving wild animal life within their borders only in ways consistent with the basic principle that the pertinent economic unit is the Nation; and when a wild animal becomes an article of commerce, its use cannot be limited to the citizens of one State to the exclusion of citizens of another State." Despite abolishing Geer, the Hughes decision pointedly reaffirmed what by then were long-standing state rights to regulate and manage wild game in behalf of the public: "[T]he general rule we adopt in this case makes ample allowance for preserving, in ways not [441 U.S. 322, 336] inconsistent with the Commerce Clause, the legitimate state concerns for conservation and protection of wild animals underlying the 19th-century legal fiction of state ownership." It was this broad mandate for conservation—premised on historical notions of common property and the public good—that would make *Geer v. Connecticut* such an influential ecological force during the twentieth century.

After Geer, President Theodore Roosevelt, himself an avid sportsman who founded the Boone and Crockett Club, urged state governors to enact or strengthen laws that required hunters to purchase licenses, established a short hunting season, set bag limits, and restricted the killing of does.[32] With these tools, the states successfully converted deer hunting from unregulated subsistence and market activities into a fully regulated sport.[33] During the next sixty years deer herds rebounded. By the early 1960s, deer populations in the Kickapoo Valley had grown to at least 11 deer per square mile. At that time Wisconsin policy shifted focus from herd recovery to herd maximization with an all-out bureaucratic and biological effort to increase hunting opportunities. The effort paid off. The deer population in agricultural areas grew from fewer than 100,000 animals in 1962 to nearly 600,000 in 1995. Statewide the herd has now reached 1.6 million deer, while 30 percent of all Wisconsin men hold hunting licenses.[34]

Modern state policy exacerbated the problem of oak regeneration. Wisconsin's natural resource agencies manipulated deer populations to achieve what they called a maximum sustainable harvest. They wanted to produce the highest number of fawns in the spring. The larger objective was to make deer hunting big business in the state, and the policy succeeded. In 1996, according to the Department of Natural Resources, 676,000 deer hunters spent $897 million in Wisconsin on licenses, food, lodging, transportation, and equipment. The venison itself was worth approximately $35 million. By adding indirect profits from wages and taxes to the total, state accountants estimated that deer hunting generated more than $2.6 billion of economic activity in just that one year.[35] Hunters in turn became one of Wisconsin's most powerful lobbying groups. Their role in setting policy had long been institutionalized in an organization called the Wisconsin Conservation Congress, a quasi-governmental citizens group established in 1934. The Congress's 360 delegates (mostly sportsmen elected in each of the state's seventy-two counties) were charged with making recommendations to the Department of Natural Resources on conservation policies. As the state became more active in managing the deer population, the Conservation Congress's role also expanded. It proposed deer harvest quotas, the length of the hunting season, licensing fees, and public land management for wildlife habitat. In addition to the Congress, hunters harboring any suspicion that the state had lowballed population goals, a common gripe, were quite willing to confront their county DNR wildlife biologist.[36] State wildlife biologists risked political mutiny if they attempted to manage deer for ecological outcomes. Yet the persistence of many forest ecosystems, including oak-hickory, may hinge on the enactment of just such a policy.

There was another kind of mutiny taking hold in Wisconsin. Rural communities had come to resent the hunting scene—the bell that opened the gate to a crush of deer enthusiasts racing onto rural landscapes. Proud hunters, said one Valley resident, thought that "their license gave them the right to cut fences, leave gates open, shoot hereford cattle in deer season (some of them did not know that with a deer the white is on the opposite end of the animal), to overrun the land without regard or respect."[37] The DNR was thus forced to confront growing conflict between deer hunters and landowners. To sportsmen canvassing prospective hunting grounds, the area around Stark must have seemed ideal. Deer were abundant and the reserve was open to the public for hunting. Vernon County DNR wildlife biologist Dave Matheys described the reserve as a hunting sink.[38] He was adapting the biological term "population sink," which loosely means a place that sustains large numbers of a species—only Matheys was referring to the hunters! Inviting though it was on a map, the reserve could not hold everyone who wanted to hunt there. If ever an enforcement presence was apparent, it was during deer season—the one time when people became reluctant to take their vehicles onto the land illegally. This posed a physical limitation that reduced the usable scale of the landscape. How many hunters, Matheys asked rhetorically, would willingly hunt more than a few hundred yards into the reserve having to haul out a deer over rough terrain? The reserve helped concentrate hunters in Stark, but uncomfortable standing elbow to elbow with their fellows, many hunted deer elsewhere, on private land.[39]

As deer hunting took off in the Kickapoo Valley, residents began posting their land to rebuff fervent, trespassing sportsmen. Some people decided to lease their land for hunting, partly for the income and partly because lessees would help minimize trespass. "Who wants to confront a group of drunk men with guns?" asked a landowner who chose this method to control access to his land during deer season. This was all a byproduct of the state's "military-industrial hunting complex," he added. Plenty of landless hunters went where they could. The suburbanite turned hunter for nine days—the same person who might have chided a neighbor crossing his backyard at home—temporarily adjusted his ideas about private property while crossing another stranger's rural backyard. The farmer who hunted, the absentee owner who did not hunt, the absentee owner who bought land so that she could hunt, all started to complain. "The materialistic greed of our lawmakers has spilled over upon the participants of this fiasco," said the *La Farge Epitaph*. "And he who spends bucks expects "Buck" and will pursue his course with rugged determination involving trespass and illegalities with no love or thought of safety for his fellow man."[40]

Social conflict over deer was not new to state policy makers. In agricultural regions where biological carrying capacity did not limit herd size, the aim of modern deer management was always straightforward: Expand opportunities for sportsmen up to the point where local communities or the larger public no longer accepted the costs. The DNR's Bureau of Wildlife Management called this "social carrying capacity." Wildlife managers would consider social carrying capacity before settling on final population goals for the next year. Until the detection of Lyme disease borne by deer ticks, and more recently, chronic wasting disease in the deer herd, the most important social considerations were crop damage and collision rates between deer and motorists. In direct response to angry farmers, Wisconsin established the 1983 Wildlife Damage Abatement and Claims Program, a successor to other programs going back to 1931.[41] Under this program the state would compensate farmers for crop damage, and it would issue out-of-season permits to shoot nuisance anterless deer. The program raised landowner tolerance only so far. One farmer in Stark felt frowned upon by her neighbors when she took out a nuisance permit. The real problem, she believed, did not come from two or three animals, but from the sheer size and concentration of the herd. Creating another disincentive, the legislature linked the program to its goal of expanding public access to hunting land. Anyone who signed up must allow hunters on their property during the open season. When the Wisconsin legislature strengthened the DNR's ability to enforce this provision in 1993, enrollment in the program dropped by more than half.[42] As of 2003, only one landowner in Stark was enrolled.

Along with crop damage, landowner tolerance for hunters had become a mainstay in the political balancing act of deer management policy. A 1995 change in state statutes on trespass suggested that the limits of this tolerance had been reached.[43] Wisconsin law once read that for unmarked private land, landowners were responsible for informing you that you had entered private property. You were not trespassing unless you were already aware of the property lines. Under intense pressure from fed-up landowners, the Wisconsin legislature changed this statute, making it the visitor's responsibility to know the property boundaries. Ignorance was no longer a legal excuse for trespass, and buying a hunting license was no longer a seasonal passport onto land normally off limits.

State game policy stacked seasonal and ecological layers onto the Kickapoo Valley's complex mosaic of private and public property. The mosaic had been in constant flux. Its fluid quality is the key to understanding the deeper significance of Stark's history. To explain with a brief recap: Land ownership was fluid. Many thousands of acres of private land became public land; and landowners who did not live in the township or even in the Valley replaced local farmers. The reserve's new status as public land cultivated a very different looking landscape, wilder, more forested. It retarded forest succession to maple but expedited old-field succession. Off the reserve, a small amount of farmland endured in the midst of a private recreational landscape.

Basic changes in landownership also had cultural consequences. As the land's status changed, people treated it differently. Their ideas and actions were as fluid as property was. On the reserve some people went berserk to an extent they would never have dreamed of on Great Uncle Eli's back forty. As for private land, it became considerably less private every autumn. Hunting season was when you might have felt justified in rebelling against someone's legal prerogative to exclude you from her land. Though landowners found it annoying, the attitude came out of traditions honoring some sort of public access to common property, which by definition no *one* owns. The state itself nurtured this ancient idea with modern game management and hunting regulations.

We return then to questions of land ownership and property. Nothing more clearly illustrates that property is not simply the adjacent rectangles on a map than Stark's history. Indeed this history, which is a history of property, consists almost entirely of changing relationships and shifting negotiations. The relationships form a triangle of sorts: people, the government, and the land itself. Within the triangle people negotiate who controls what land, who else gets access, and under which conditions. Today we call these negotiations "property debates," but that is not quite right. A debate implies a single conflict that can be settled one way or another. A negotiation denotes the open-ended condition of society establishing relationships around land and then adjusting them as new (or old) ideas take hold. Negotiation is a process, not a debate. The process is fluid.

During the process the state can assume the role of mediator, of partisan, or, in the case of deer hunting, both. A dual role will create paradoxes. The state had jurisdiction to manage deer as common property for the public good. It defined public good as maximizing the access sportsmen had to hunting land. Yet unlike deer, the state and hunters could not ignore private property boundaries. The state defined public good as managing deer at the highest population that local communities would tolerate. Yet the policy precluded other public goods, such as conserving ecologically and economically valuable forests. The negotiation—the process—continues.

As for the reserve, it became the beneficiary of an amazing change of mindset. People in Stark were still irate over its existence. But the destructive behavior of a few people had a curious effect: Other members of the community started to feel protective toward the land. At first people talked about what they did not want. They did not want free-range trucks; they did not want chaotic paths fragmenting the forest into ever-smaller pieces; they did not want a massive invasion of exotic plants; they did not want old refrigerators, feral dogs, or scary people. What they did want was a say in the land's future. Here was a small chrysalis of a new vision, but what would it transform into? Who would negotiate for it and what prerogatives would they try to assert—private, public, community? Or something else altogether?

8

(Re)Enter the Ho-Chunk

The reserve languished in administrative limbo throughout the 1980s. No one could agree on its purpose, its management, or its future. Many people continued to deplore the passing of the La Farge dam. At times their rhetoric sounded like a midwestern replay of old western land wars between the federal government and local people. But this saga had a few twists left. Oblivious to any irony in the Kickapoo Valley, the Corps of Engineers had adopted new language in the 1980s to publicize its mission. "Project delivery is the Corps' business," a glossy brochure announced. "From conception of a project until its completion and turnover to the ultimate user; the Corps provides complete project management services." Rather than districts, or engineers, or planners, the Corps now used, according to the brochure, "Corps Life Cycle Project Managers," who served "as points of contact for customers to ensure that they are fully informed and involved, forecast trends and resolve problems, and oversee all phases of project development, ensuring the delivery of 'a quality product, on time and within budget.'"[1] This advertisement is significant not because it embraced the new business jargon of the times but because project completion and turnover were precisely the aims for anyone interested in the reserve, which meant everyone who lived in Stark.

In 1993, residents across the Kickapoo Valley began meeting to develop a plan. They wanted the Corps to complete the La Farge dam's life cycle, even if the dam itself must remain unfinished. They hoped to convince the federal government to transfer the reserve to the state, after which they hoped the state would appoint a local board to manage it.[2] Doing its part to resolve the long-festering issue, Wisconsin petitioned for the land's release from federal control.

It is worth pondering the implication of the local plan and the state's request. Wisconsin was asking Congress to devolve control over a highly contested piece of public land, something state governors have expressed interest in for a hundred years. They have rarely succeeded. The general purpose of federal lands—the question of who makes up their legitimate constituents—has always been a point of contention in the country, but devolution is a more sensitive topic yet. The negotiations involved would entail competition between levels of government, agencies, users, local communities, and nonlocal interests of every kind.

Apart from the political arena of Congress, there was another process available for settling the status of the reserve. When federal land is not in use for ten years or more it becomes classified as "excess real property." Upon this designation the U.S. General Services Administration (GSA) will search for a new custodian. There is a pecking order in the search. The GSA will look first to other federal agencies, which have the right of refusal. Only then will the GSA designate the property "surplus." Then state and local governments or certain nonprofit organizations can step forward.[3] No doubt Kickapoo Valley communities did not want to watch from afar as one federal agency, the Army Corps of Engineers, transferred its land to another federal agency. They did not want to wake up and find a national park in their midst.

Not to put too fine a point on the matter, the La Farge dam fiasco still burned in the local psyche. Any hint of a federal alternative to the Corps would have fueled the political equivalent of a forest crown fire. Devolution was what people wanted, emphatically. This was clear to all the politicians who found themselves engulfed by the issue. Russell Feingold had been trapped on the very day he was first elected U.S. senator, when a constituent approached him in his own garage and asked him to introduce legislation transferring the Corps land to the state of Wisconsin.[4] Feingold responded to his constituent with impressive alacrity. He drafted a provision to deauthorize the La Farge dam project with language setting the terms of the transfer in the Water Resources Development Act of 1994. He was unsuccessful in inserting the language that year, so he planned to try again in the 1996 act. In this way the reserve would become an exception to the rule against political rather than administrative devolution in our system of federal holdings. (Although making an exception establishes a process others may follow in the future.)

While Feingold was working on federal legislation, Governor Tommy Thompson had to decide which of his agencies would eventually house the reserve. He chose the Department of Tourism. This was a strange home, but there was too much antipathy toward Thompson's other choice, the Department of Natural Resources. Even DNR Secretary George Meyer agreed. "With the history out there, [DNR ownership] would never work," he said.[5] Then Thompson had the delicate task of arranging for the reserve's future management. Here he became the consummate diplomat. Thompson settled on a board of local and state citizens who would oversee a newly christened Kickapoo Valley Reserve.[6] Four members would come from the townships of Stark and Whitestown and the villages of La Farge and Ontario, which respectively encompassed and bordered the reserve. Two more members would represent the greater Kickapoo Valley watershed. Though local communities would not have complete control over the land, they would have a majority at the table, and just as important, the table would be in La Farge.

A form of public land tenure unique in the country was taking shape. Valley residents anticipated terrific possibilities. A few hoped that a future board would return some land to previous owners. But after a quarter century, that would have provoked questions about previous compensation, land values, heirs, and so forth. Other people wanted to use the land for economic development, perhaps small industry or agricultural leasing. Still others wanted to designate the reserve a biological core area. This would be the ideal way, they said, to pursue ecological restoration and to sustain important regional ecosystems. Between the poles of economic and environmental sustainability, hopes ran high that the reserve would become a mecca for ecotourism, a winning hybrid of recreational development and environmental protection.[7]

But the actual Water Resources Development Act of 1996 laid out a fourth, unanticipated path for the property. Congress did agree to devolve control, only it added a caveat. Twelve hundred acres with "culturally and religiously significant sites," the act decreed, would go to the Ho-Chunk Nation, formerly known as the Wisconsin Winnebago. The law left open the possibility that additional sites, meaning more land, could be reserved for the Ho-Chunk after ten years. Management decisions for the entire property, moreover, must include the Ho-Chunk, who would appoint two of their own representatives to the board. The La Farge dam had just generated another surprising spillover.

People in the Kickapoo Valley were incredulous. Where in the world did the Ho-Chunk come from? some of them asked. What right did they have to any of the land? They didn't even live in the Valley![8] The Ho-Chunk seemed to appear out of nowhere. Yet signs of earlier occupants were strewn across the reserve in the four-hundred-and-fifty-plus archeological sites the Corps of Engineers had catalogued since 1960.[9] So the more apt question might have been, *when* did the Ho-Chunk become involved with this land?

In 1825 and 1827, United States–Indian treaties mapped tribal territories in the Great Lakes region in order "to promote peace among these tribes, and to establish boundaries among them and the other tribes who live in their vicinity, and thereby to remove all causes of future difficulty."[10] With these words President John Quincy Adams allocated to the Winnebago the territory they already occupied. This was most of the land in southwestern and southern Wisconsin contiguous with a smaller area in northwestern Illinois.[11]

Unfortunately for the tribe, the 1825 treaty coincided almost exactly with white discovery of lead on the Fever River in Galena, Illinois, the southernmost part of their territory. Miners began flooding the region, violently usurping Indian land and resources. Winnebago chief Four Legs brought up the incursions during negotiations for the 1827 treaty on boundaries. "Father," he began, " . . . you have always told us to be still, to raise our children, provide for our families, and not be afraid of your men. But I am afraid of your young men at the mines. There are a great many Americans on our land, working it without our permission, and I want you to tell our Great Father to stop it—to reach out his long arm and draw them back."[12] The following year another Winnebago chief, Old Grayheaded Decora, described the same scene in more detail: "When some lead is found, and it was known down the Mississippi, white men came flocking to Fever River like the wolves in the plains to the dead buffalo. . . . They spread out in every direction and began to dig and find and carry off lead on the Winnebago lands. We said, 'if we do not stop them soon, it will be too late. More and more are coming every day—the game and furs are leaving the country, and the Indians cannot live in it any longer, if we do not stop the white men from coming over the line into our country.'"[13] The line, however—the Winnebago property line as established by the United States government—had been breached. President Adams had no intention of removing the lead miners. Unlike the Winnebago, the miners had powerful armaments and still more powerful political connections.[14]

By fixing legal boundaries among Indian tribes, the treaties of 1825 and 1827 accomplished something quite different than the Winnebago could have imagined. The treaties provided the legal foundation on which the U.S. government could begin negotiating land cessions. What this means is that the treaties defined the proper ownership for any lawful transfer of land from one nation to another. Only one year after their territory became defined and codified in U.S. law, the Winnebago found them-selves negotiating a transitional treaty with the United States. Now, according to the subsequent treaty in 1828, "it is fully understood, that the United States may freely occupy the country . . . until a treaty shall be held with the Indians for its cession; which treaty, it is presumed, will be held in the year 1829." What's more, the document insisted, "it is expressly understood and agreed, that if any white person shall cross the line herein described, and pass into the Indian country, for the purpose of mining, or for any other purpose whatever, the Indians shall not interfere with nor molest such persons."[15] The next year the Winnebago began ceding their land to the United States, in three parts and three treaties of cession.[16]

First on the table was the lead mining area in Illinois along with adja-cent land running north into Wisconsin, a total of 2,530,000 acres. The great Winnebago orator Little Elk was stunned at the amount of land the government demanded from the tribe. "Why do you wish to add our small country to yours, already so large?" he asked. "Do you want our country? Yours is larger than ours! Do you want our wigwams? You live in palaces! Do you want our women? Yours now sitting behind you are handsome and dressed better than ours! Look at them yonder! Why, fathers, what can be your motive?"[17] Though Little Elk did not realize it yet, the answer to one of his questions—Do you want our country?—was yes. For a large portion of their whole country the government forced the Winnebago to accept $18,000 annually for thirty years, another $30,000 in goods imme-diately, and an annual delivery of three thousand pounds of tobacco and fifty barrels of salt for thirty years.

At the gathering where Little Elk and his fellow chiefs agreed to the treaty's terms, U.S. Commissioner Caleb Atwater turned his gaze on an unhappy female onlooker. Some kind of exchange ensued. Regrettably the woman's actual words were not recorded. But Atwater's harsh account of her—as a woman and as an Indian—is a reminder that many of the people most profoundly affected by these events had little say in them. "As I passed through the open spaces between the ranks," Atwater began, "my attention was forcibly drawn to a particular spot by a constant snarling, hissing noise of some miserable human being, on whom approaching her, I ascertained to be an Indian woman, shriveled, haggard and old, though remarkably neat in her person and dress." Saying he wanted to please all the Indians and "especially the ladies," Atwater recounted his effort to address this woman. "I told her that her great father, the President, had specially ordered me, so far as in me lay, to please all, and to see that no one went home dissatisfied. At that moment she returned upon me a volley of epithets too degrading to be repeated, even though applied to myself, as I felt conscious of not deserving them." He sought an explanation for her animosity anywhere but in the occasion of the treaty itself: "Turning around to see some females who were politely sitting on the ground behind me, I learned the fault finder *was an old maid* (unmarried men at sixty years of age I will call bachelors, but ladies never), and that the only distinguishing mark of attention she had ever received from any man was a smart blow with a flat hand on her right ear" (emphasis in original). Sure of his explanation, Atwater dismissed the episode, saying, "as I never could endure the ideas conveyed to my mind by a rattlesnake, a heartless politician, an iceberg and a cold hearted woman, I turned away from her in disgust, and never saw her more nor inquired her name, for fear I should remember it." As Atwater saw it, "She was the only person who left the treaty ground dissatisfied with the commissioners."[18]

Because she was a woman, the name of Atwater's fleeting antagonist does not appear on the treaty. What a shame. Though we will never know what instigated the argument, or what the nature of her complaint was, it is not unreasonable to suppose that she was giving voice to an agonizing process for Winnebago women. She and her companions could only bear witness to decisions that would irrevocably change their lives but were entirely outside their control. Their position had not always been so marginal. Through intermarriage with Europeans, Indian women had been important cultural intermediaries—"influential creators of the middle ground"—as historian Richard White described Algonquian women.[19] Cession treaties with the Winnebago were part of the erasure of the middle ground, where Indians and Europeans had found mutual accommodation, and where Indian women had held an influential place. In Atwater's one-sided and even misogynistic account, there are hints that one woman's words, at least, were still powerful, if not her influence. Her words were certainly disturbing enough to Atwater, who got some revenge by distorting her image and rendering her nameless. Meanwhile the process of rendering her people landless had just started.

Next went the easternmost half of the territory in Wisconsin, up to Lake Winnebago. By this time an alliance between the Sauk war leader,

Black Hawk, and the chief of a band of mixed blood Winnebago and Sauk, known as the Winnebago Prophet, had culminated in the Black Hawk War of 1832. Back Hawk and his followers had wanted to return to their ancestral village Saukenuk, which lay within territory ceded to the U.S. government in 1804. Black Hawk's anti-American uprising was ruinous for his people; after tracking the band through the valleys of southwestern Wisconsin and across the Kickapoo River, the government slew as many as four hundred at the mouth of the Bad Axe River on August 2, 1832.[20] Most Winnebago bands had not supported Black Hawk and the Winnebago Prophet. Indeed Winnebago had persuaded the two to surrender. In handing over Black Hawk to the Americans, Winnebago leader One-eyed Decora said, "My father, we deliver these men into your hands. . . . We want you to keep them safe; if they are to be hurt, we do not wish to see it—wait until we are gone before it is done. . . ."[21] Rather than executing their Indian prisoners, the Americans exacted a different kind of price for the Black Hawk War. Arguing for a bigger separation between whites and Winnebago, to avoid "quarrels and wars," the government demanded a second treaty of cession. In return for an unfamiliar place to live west of the Mississippi River, also for $10,000 annually over twenty-seven years, for a boarding school to educate Winnebago children, and for sundry tokens including the relocation of a blacksmith's shop, the Winnebago relinquished almost half of their land in Wisconsin. Still remaining was the westernmost part of their territory, which encompassed the Kickapoo Valley.

In the summer of 1836 a smallpox epidemic devastated the Winnebago, killing one thousand people, nearly one-third of the tribe, including many important chiefs. This was the moment when territorial governor Henry Dodge asked the Winnebago to sell the last of their lands in Wisconsin. At the time, Waukon Decora led a Winnebago band that resided at the mouth of the Kickapoo River. His village had been large. One explorer recalled that the band cultivated a hundred acres of pumpkins, potatoes, squashes, and wild tobacco.[22] A smaller Winnebago settlement lay farther upstream. From their agricultural locus, small parties ranged along the river and through Valley forests, hunting and trapping and gathering wild berries and nuts. The towering, uneven bluffs on what is today the Kickapoo Valley Reserve sheltered Winnebago hunters, who butchered and cooked deer under their rocky overhangs.[23] Later residents called these bluffs the Oocooch Mountains, possibly a mispronunciation of Ho-Chunk.[24]

Waukon Decora spoke for the entire tribe in rebuffing a third and final cession. Reading even a fragment of his speech, you cannot fail to appreciate the anguish of a people faced with losing their land, their livelihoods, and many of their lives in a single year. "All our chiefs and forefathers have died upon the land we are now living upon," he said. "Many of our principal men died here last summer; their bones are buried here, and it seems hard for us to leave them." This was the last vestige of Winnebago land in Wisconsin. "We had one tract of land which did not suit us so well as this, and we sold it. But we did not tell our Great Father we would sell this country—not a foot of it."[25] Yet the next year in Washington, D.C., the Winnebago unwittingly ceded their last holdings. The lopsided setting was this: The tribe had sent a delegation to Washington, D.C., not to relinquish their lands but to try and hold on to them. It is probable that some of those in the delegation did not have tribal authority to sign a final agreement. During the trip, Indian agent Thomas A. B. Boyd withheld funds from the delegation and appeared to have used them on liquor and prostitutes for himself. Finally, the Winnebago present believed that the treaty stipulated an eight-year grace period before they must leave the territory, when it really gave them eight months to relocate west of the Mississippi River.

After the Winnebago signed this third treaty of cession, their connection to the land of southwestern Wisconsin did not end; it simply entered a treacherous new phase. What followed during the next twenty-five years was a series of relocations, land cessions, and removals to reservations ever farther from Wisconsin. In 1840, Winnebago who abided by the treaties went first to the "Neutral Ground" on the Turkey River in Iowa, a place that was not neutral at all but a repository for warring Dakota and Sauk (between which the Winnebago were sandwiched). In 1846, the United States government moved the Winnebago to north central Minnesota, where they again became a buffer between warring tribes, this time Dakota and Ojibwe; then to southern Minnesota in 1855 after another treaty of cession; followed by a tortuous forced march to the Crow Creek Reserve in South Dakota, during which five hundred Winnebago died; and ultimately to Nebraska.[26] At every point Winnebago slipped out from under government surveillance to return to Wisconsin. These were the "disaffected bands," the "dwellers among the pines" (*Wazijaci*), who hid in the region despite a military policy to round them up and evict them from the state.[27] The period marks what would eventually become a durable split between the treaty-abiding faction, which settled on the Nebraska

Winnebago Reservation, and the Wisconsin Winnebago—later the Ho-Chunk—who never had their own reservation.

Their enduring sense of place made its way into Kickapoo Valley and Vernon County lore. Sometime during the 1860s, a poet using the *nom de plume* of Esmerelda composed the following tribute to Winnebago expatriates.[28]

THE INDIAN

Oh! Lone Winnebago,
How sadly you weep
O'er the bones of thy loved ones
In their desolate sleep;
The white man hath robbed thee
Of thine own native soil,
And the graves of they fathers
Are sunk neath their toil,

How sad is thy journey,
As thou goest alone
Through these wide rolling prairies,
That were once all thine own,
'Mid the homes of the white man
No more thou art free;
Scarce a grave for thy dead
Will they grant unto thee.

No more o'er these bluffs
Shall thou roam with delight,
Nor chase the wild deer
With fleet step and light,
Nor 'round the great council fire
Recline at thine ease,
Nor smoke with thy kindred
The calumet of peace.

No more shall thou fish
In this bright, silver stream,
No more shall the blade

Of the tomahawk gleam;
No more shall thine arrow
The water-fowl cleave;
At the bidding of white men.
All these thou must leave.

Oh! Sad Winnebago,
We grieve for thy fate,
Thy wrongs by the White man
Hath earned them thy hate.
May the spirit thou worship
Yet grant unto thee
A portion with braves
And home with the free.

A later account avowed that "the Winnebagos were so deeply attached to their Kickapoo valley that the government had to move them off time after time. They would come creeping back the next year, to hide in the swampy lands along a smaller river pouring into the Kickapoo. 'Hiding in the Kickapoo' became a specific term."[29]

Periodic roundups notwithstanding, the Wisconsin bands grew to one thousand people by 1873. In that year the Wisconsin legislature initiated the most notorious of the forced relocations. The first phase of the removal took place at Portage City. According to a Winnebago depiction, eighty people, including women with nursing babies back at home, were "pressed with the bayonet aboard the [railroad] cars waiting for them at that place."[30] Not all white residents supported the cruel policy. One group of citizens protected Blue Wing and his family from soldiers who were about to force them on a train. In the end, however, the state succeeded in shipping nine hundred people west to Nebraska through the winter of 1873–74.

Their removal proved still more catastrophic once they arrived in Nebraska. Out of desperation Winnebago chiefs sent news of their plight to President Grant. "We respectfully show to your excellency that there are now on their [Nebraska Winnebago] reservation nine hundred of our people, and we are poor and in need of help. Very many of our people are dying from want and exposure. Thirty of them have been buried within the past nine days." Comparing their destitution to better conditions in Wisconsin, where they had "lived like white people," the chiefs warned the president, "We cannot live here in this way and unless you do some-thing for us, we shall go back to Wisconsin where we can hunt and fish."[31] By spring almost all the survivors had returned to Wisconsin.

Though the Wisconsin bands never gained reservation land in the state, their presence did finally win grudging acceptance. In 1881, special legisla-tion allowed individual Winnebago Indians to buy forty-acre homesteads as long as they abandoned any claim to the Nebraska reservation.[32] Of course the land was not free; nor was it good land for farming and hunt-ing, since Euro-American settlers had already purchased the best tracts; nor did the land become government-sanctioned tribal property. Even so, the Winnebago had acquired a lawful place in southwestern Wisconsin. They clustered in northern parts of the region, near Black River Falls. Their presence dwindled farther south, in the Kickapoo Valley. At the end of the century residents noted that the Valley "is some times visited by small bands of Indians, but even this is getting to be rare."[33] A local perception settled in that the Winnebago had faded away into the night of history.

Where land is concerned this is not an uncommon narrative of con-quering peoples. Examples abound the world over. Where some indige-nous group was on the scene first, then displaced by another group, the displacers must dispose of the earlier residents in order to assert their own primacy over the place—in other words to assert their right to the land. Obviously the Winnebago were physically displaced, although that is not precisely my point here. After all, when one group loses land in a war, it might try to reclaim the land with force. Both sides see the logic of the claim, even when they are fighting over it. The kind of displacement I am referring to is more beguiling than war. It is the displacement that occurs in the cultural narratives of invaders. They must incorporate earlier groups into their own stories of arrival, and yet find a way to wipe the slate clean, to become *first* in a place. Perhaps, goes one story, the earlier people were not civilized. Dehumanizing predecessors is a typical way of justifying ter-ritorial conquest. You find colonial versions of it in Africa, Asia, and South America too.[34] Or an alternative story: Earlier people were admirable in their spirituality and closeness to the land, but sadly they waned into oblivion leaving only traces for us to honor. Both are forms of origin sto-ries. Just as importantly they are cultural claims to land. The question is, what happens when circumstances change for the people who have been displaced? What happens when a group believed entirely out of the pic-ture returns to reassert its own cultural stories and claims?

The Winnebago had long been memorialized and then disposed of in written histories of Wisconsin counties and townships. As a result, few non-Indians understood that in the *present-day* Kickapoo Valley the Winnebago still mattered. Admittedly, their memories of home and displacement were not confined to the same kind of boundaries that held sway among non-Indians in Stark. Their history could never be limited to a homestead parcel or a township or a county or a reserve. But under the right circumstances they had the power to shape a public reserve and a township, even if those particular boundaries had not previously held any meaning.

Jump ahead nearly one hundred years to the 1960s, and two events in Winnebago history converge. The first of these occurred in 1963, when the Wisconsin Winnebago established a formal government under the Indian Reorganization Act of 1934. This act was an attempt to reverse the General Allotment Act of 1887, a spectacular failure in Indian land policy. Under the policy of allotment, Indian tribes had lost two-thirds of their reservation lands. The 1934 act gave tribes more control over assets, and it compelled federal and state governments to respect tribal constitutions. Because they had internal disagreements, and because they also feared abrogating long-standing claims against the federal government, the Wisconsin Winnebago declined to organize in 1934.[35]

They had a number of reasons for changing their position three decades later. A document from the Wisconsin Winnebago Business Committee observed that the moment had come when Indians around the country "generally desire recognition as Indian tribes and seek improvement on a tribal level rather than assimilation and loss of ethnic identity."[36] There was a more place-specific reason to organize as well. As a nonreservation people, the Wisconsin Winnebago resided on taxable lands, or private property, whereas the federal government's fiscal obligation to tribes centered almost entirely on reservations. The result, according to Mitchell Whiterabbit, was that, "We, the Wisconsin Winnebagoes, who do not reside on any reservation, and who, the greater number of us now reside on taxable lands and who need federal assistance, have often been excluded from receiving Federal aids and benefits."[37] Although federal recognition would not achieve the aim that all aid "extended to Indians residing on reservations . . . be equally extended to us," it would give the Wisconsin Winnebago a stronger institutional position from which to negotiate the problem. In January of 1963, the Wisconsin Winnebago voted *en masse* in favor of their new constitution: 514 people for organization, 5 people against.[38] In 1994, they changed their name from Winnebago—which other tribes had imposed on them centuries before—to the Ho-Chunk Sovereign Nation. They thus proclaimed their identity as "People of the Big Voice."[39]

Just prior to the 1963 vote on organization, Mrs. Helen L. Peterson, a member of the Oglala-Sioux Tribe, addressed the Wisconsin Winnebago General Council Meeting about the Indian Reorganization Act. She took care to explain that the act would not benefit the Wisconsin Winnebago as much as it had other tribes because of their nonreservation status. Still, Mrs. Peterson felt strongly that the tribe should organize. One of her central arguments was so shrewd that it seems worthwhile to quote it at length. She drew the attention of everyone present to section 17 of the act, which allowed tribes to obtain federal charters for incorporation. "You know and I know," she said, "that 'corporations' seem like such a complicated concept for most of us who have had little or no business experience that any discussion of this seems above our heads. You know, yourselves, however, that this is a common form of doing business today and that we all ought to inform ourselves better on what corporations are, what advantages they offer, and so on. In many instances it takes a corporation legal structure to conduct business enterprises advantageously." Gesturing to their impoverished condition, Mrs. Peterson allowed that, "With no land, no money, or no resources, you may feel this provision or possibility wouldn't be important today." But think ahead, she prodded, "Maybe you *don't* have much of anything right now, but perhaps you will someday."[40]

Helen Peterson had just unknowingly foreshadowed Indian gaming. In 1987, the U.S. Supreme Court ruled that state law cannot ban gambling on Indian land if it permits and regulates gaming otherwise.[41] Congress followed with the 1988 Indian Gaming and Regulatory Act, under which states must negotiate gaming compacts in good faith. By the 1990s, the Ho-Chunk Nation had proven Helen Peterson prophetic, having become a large corporation whose holdings included three successful casinos. Once one of the poorest tribes in the state, the Ho-Chunk were now the most economically influential.[42]

Their newfound bureaucratic organization and wealth made it easier for the Ho-Chunk to focus on cultural matters of the highest importance, specifically, the inventory and care of archeological sites. By 1993 the Ho-Chunk had already initiated a project to map hundreds of effigy mounds in southern Wisconsin. On one site beside the Wisconsin River, they planned to spend $700,000 to buy land and conduct archeological research.[43] Beside another river, the Kickapoo, their ancestors had cooked deer in rock shelters, carved petroglyphs in soft sandstone bluffs, and built burial mounds for their kin. Present-day Ho-Chunk had a sacred obliga- tion to the place, which extended even to the physical remains of still ear- lier cultures. With the reserve's status in flux, the Ho-Chunk saw a window of opportunity. They now had the political sophistication and the finan- cial clout to make a modern land claim.

In Washington, D.C., Senator Feingold's staff had been working hard on the part of the senate budget bill that would deauthorize the La Farge dam project. Feingold was almost ready with freestanding language to transfer the land to the state. His office had been in regular contact with the Kickpaoo Valley citizens group, and no substantive concerns had arisen. But the senator wanted to know if the Corps of Engineers would also support the bill's language. He got a most unexpected reply from the Corps. This bill, the agency said, may abrogate the rights of the Ho- Chunk Nation.

Feingold's staff was stunned. No one had been aware that the Ho- Chunk Nation had any connection to the land. What the senator's office learned on further research changed the way they all thought about the reserve. It emerged that a previous president of the tribe had written the Bureau of Indian Affairs—a federal agency—and asked the Bureau to make a claim should the General Services Administration declare land from the La Farge dam excess property—a claim, by the way, for the entire property.[44] This told the senator two things. One was that the Ho-Chunk Nation had maintained an active interest in the land, to the point that it had tried to ensure its own future role as owner. And second, the legis- lation as it stood could usurp the Ho-Chunk's claim. The question that followed was whether or not state and local officials and Kickapoo Valley communities had been aware of the claim and had pursued legislation as a way to bypass the Ho-Chunk Nation. The senator's staff never satisfied themselves either way on that point, but it became clear that no formal discussions had taken place with the Ho-Chunk during community meet- ings on the reserve's status.[45] The Ho-Chunk had not been an official part of the process.

Senator Feingold could have responded in a number of ways. He could have gone ahead with the language already developed for the Water Re- sources Development Act of 1996. If a political fight arose, however, this approach might put the legislation at risk. Alternatively, Feingold could have inserted explicit language in the bill to protect cultural sites, thereby addressing Ho-Chunk concerns but not actively promoting their further involvement. Instead, Senator Feingold stopped the project altogether in order to confer with the Ho-Chunk. Chloris Lowe Jr., then president of the Ho-Chunk Nation, traveled to Washington with a map of archeological sites on the reserve that looked, according to one person present, as if someone had thrown rice at it and all the grains stuck. Feingold decided to allocate some of the reserve to the Ho-Chunk, but he needed a specific number of acres for the bill. Lowe proposed twelve hundred acres and the senator agreed (the agreement would later infuriate Ho-Chunk elders).[46]

That the federal government was planning to devolve so much land to the state was notable. More notable yet, for the first time in U.S. history the federal government would return some of the land the Ho-Chunk had once controlled. "My dream has been to have this area . . . set aside and reserved in perpetuity for Ho-Chunk people and their descendents," said Lowe. "At the same time," he continued, acknowledging the land's recent history, "I am happy the nation has been able to assist in ending the suffering the people of the Kickapoo Valley have experienced for decades because of the La Farge Dam project."[47]

The 1996 act included a number of conditions, any one of which could derail the transfer. Foremost was the requirement that the Ho-Chunk Nation and the State of Wisconsin sign a formal Memorandum of Understanding on their respective property boundaries within the reserve, as well as agree on a management plan for all the land.[48] They had to reach an agreement on or before October 31, 1997, only one year and one day after the law had passed, and after which the law would expire. At the same time, the U.S. Army Corps of Engineers had to sign a Programmatic Agreement with the State of Wisconsin in order to comply with a different law, the National Historic Preservation Act.[49] Under this law, before the Corps could relinquish any land it must provide for the protection of archeological sites listed in or eligible for the National Register. Likewise the Corps must take precautions to protect any undiscovered sites from future harm. The problem for the agency was that federal law mandated a much higher level of protection on federal land than Wisconsin state law mandated on state land. The Corps could not act until the state addressed the adverse effects its ownership might have on archeological sites.

The requirements of the National Historic Preservation Act put the St. Paul District Corps of Engineers in an uncharacteristic position. Whereas the district had once worked to inundate the area, now it was the principal custodian of valuable and sacred cultural resources. Whereas the criterion for success had once been completing the La Farge dam, now it was completing a land transfer. The new goal was as straightforward as the Corps could ever want in a project. The only obstacle was obtaining consensus among representatives of the State of Wisconsin, the Ho-Chunk Nation, the State Historic Preservation Office, the Kickapoo Reserve Management Board, and the Bureau of Indian Affairs. Because this was a social challenge rather than an engineering problem, a nonengineer and nonofficer in the St. Paul District stepped forward to coordinate the process. John Anfinson was a historian and the District's Chief of Cultural Resources. The detailed minutes he recorded at meetings on deauthorization provide a rich portrait of negotiations whose outcome was never certain. Likewise, his words touch on the drama that always hovered over the reserve. Through Anfinson's work in this setting, the St. Paul District became, for a brief moment, what the Corps liked to profess itself: a relatively objective observer and mediator.

The Programmatic Agreement was in effect a contract outlining the property rights the State of Wisconsin would hold once it assumed ownership of the reserve. The same was true for the Memorandum of Understanding between the Ho-Chunk and the state. These were separate documents, but the negotiations over both would be inseparable. Discussions throughout the year revolved around three interwoven problems. First was defining the boundaries of the Ho-Chunk's twelve hundred acres. Second was how to safeguard archeological sites when the state took over its part of the reserve. And third was whether or not the Ho-Chunk would claim additional land later, a possibility the Water Resources Development Act had left open. Always pressing on the negotiations was the October 31 deadline for signing an agreement.

The Ho-Chunk needed to delineate twelve hundred acres, an obligation that immediately became a sore point. Why the short deadline? asked Ho-Chunk negotiators.[50] Earlier archeological work notwithstanding, they must have a chance to assess the property themselves. The research could not be accomplished in a single year, and they wanted to be very cautious because tribes throughout the country were watching the process.[51] Compounding Ho-Chunk frustration was a deep-seated anger over the amount of land involved. In settling on twelve hundred acres, their former president had gone beyond his authority, they asserted. He had not represented the tribe.[52] Minutes from one meeting paraphrased the feeling: "It did not matter whether a site had one flake or a variety of cultural resources. All the sites were significant; the whole valley was sacred. [The Ho-Chunk] may, therefore, ask for all the sites, regardless of which are significant from a National Register Perspective."[53] Ho-Chunk negotiators, said John Anfinson, "never gave up the point that there is no 1200 acres—it's all sacred."[54] By October, however, the Ho-Chunk had acted on the twelve hundred acres guaranteed them. They decided against sites scattered across the reserve as Chloris Lowe had originally calculated. The tribe settled instead on two large parcels, one in the township of Whitestown, the other in the township of Stark.

Along with Ho-Chunk property boundaries came the question of how to ensure a high level of protection for cultural sites on the remaining land. Over several meetings Richard Dexter, of the State Historic Preservation Office, argued for a covenant, while Ho-Chunk attorney Glen Reynolds preferred a conservation easement held by the Bureau of Indian Affairs. Rich Berg of the Bureau of Indian Affairs was unhappy at the prospect of enforcing an easement. For their part Corps representatives reported that the precise instrument did not matter: Corps Headquarters Real Estate in Washington would reject an easement and a covenant because both would keep the federal government involved in the property.[55] This was a dispute over the means to an agreed-upon end.

Negotiators for the State of Wisconsin went straight to the real schism that easements and covenants exposed. Why do the Ho-Chunk need title to any land if an easement can protect the entire property? one of them asked. For him the Ho-Chunk's attorney gave a brief history lesson. Another state negotiator presented the flip side of the same question. Whether by covenant or easement, aren't the Ho-Chunk "getting their cake and getting to eat it too?" That was to say, the tribe would own twelve hundred acres outright while directing how the state managed the rest. Still a third state negotiator, who was assigned to represent local interests around the reserve, wondered how he could convince local citizens to go along with an easement.[56] His anxiety was well founded. Residents were closely following the negotiations. At one meeting a member of the property rights group PLOW (Private Landowners of Wisconsin) had disputed the constitutionality of the whole deal. On a bridge across the reserve, anti-Indian graffiti stared drivers in the face.

In the end the negotiators decided against an easement or a covenant. Instead they combined a National Register historic district nomination with a formal Cultural Resources Management Plan.[57] Together the two would provide the same level of protection as federal law. Although they came to naught, the discussions over easements and covenants put a spot-light on the ambiguous meaning of public property. It was a hollow idea until all the interested parties gave it some form, working out parameters for access to and control of the land.

Not yet resolved was the part of the Water Resources Development Act that enabled the Ho-Chunk to request additional land after ten years. With only three weeks left to reach an agreement, the Ho-Chunk introduced the topic. They wanted specific criteria in the Memorandum of Under-standing for future land transfers to the tribe. According to meeting min-utes, "This led to a 3 hour break down in the negotiations. The State team was extremely upset."[58] For months the five-member commission negoti-ating for the state had tried to ensure that the Ho-Chunk would not claim more land. Doubtless this was their biggest concern all along. No wonder then, when nearly every other issue had been resolved, that this remained the deal-breaker. "It was like push and shove," said Ho-Chunk attorney Glenn Reynolds. Both sides had a lot of land to lose, but together they would lose it all if they did not come to terms.

At some point during their struggle, at some breaking point, the nego-tiators moved beyond the specific property debate. They left it behind and moved toward weary acceptance that the process of negotiation would continue long, long after they were done, and so their solution was very wise. They left open the possibility of a future shift in property bound-aries. And they also left open the possibility that the boundaries would stay fixed in place. On the issue of additional transfers, the Memorandum of Understanding ultimately read, "the State, through the [Kickapoo Reserve Management] Board, agrees to consider future transfers of land . . . which contain sites, discovered subsequent to the transfer of the initial 1200 acres . . . of cultural or religious significance."[59] After specifying how the Board would evaluate Ho-Chunk requests, the Memorandum made plain that "future land transfers are not guaranteed under any circumstances, but will be given fair consideration." Nor would the Board guarantee that any property line would be sacrosanct or fixed for all time (though some property lines may well be remembered for all time).

The negotiators barely met their deadline for an agreement, a triumph nonetheless. In one year they had made peace with the tensions inherent in the reserve and in the process had negotiated a new form of public-private-community and federal-state-local land tenure. As defined by the communities of the Kickapoo Valley, the Ho-Chunk Nation, the State of Wisconsin, the Corps of Engineers, the Kickapoo Reserve Management

Board, the Bureau of Indian Affairs, the State Historical Society, the Water Resources Development Act, and the National Historic Preservation Act, the Kickapoo Valley Reserve represented a hybrid of public and private ownership; a partnership between historic antagonists; a source of empowerment for local people and the Ho-Chunk; a sacred space; and several new land titles.

A note of caution to anyone interested in applying a similar devolutionary model to other public lands: Conflict over the reserve had centered on who would hold title to the property and what the precise property boundaries would be. But when negotiators had discussed the actual land, there was little discord. None of them proposed, for example, that the reserve become a site for commercial resource extraction. The Ho-Chunk presence might have set tacit limits. Or perhaps the strict deadline encouraged negotiators to focus on shared values, rather than on values that would have separated them. It was probably both. Within this context everyone was united by a vision that was at once cultural and ecological. Quoting from their joint plan, the Ho-Chunk Nation and the state agreed to:

Both symbol and artifact. The Kickapoo Valley Reserve management board decided to preserve the La Farge dam intake tower because of its historical significance. (Lynne Heasley)

protect the reserve and all it contains with special protections for significant
cultural and environmental resources;

provide for managed public access to balance various user groups with the overriding mission to protect the reserve;

cherish the history of the reserve, its resources and the lives of the people that
have been affected by the political and natural occurrences which ultimately
led to this project.

The plan outlined more specific principles as well. "The management of
the Reserve shall: Protect the Reserve's aesthetic, cultural, scenic and wild
qualities as well as the native wildlife and plant communities."[60] Though
protection was the main theme (no more pickup trucks), the plan did
not adopt a hands-off approach. It noted the presence of "poorly managed
cultivated forests that need selective harvesting, as well as areas in need
of reforestation" (there will be some eco-logging, therefore). The Board
would also "make recommendations for appropriate restoration of oak
savannas, prairies or other native habitats" (perhaps some eco-plowing, too,

A landscape vision—a communitywide agreement to "protect the reserve and all it
contains with special protections for significant cultural and environmental
resources." (Courtesy of Wolfgang Hoffmann)

or at least herbicide applications to make room for prairie plants). Tourism would be the primary human activity on the reserve, but it "should have as little effect on the land as possible" (silent sports especially welcome, but we won't shut out hunters). With this plan the negotiators laid out their intent to shape the landscape of the future. Conversely, they specified ways in which the nonhuman nature of the place would shape management.

By approaching the reserve as property, the negotiators had established new social relationships on the land. By approaching it as nature worthy of care in its own right, they had made room for important ecosystem dynamics—a sustainable wildness, you might say. By approaching it as part of a long and contentious human history, they helped old combatants reconcile. There was the Ho-Chunk's erstwhile grievance with the U.S. government. There was also the more recent rancor between the Sierra Club and locals who had fought for the La Farge dam. All these groups accepted the Programmatic Agreement, the Memorandum of Understanding, and the Joint Management Plan. All that remained was for Ho-Chunk president Jacob LoneTree and Wisconsin Governor Tommy Thompson to sign the final documents. "It came right down to October 30," Anfinson said.[61]

More than twenty-five years earlier, residents in Stark had celebrated the ground breaking for the La Farge dam. Some twenty years before they had burned Senator Proxmire in effigy when he came to town and announced the end of the project. Now it was October 30, 1997, and they were preparing a big welcome for the governor and the Ho-Chunk Nation at the signing ceremony in La Farge. "They had the town hall all decked out, cookies and coffee, everyone was waiting," recalled Anfinson. "Then . . . ," Anfinson paused. "The governor called and said he wasn't coming." The governor did not want to land his plane in the dangerous coulee country around La Farge. Even at this most human moment it seemed that the Valley landscape must be part of the finale. "I felt so bad for the town," Anfinson said. "They were stood up."[62]

Besides the slight, and some did feel it as a slight, the law deauthorizing the reserve was about to expire. Governor Thompson changed his mind about the trip after Marcy West, executive director of the Kickapoo Valley Reserve, spoke with him by phone. "We discussed options," West said tactfully of the conversation.[63] She tried to convince the governor to make the two-hour drive from Madison. He decided to fly to La Crosse instead, about a forty-minute drive from La Farge on a winding two-lane highway. "We all jumped in our cars and raced over to La Crosse," said

Anfinson (energetically). "There was tension down to the last minute. The Ho-Chunk were threatening to leave." Many Valley residents were in the caravan. "There were some people that needed to witness it," said West.

Despite all the drama, and because of it, the Ho-Chunk did participate in the signing. Afterward they joined some of the St. Paul District staff for dinner at a local restaurant. Forced off their land 160 years earlier, the Ho-Chunk had returned to claim their history and their property. On this occasion, both the government and Kickapoo Valley communities welcomed them back.

Conclusion

Claims on Paradise

In writing this book my hope is that people concerned with rural places—especially those who live in them—will be empowered by their own complicated histories. The historical tension between individual and community prerogatives on the land is the central problem this book has explored. Making sense of this tension is crucial to understanding rural transformation in the twentieth century. Like many rural places, the Kickapoo Valley has moved away from local farm economies and landscapes and toward regional diversity, both social and ecological. We could use many lenses to view these changes. Macrolevel lenses include capitalist development, globalization of agriculture, and demographic trends reshaping country, city, and suburb. At a microlevel we could focus on social dynamics such as class, ethnicity, race, and gender. All of these are important analytical lenses and many of them have a place in this book. But the book has been primarily concerned with property—as an institution, a cultural prism, and an ecological force. Property is a locus where society and the natural world reshape each other, and where society's deeper values surface.

My approach to the problem of individual and community prerogatives has involved examining the historical interplay between property regimes and landscapes using case studies—the townships of Liberty, Clinton, and Stark. This required tracing ecological outcomes in changing landscapes and cultural outcomes in changing narratives about property and the environment. This was more challenging than it sounds, because the events that influenced outcomes in the Valley took place on many levels: local, regional, and national; and ecological, cultural, and legal. The most striking result was the divergence of the three townships. Since the 1930s, clear differences have emerged in their landscape patterns of fields, forest, and pasture and in their vernacular landscapes of farmhouses and outbuildings, second homes and bed-and-breakfasts, fence lines and sawmills, ancient pictographs and springhouse ruins.

Twin landscape and ownership histories have shaped the townships' dominant property narratives, which likewise diverged. Liberty, for example, showed a basic schism by 1995. A mosaic of large parcels surrounded a cluster of small ones. While beef ranching and recreational land speculation established the two patterns, their roots go back to earlier federal policies like the Soil Bank program. Today, local narratives reflect widespread familiarity with the ownership trends; there is almost nowhere in rural America where concentration, fragmentation, and absentee ownership are not happening in one form or another. But the narratives have also obscured the actual policies and people that spurred the changes in Liberty. In retrospect the changes *appear* inevitable and natural, a product of the proverbial invisible hand of the market. Quite differently in Clinton, residents understand their own recent history through an ethnic narrative. A sense of territory, demarcated by cultural outsiders, now overlays private property boundaries. (The Amish made up one group of outsiders, the Air National Guard another.) This narrative, too, is familiar in many rural places, though it takes on other guises depending on the ethnicity or nationality of the newcomers. And in Stark, the community views much of its history through the prism of property if for no other reason than its residents keep local ownership histories so alive in the present. Any stranger could spend two days in the township and come away with the conviction that the unfinished La Farge dam was a defining event. Stark's history would surely resonate with rural communities that feel they have come out on the losing end of their dealings with the federal government and make this one of their central narratives.

I have also attempted to test philosophical ideas about property using the Kickapoo Valley's environmental history. Returning to the book's introduction, these ideas include the purpose of property—which of society's values it serves; whether the terms of holding property are primarily fluid or static; and the model of land ownership that most aptly expresses land use policy. Taking the ideas one by one:

In terms of the purpose of property, both private and public regimes have borne a heavy burden. The burden consists of the sheer diversity of values that have shaped how people approach land ownership. In Liberty, economic freedom and individual autonomy were core values that dominated hands-off approaches to real estate speculators and corporate beef ranchers. Liberty's town board was also concerned about any unfairness to landowners in restricting unexpected new land uses, especially in the case of the motocross, and so fairness was a local value that became entwined with freedom of action. The Amish looked at the same values differently, and expanded on them. Though important, economic prosperity was merely a means to their deepest values of community well-being and religious freedom and fidelity. Also deeper than economic values were land stewardship and separation from American cultural life. As for individual autonomy, it was always secondary to the health of the community. For its part, the La Farge dam controversy spanned the poles of economic development and environmental protection. But under the surface La Farge Lake was really supposed to help Valley communities achieve some measure of stability and security as well as local autonomy (much like the Amish). Stability, security, autonomy, these were the shared values that prompted Valley communities to support the conversion of private to public land, and to accept the severe environmental costs of the dam. They overrode both landowner prerogatives and environmental values. The irony was that both environmental and economic values prevailed: NEPA forced the Corps of Engineers to make environmental costs public, while unfavorable economic cost-benefit analyses doomed the project once and for all. In another twist of values, the Kickapoo Valley Reserve, born, it seemed to residents, out of the charred ruins of their own dreams, came to embody the very deepest noneconomic meanings that can be invested in property of any kind. Care of the land and care of cultural tradition became its twin purpose. The Reserve became a place in which to honor many histories, ecological and human.

In the Kickapoo Valley, the terms of holding property have been decidedly fluid. Here especially the Valley is representative of most rural regions. To argue otherwise is to conceal history. Soil conservation was just one of many examples in which different property rights—metaphorical sticks— became redistributed among the ownership bundles of farmers, state and local governments, and federal agencies. State game policies likewise inserted notions of common property into private and public land ownership. The Kickapoo Valley Reserve is emblematic of the ways in which property can evolve. It became an entirely new form of public property, jointly managed by the state of Wisconsin, local communities, and the Ho-Chunk Nation.

The very fluidity of property arrangements in the Valley tells us a lot about the ownership models that shaped those arrangements. No doubt the classical model had and continues to have tremendous influence. It provides the ubiquitous backdrop, a local approach to property that acknowledges a primary relationship between a landowner and his, her, or its land. Yet the history of landownership in the Kickapoo Valley has come much closer to Joseph Singer's social relations model of property than many of its own residents might recognize. Property rights have been contingent not only on their social context (as per Singer's model) but on their environmental context too. Whether the land use question was soil conservation and contour strips, forest management and livestock grazing, a dam and endangered species, deer hunting and oak regeneration; whether the land ownership question was shady real estate developers, Amish settlement, seasonal trespass, Ho-Chunk land claims, devolution of public land, and most recently, state-mandated Smart Growth zoning, together the individual stories make up a much larger history of constant negotiation. In other words, the stories make up a history of changing relationships.

This, then, is a central insight of the book: alongside economically centered and individualistic notions of property, democratic and fluid visions of property have also been powerful. If we look across philosophical divides we will see individual and community approaches coexisting, and changing. The special contribution of Liberty, Clinton, and Stark is that they present adjacent historical scenarios. Their different outcomes offer the ideal opportunity to compare and weigh ideas about property. The challenge is deciding how to assess the townships, which criteria to use. Inevitably the choice will affect the lessons people draw. Four criteria in particular can help us derive lessons from these complex township histories.

(1) The first and most obvious criterion is a community's ability to achieve its desired outcomes. By this measure the Cashton settlement of Amish in Clinton was highly successful. Every time the community mobilized toward a particular end, it succeeded: first with its settlement and expansion; then with its cheese factory; and finally, when it defeated the Air National Guard's plan for low-level flights over the Kickapoo Valley. The Ho-Chunk Nation was similarly successful in Stark and neighboring Whitestown. The group reclaimed rights in land it once held in southwestern Wisconsin. By precisely the same measure, however, Stark's longtime residents still view their own mobilization for the La Farge dam in a harsh light. They did not accomplish their hard-fought end, and on top of that they paid dearly in thousands of acres of unwanted public land. Because Stark represented a concerted effort that failed, it also represented

what local communities felt at the time to be a loss of their viability. But this criterion, which we (or they) might use to lament Stark's history, butts up against a second obvious criterion.

(2) Environmental outcomes offer another yardstick for assessing the townships. From an environmental perspective Stark's history doesn't look so depressing, even to local communities. In 1935, the Kickapoo River overflowed its banks and inundated the village of La Farge. Sixty years later, once-agricultural riparian land traversing the Kickapoo Valley Reserve had grown to lowland forest and wet meadow. In recent years nearby residents have noticed less flood damage downstream. Is this a coincidence, they wonder, or is the land along the river absorbing more water? In terms of biological diversity, a standard environmental yardstick, Stark is moving at crosscurrents. So far the township has sustained oak-hickory forests on the reserve and even on some private land around the reserve. It is also home to endemic endangered plants. At the same time, the area's high deer population is simplifying forest ecosystems. Still, because of the reserve, biologists and ecologists anticipate a level of ecological diversity—of wildness—unusual in the Midwest.

Liberty's land ownership history had environmental consequences that were also present in Stark and Clinton but not as pronounced in those townships. One was the construction of second homes on steep slopes with their driveways cutting straight uphill. Severe recurring soil erosion resulted, making recreational development one of Liberty's biggest environmental problems. This is part of a historical trend in Liberty toward landscape fragmentation. Of course Liberty is not alone. Clinton's forest ecosystems are fragmented too. Both townships have lost oak-hickory communities to a greater extent than Stark. Yet the scene is complicated. Not every ecological outcome has been negative. A great deal of agricultural land in Liberty has regenerated to forest. Many people consider reforestation one positive result of changing land ownership. A reasonable conclusion about Liberty might be that accelerated land turnover and absentee ownership have produced diverse land uses, which in turn have made its landscape more heterogeneous, or fragmented, and in some respects more ecologically impoverished.

Alone among the three townships, Clinton has remained primarily agricultural. Amish farming may well be Clinton's most compelling environmental outcome. We should therefore consider Clinton in agroecological terms. Whereas Liberty stands out for its diversity of land uses, and Stark stands out for the biological diversity of its forests, Clinton stands out for its agricultural diversity—a variety of farm animals, crops, fruits, and vegetables. Like beef cattle in Liberty, Amish dairy cattle degraded streams and forests. Clinton's herds, however, were much smaller and more dispersed. Even today one farm might have as few as twelve cows. Fully integrated into Amish farms, forests make the agricultural scene still more diverse. The Amish harvest timber in their forests, but they also tend to what foresters call nontimber forest products like wild game, wild mushrooms, and native ginseng. The result ecologically speaking is an anthropogenic (human dominated) "disturbance regime"—in other words, heavily used second-growth forests whose canopy structure and species distribution are less diverse than forests in the nearby Kickapoo Valley Reserve but which enrich the agricultural landscape nonetheless.

However valid the first two criteria (achievement of local goals, environmental quality), they can lead to opposing perspectives. Stark might be a brilliant success of a place, or it might be a pitiful failure. Separately, the measures encompass restricted sets of values, which under the right conditions—the La Farge dam, for example—will be mutually exclusive. In just this way, old property debates return again and again, reduced not to low but to narrow denominators. If Stark, Liberty, and Clinton are to take us beyond the axiom that beauty is in the eye of the beholder, we must seek additional measures for weighing them. A third criterion builds a bridge between these first two.

(3) We can weigh the townships by the following question: *Which communities self-consciously accommodated the widest array of values in their decisions?* Here the Amish community in Clinton looks successful indeed. It honored individual land ownership and community well-being, though it gave priority to the community. It honored economic prosperity for its members, but tempered by personal humility and frugality; an agricultural way of life, but only in a form that allowed stewardship of God's creation; cultural separation, but peace with all neighbors. The list could go on, but the important feature is its complexity. The Amish have not taken an either/or approach to their values. Rather, they have taken on the hard work of organizing *all* their values into a coherent worldview. The results are carved in the land itself for us to consider.

(4) A fourth criterion for assessing the townships takes us back to Stark and Liberty. Rather than focusing on a community's ability to achieve particular outcomes, we could measure how successful it has been in formulating a shared vision. This is different from vying for something concrete like the La Farge dam. Developing a vision means not assuming particular

ends at the outset. The shared part probably means redefining the community, enlarging the table at which people sit. In this regard it would be hard to imagine a more dramatic example of success than the eventual consensus in La Farge over the Corps of Engineers land. The Water Resources Development Act of 1996 brought antagonistic stakeholders together. No one could impose prior assumptions on the others. Thus began a truly inclusive process that forged permanent ties between local communities and the Ho-Chunk Nation. The Kickapoo Valley Reserve is the environmental manifestation of their shared vision. More recently in Liberty, the town board approached local zoning as a democratic process. Before undertaking a new ordinance, the board facilitated a dialogue among all its landowners and residents. The board asked people to reimagine Liberty and their place in it. The ordinance would be an expression of the process, and a vision for the future.

In their distinct ways, each of these townships has something important to say. But their separateness is not where the most profound lessons lie. Taken together, Liberty, Clinton, and Stark occupy a total area twelve miles across and sixteen miles in length. From this vantage the townships are not separate at all. In fact the stories that I have relegated to one township or another are stories that residents feel they hold in common. Together, the townships are part of a single place whose environmental history reveals a remarkably wide and tangled array of values. But where do we go with these values? How do we ultimately weigh the tangled and contested history of rural America?

There are risks and opportunities in framing the lessons of the Kickapoo Valley in terms of values. Yet that is how people have approached property rights and the environment and rural history—in the language of values. The risk is that values can become a straitjacket for enforcing conformity, or a cudgel for brutally achieving ends to which others disagree. Take "community values." Community might mean that the majority rules, or the majority tyrannizes. Sometimes a great unity of values can lead to repression.

Invoking community values can be as divisive as it is unifying. This is apparent in the distinction some self-identified conservatives and some self-identified liberals make between themselves: fear among conservatives of radical (i.e., immoral) individualism gone amok and fear among liberals of restrictions on individual freedom and rights. This is the paradox of the property rights movement. It has championed maximum freedom and rights to the individual with minimal imposition from a larger community whose interests will not always coincide with those of individual landowners.

Even so, the language of community values allows people to make their case for alternative scenarios. In the Kickapoo Valley, few residents feel that land ownership is entirely relative, with a Woodland Farms being no better or worse than an Amish farm. They have preferences. They understand the morality of different kinds of land uses. The language of a value like "community" helps people articulate why their collective viewpoint should be honored. The argument goes something like this:

> An entirely individualistic, present-minded, hands-off approach deprives people in places like Liberty of any meaningful say in their own quality of life and environmental integrity. When it comes to rural well-being (social and environmental), moderating the dominance, even triumph, of radical individualism must be part of the discussion.

Likewise, the language of a value like "local democracy" helps people articulate how their collective viewpoint should be honored, along the following lines:

> This is not to argue for the obliteration of individual needs or desires, but for the ability to negotiate at both individual and collective levels. Local democracies must take all their members into account, as de Tocqueville saw so clearly in the nineteenth century. This means balancing an allegiance to individual rights with an allegiance to the community. The best approach, then, is an open and democratic assessment of when and how individual landowners will defer to community needs and values.

But what happens if community values *are* primarily individualistic and economically centered? This is where a place's history and culture come in. In the Kickapoo Valley, history shows that such values have never been exclusive; they have always served alongside other core values. In fact, for more than 150 years a radiant environmental aesthetic has suffused local Valley culture. In 1856 the Nuzum family settled in the Kickapoo Valley. A century later in his book *Here on the Kickapoo,* Ralph Nuzum mused about his parents' choice of home:

> Nobody knows why these early settlers passed up the level lands of Illinois and Indiana, or even the prairie country southwest of Viroqua, but they came from

a hilly and wooded section, and were always looking for plenty of fire-wood, as near as possible to a spring. That's why they settled in the Ozarks of Wisconsin among the harmonious hills of the Kickapoo, and why we happen to be living in this quiet and restful spot . . . this western wildwood.[1]

Nuzum usually described the Kickapoo Valley in blissful terms. To him it was a "lotus land," a "maiden's dream," an "enchanted coulee land," a "friendly and hospitable paradise"—"plumb peaceful"—"the most heavenly spot this side the stars!" And these were from just one of the four books he self-published about the place.[2] Nuzum, by the way, owned the largest, most profitable sawmill in the Valley.

In *Among the Hills,* beloved local author Josie Churchill reminisced about her brother Vincent, who was born in 1897. The natural world of the Valley was inextricably tied to her memories of Vincent.

He was a naturalist from the time he was a little boy and Papa led him by the hand through the deep woods and along the streams. My father, always living off the land was a naturalist himself and I've often wondered how he knew so much about all the wild things around us. Vincent was a gleaner in our fields of nature and remained a bachelor all his life.[3]

Kickapoo Valley storyteller Ben Logan recalled his 1930s childhood in an exquisite book, *The Land Remembers:*

The seven of us, and the land with all its living things, were like a hive of bees. No matter how fiercely independent any one of us might be, we were each a dependent part of the whole, and we knew that.[4]

Also weaving together Valley people and landscape, Robert E. Gard and Dale O'Brien wrote that:

Folks around here understand what it means to just stand and look out over the land. These people are still kind of dreamers, practical though many of 'em are too, and they appreciate a great view. These farmers know what it means when you say save nature. They're not so much scholars of ecology; but they are ready to pitch in and make the land as good as it can be.[5]

These are but a sampling of literary exertions from the Kickapoo Valley. What they all share is a profound sense of place, and this sensibility clarifies values important to people in the Valley: love of place, desire to be *in* place, people as a meaningful part of the land, care for the natural world.

To Valley residents, their collective aesthetic is a spiritual fact. But the aesthetic is not *always* an ecological fact, or a community fact. Like rural people anywhere, many will still default to landowner prerogatives—property rights in shorthand. Sometimes people default this way from a position of insecurity (landowners fearful of losing their jobs, their health, or their land), sometimes from a position of influence (investors maximizing their value). Often the argument falls under the ideological guise of "no government interference," but really it means no community or even no local democracy. The challenge is how to help people who want to stay on the land gain some security while protecting the land itself through a succession of different owners.

The language of values can offer real hope when it becomes a touchstone for local decision making and a starting point for negotiating outcomes. It may be the only way to envision an ideal or even an acceptable rural landscape. Developing the language of values is a necessary first step in revitalizing the idea and practice of community in rural places. By bringing values into the open, people can speak more clearly.

Last words from the Kickapoo Valley. (Lynne Heasley)

NOTES
BIBLIOGRAPHY
INDEX

Notes

Introduction

1. See John Locke, *Two Treatises of Government* (1988).

2. One of the most formidable contemporary craftsmen of Locke's ideas is libertarian scholar Richard Epstein, whose *Takings: Private Property and the Power of Eminent Domain* (1985) has become the textbook for this position on property's core functions. Also influential has been the work of John McClaughry, former Vermont senator and president of the Ethan Allen Institute. See John McClaughry, "The New Feudalism," *Environmental Law* 5 (1975): 675–702. For helpful surveys of Epstein and like-minded thinkers, see James W. Ely Jr., *The Guardian of Every Other Right: A Constitutional History of Property Rights* (1992); and Eric T. Freyfogle, *Bounded People, Boundless Lands: Envisioning a New Land Ethic* (1998), 97–105.

3. For Jefferson, says Arthur McEvoy, "private property was the key to a political ideology of civic republicanism that valued participation with other citizens in self-government as the highest good." Land ownership according to Jefferson, add Charles Geisler and Gail Daneker, "is as much a social as an economic asset." Arthur McEvoy, "Markets and Ethics in U.S. Property Law," in *Who Owns America? Social Conflict Over Property Rights,* ed. Harvey M. Jacobs (1998), 100; Geisler and Daneker, *Property and Values* (2000), xiv–xv; also, Donald Last, "Private Property Rights with Responsibilities: What Would Thomas Jefferson Say about the 'Wise Use' Movement?" in Jacobs, *Who Owns America?* 45–53. Another helpful summary of this second tradition is Freyfogle, *Bounded People, Boundless Lands,* 73–74, 105–7. For a critical vetting of whom or what property has served—and whom or what it should serve—see John Christman, *The Myth of Property: Toward an Egalitarian Theory of Ownership* (1995).

4. Brazil offers the classic case of concentrated political power being derived from concentrated land ownership and vice versa. Under its *latifundista* property system a small number of wealthy owners control most of the country's productive land at the expense of both impoverished Brazilians and the environment. These same landowners exercise great, and often brutal, power over Brazil's political system at local and national levels. A valuable appraisal by one of the leading thinkers on land tenure and

land reform is William C. Thiesenhusen's *Broken Promises: Agrarian Reform and the Latin American Campesino* (1995).

Scholars have documented highly skewed (and politicized) land ownership in this country too. See especially, Appalachian Land Ownership Task Force, *Who Owns Appalachia? Land Ownership and Its Impact* (1983); also Louise Fortmann, "Bonanza! The Unasked Questions: Domestic Land Tenure through International Lenses," in Jacobs, *Who Owns America?* 11–12; and Ingolf Vogeler, *The Myth of the Family Farm: Agribusiness Dominance of U.S. Agriculture* (1981), 85.

5. McEvoy, "Markets and Ethics in U.S. Property Law," 94–113.

6. Alan M. Gottlieb, ed., *The Wise Use Agenda* (1989).

7. It was Dr. W. J. McGee, Pinchot's long-time colleague and collaborator, who coined this influential and enduring definition of conservation. See Gifford Pinchot, *Breaking New Ground* (1947; reprint, 1998), 326.

8. Char Miller and V. Alaric Sample, "Gifford Pinchot and the Conservation Spirit," in *Breaking New Ground,* ed. Char Miller and V. Alaric Sample (1998), xi–xvii.

9. Nor did the *Agenda* share Pinchot's great faith in public land management for a higher public good. Harvey Jacobs provides a fine overview of the wise use movement in "The 'Wisdom,' but Uncertain Future, of the Wise Use Movement," in Jacobs, *Who Owns America?* 29–44. For a follow-up to *The Wise Use Agenda,* see Ron Arnold and Alan Gottlieb, *Trashing the Environment: How Runaway Environmentalism is Wrecking America* (1993).

10. Epstein, *Takings;* Arnold and Gottlieb, *Trashing the Environment.*

11. Daniel Bromley, "Regulatory Takings: Coherent Concept or Logical Contradiction?" *Vermont Law Review* 17, no. 3 (1993): 647–82; Daniel Bromley, "Rousseau's Revenge: The Demise of the Freehold Estate," in Jacobs, *Who Owns America?* 19–28; Eric T. Freyfogle, "The Owning and Taking of Sensitive Lands," *UCLA Law Review* 77 (1995): 77–138; Christman, *The Myth of Property.*

12. Joseph W. Singer, "Property and Social Relations: From Title to Entitlement," in *Property and Values,* ed. Charles Geisler and Gail Daneker (2000), 4–8.

13. Ibid. Also Freyfogle, *Bounded People, Boundless Lands,* 101–5. Freyfogle reviews United States Supreme Court Justice Antonin Scalia's influential role in reinforcing this model through important Supreme Court cases such as *Nollan v. California Coastal Commission,* 107 Sup. Ct. 3141 (1987); and *Lucas v. South Carolina Coastal Council,* 112 Sup. Ct. 2886 (1992). The court decision in *Nollan* held that, "Requiring grant of public easement across beachfront section of private property, as condition of granting permit to build house on property, held to effect taking of property without just compensation in violation of Fifth Amendment."

14. Singer, "Property and Social Relations," 7.

15. Ibid., 10–11.

16. Ibid., 15–16.

17. Bromley, "Rousseau's Revenge," 25.

18. The Fifth Amendment to the U.S. Constitution is the source of the takings debate in American law and culture. Its closing clause reads, *nor shall private property be taken for public use, without just compensation.* The critical questions are: Should public regulations that define acceptable and unacceptable land uses ever be considered a

taking of private property? And, if so, at what threshold does a reduction in land value constitute a regulatory taking? C. Ford Runge et al. make the important point that government regulations can both reduce *and* add value to land. Landowners may benefit from "givings," not just suffer from takings. This being the case, the authors ask, should society tax the "givings," the added value an owner receives from the government? See C. Ford Runge et al., "Public Sector Contributions to Private Land Value: Looking at the Ledger," in Geisler and Daneker, *Property and Values,* 41–62; also Bromley, "Regulatory Takings," 647–82; and on the other side of the issue, Epstein, *Takings.*

19. Gertrude Frazier and Rose Poff, *The Kickapoo Valley: The Gem of Wisconsin* (1896), 4–5 (misspellings in original).

20. Vernon County Historical Society files, Martha Ady (Mattie) Dawson journal, 1913 entry, 100.

21. Ralph E. Nuzum, *Here on the Kickapoo* (1955), 59.

22. Quoted in University of Wisconsin–Madison College of Agriculture and Life Sciences, *The Kickapoo Valley Reforestation Fund* (2002), http://www.cals.wisc.edu/snr/kick.html.

23. Readers might start with Donald Worster, "Doing Environmental History," in *The Ends of the Earth: Perspectives on Modern Environmental History,* ed. Donald Worster (1988).

24. Stephen J. Pyne, "Smokechasing: The Search for a Usable Place," *Environmental History* 6, no. 4 (2001): 535.

25. David M. Hix and Craig G. Lorimer, "Growth-Competition Relationships in Young Hardwood Stands on Two Contrasting Sites in Southwestern Wisconsin," *Forest Science* 36 (1990): 1032–49; David M. Hix and Craig G. Lorimer, "Early Stand Development on Former Oak Sites in Southwestern Wisconsin," *Forest Ecology and Management* 42 (1991): 169–93; Craig G. Lorimer, "Causes of the Oak Regeneration Problem," in *Oak Regeneration: Serious Problems, Practical Recommendations,* ed. D. L. Loftis and C. E. McGee (1993), 14–39.

26. Matthew Turner addressed the issue in his introduction to a superb paper at the 2002 Environmental History meeting: "Spatial Contingency in Sahelian Environmental History and Its Filtered Revelation by Remote Sensing/GIS," American Society for Environmental History Annual Meeting (March 20–24, 2002).

27. Lynne Heasley, "Shifting Boundaries on a Wisconsin Landscape: Can GIS Help Historians Tell a Complicated Story?" *Human Ecology* 31 (2003): 183–211. For more on historians using GIS, see Anne Kelly Knowles, ed., *Past Time, Past Place: GIS for History* (2002); and Anne Kelly Knowles, ed., "Historical GIS: The Spatial Turn in Social Science History," special theme issue of *Social Science History* 24 (2000). For examples of social scientists integrating GIS and landscape ecology, see D. R. Field et al., "Reaffirming Social Landscape Analysis in Landscape Ecology: A Conceptual Framework," *Society and Natural Resources* 16, no. 4 (2003): 349–61; T. K. Kuczenski et al., "Integrating Demographic and Landsat (TM) Data at a Watershed Scale," *Journal of the American Water Resources Association* 36, no. 1 (2000): 215–28.

28. In our case, if we wanted a high level of ownership *and* landscape detail, then how many dates could we afford to re-create? If we wanted to tackle several dates, then how much of the landscape could we cover? If we wanted to cover a broad cultural

landscape rather than, say, a few illustrative properties, then in how much detail and for how many dates could we realistically accomplish this? In the end we kept to a relatively fine grain of detail. We also settled on six dates from 1930 to 1995, in itself an ambitious undertaking.

29. Alexis de Tocqueville, *Democracy in America,* vol. 1, ed. Phillips Bradley (1945), 67.

30. Ibid., 69–70.

31. I am making a general observation across a number of disciplines concerned with rural places. Forests in many agricultural regions are tightly woven into the rural fabric, socially and ecologically. Even so, when forests are present in the same unit of analysis as agricultural fields (e.g., the "farm"), it is often the cropping and livestock systems that receive the lion's share of attention, undoubtedly because they are a continuous part of the formal economy. By contrast, farm woodlots are fully integrated into informal economic networks involving hunting, firewood gathering, mushroom hunting and the like, but they contribute their timber only sporadically to the formal economy.

In addition, there are forest-agriculture biases in subdisciplines. For instance, a "social forester" (a sociologist who specializes in forests) will concentrate on forests. The same holds true for a forest economist, while an agricultural economist is less likely to look at forests. Within the natural sciences, ecologists and soil scientists will specialize in components of the landscape. Even in history, the rural historian and the forest historian are less likely to cross their respective borders between field and forest. This is one of the reasons why environmental history and geography (as well as their counterpart in the natural sciences, landscape ecology) are so important in both rural and environmental studies; they tackle whole pieces of cloth, not just separate patches. For an excellent example of a holistic approach to farms and forests, see Louis S. Warren, *The Hunter's Game: Poachers and Conservationists in Twentieth-Century America* (1997), 48–70; and William Cronon's classic *Changes in the Land: Indians, Colonists, and the Ecology of New England* (1983).

32. William Cronon, *Nature's Metropolis: Chicago and the Great West* (1991), 148–206.

33. William Least Heat-Moon, *Prairy Erth* (1991).

34. Carol M. Rose, "Property as Storytelling: Perspectives from Game Theory, Narrative Theory, Feminist Theory," *Yale Journal of Law and the Humanities* 2, no. 1 (1990): 37–57; and Freyfogle, *Bounded People, Boundless Lands,* 91–113.

Prologue: Weekend Drive, Summer 2002

1. The Driftless region spans southwestern Wisconsin and small parts of southeastern Minnesota and northeastern Iowa. Lawrence Martin, *The Physical Geography of Wisconsin* (1939; reprint, 1965); also W. O. Blanchard, *The Physical Geography of Southwestern Wisconsin* (1924).

2. Frazier and Poff, *The Kickapoo Valley,* 7.

3. Bureau of the Census, *1990 Census of Population and Housing for Wisconsin* (1992); and John C. Leatherman, *Input-Output Analysis of the Kickapoo River Valley* (1994).

Chapter 1. Intended Consequences: Soil Conservation

1. The rise in turnover holds even after equalizing for the different lengths of time represented. Flip the analysis to focus on stability in ownership rather than change and you still have a shift after 1955: from 1930 to 1955, 21 percent of Liberty's land remained with the same owner, while from 1955 to 1978 it was only 11 percent.

2. For this and other quotes from Danny Deaver, personal communication, July 1, 2002, and July 10, 2002.

3. A report from the National Resources Board to President Roosevelt said of erosion, "This wastage of the most basic and indispensable resource of the country—the soil—has become one of the most important problems confronting the Nation." The report goes on, "The past practice of clearing and cultivating land without regard to risks of wastage of soil and water resources has been nothing short of suicidal agriculture." National Resources Board, *A Report on National Planning and Public Works in Relation to Natural Resources and Including Land Use and Water Resources with Findings and Recommendations* (1934), 161, 169.

4. Ibid., 169.

5. George Perkins Marsh, *Man and Nature; or, Physical Geography as Modified by Human Action* (1864; reprint, 2003).

6. Quincy Claude Ayres, *Soil Erosion and Its Control* (1936), 3. Ayres used U.S. Department of Agriculture Soil Conservation Service data to produce a "General Distribution of Erosion." The map shows southwest Wisconsin to be among the regions with the most serious erosion in the country at that time.

7. Wisconsin State Soil Conservation Committee, *Soil Erosion Survey of Wisconsin* (1940).

8. Wisconsin State Soil and Water Conservation Committee, *Twenty-Five Years with the Soil and Water Conservation Districts in Wisconsin* (1964), 6.

9. Ibid.

10. Angus McDonald, *Early American Soil Conservationists* (1941); and Wayne D. Rasmussen, "History of Soil Conservation, Institutions, and Incentives," in *Soil Conservation Policies, Institutions, and Incentives,* ed. Harold G. Halcrow, Earl O. Heady, and Melvin L. Cotner (1982), 4.

11. Wisconsin State Board of Soil and Water Conservation Districts, *A Soil and Water Conservation Resources Program for Wisconsin* (1981), 2.

12. August Kramer observed that some crops produced less erosion than others and subsequently alternated them in strips so as to benefit from the less erosive ones. See O. R. Zeasman and I. O. Hembre, *A Brief History of Erosion Control in Wisconsin* (1963), 3–4.

13. David Rice Gardner, *The National Cooperative Soil Survey of the United States* (1957; reprint, 1998), 32, 67–70. Gardner dates the first U.S. Department of Agriculture publication on soil erosion to 1894, when it published *Washed Soils: How to Prevent and Reclaim Them.* University of Wisconsin professor of soil science F. H. King also began publishing his research on soils and soil conservation in 1894. The first official recommendation for contour strips came out in 1901 from the Bureau of Soils.

14. Melville H. Cohee, "Erosion and Land Utilization in the Driftless Area of Wisconsin," *Journal of Land and Public Utility Economics* 10, no. 3 (1934): 253.

15. In arguing that contour strips were an outcome of changing land tenure institutions (or property regimes), I concur with Colin A. M. Duncan, who says, "I have come to believe that the institutional context in which agronomic decisions are taken should be the *first* thing to be characterized in any general agricultural history. Currently it tends to be treated as an optional 'extra,' and it is conveniently forgotten that every move made in 'the economy' occurs in a context structured by legal definitions, which in turn ultimately have their roots in politics, broadly conceived." Colin A. M. Duncan, "Legal Protection for the Soil of England: The Spurious Context of Nineteenth-Century 'Progress,'" in *The History of Agriculture and the Environment*, ed. Douglas Helms and Douglas E. Bowers (1994), 76.

16. Hugh Hammond Bennett and W. R. Chapline, *Soil Erosion: A National Menace* (1928).

17. Gardner, *The National Cooperative Soil Survey*, 92–94.

18. The intricate New Deal socioenvironmental web included the Agricultural Adjustment Administration, the Soil Conservation Service, the Tennessee Valley Authority, the Resettlement Administration, the Commodity Credit Corporation, and so on.

19. *Soil Erosion Act aka Soil Conservation and Domestic Allotment Act. U.S. Statutes at Large* 49 (1935): 163.

20. Declaration of Policy, quoted in Sampson, *For Love of the Land*, 12.

21. Ibid., 14. Congress amended the Soil Erosion Act of 1935 with the *Soil Conservation and Domestic Allotment Act. U.S. Statutes at Large* 49 (1936): 1148.

22. *Agricultural Adjustment Act. U.S. Statutes at Large* 48 (1933): 31. Note that the AAA later became the Production Marketing Association (PMA) and finally the Agricultural Stabilization and Conservation Service (ASCS).

23. Leonard Johnson, *Soil Conservation in Wisconsin: Birth to Rebirth* (1991), 100. This chapter owes a debt to Johnson, a student of Otto Zeasman's and prominent in his own right in soil conservation extension. Johnson's perceptive survey has influenced my ideas on the relationships between conservation history and land tenure. One strength of Johnson's retrospective is that it tracks the complex institutional development of public soil conservation efforts at federal, state, and local levels. The central drawback to the book is that it provides no bibliographical guide for his myriad sources, including primary data, personal and public correspondence, and agency memoranda.

24. Roy Dingle, *Nothing but Conservation* (1993), 11.

25. Zeasman and Hembre, *A Brief History of Erosion Control*, 6.

26. For example, the U.S. Department of Agriculture Soil Conservation Service, *Soil and Water Conservation in Wisconsin* (1959), 5.

27. Johnson, *Soil Conservation in Wisconsin*, 90.

28. Aldo Leopold, *A Sand County Almanac* (1949; reprint, 1968).

29. Zeasman and Hembre, *A Brief History of Soil Erosion Control*, 32; and Douglas Helms, "Coon Valley, Wisconsin: A Conservation Success Story," in *Readings in the History of the Soil Conservation Service* (1992), 51–53.

30. Also quoted in H. O. Anderson and I. O. Hembre, "The Coon Valley Watershed Project—A Pioneer Venture in Good Land Use," *Journal of Soil and Water Conservation* 10, no. 4 (1955): 181.

31. C. G. Bates and O. R. Zeasman, *Soil Erosion—A Local and National Problem* (1930), 97.

32. Johnson, *Soil Conservation in Wisconsin,* 50.

33. Aldo Leopold, "Coon Valley: An Adventure in Cooperative Conservation," in *For the Health of the Land,* ed. J. Baird Callicott and Eric T. Freyfogle (1935; reprint, 1999), 49.

34. Many historians of soil conservation have made parallel arguments, though their concern was not with property *per se.* As early as 1957, when the New Deal was barely history, David Rice Gardner saw that "Among the vase [*sic*] political changes wrought, and/or recognized, by the New Deal were those involving public attitudes toward the nature and extent of the federal government's responsibility to individual farmers. The earlier 'Conservation Movement' and the national land policies which developed before 1933 dealt primarily with nonagricultural lands, and emphasized public ownership as the remedy for misuse of land. . . . The crisis conditions of the thirties, however, and the political and administrative responses to such conditions, brought forth programs of direct federal assistance to millions of *individual* farmers on hundreds of millions of acres of *private* land." See Gardner, *The National Cooperative Soil Survey,* 117 (emphasis in the original).

35. Roy Dingle is a good example of how public extension involved multiple programs. Any person with a long career in soil conservation may have had numerous affiliations—federal, state, and county. Dingle worked first for the Forest Service helping Civilian Conservation Corps crews, which the Forest Service directed in erosion control. Those functions then moved to the Soil Conservation Service, where Dingle also moved. Later he became a soil conservationist for the Richland County Soil Conservation District.

36. Dingle, *Nothing but Conservation,* 87.

37. Ibid., 33.

38. Wisconsin State Soil Conservation Committee, *Why Should I Be Interested in Soil Conservation?* (1947), 6.

39. For a comparative review of the conservation evidence for and against tenant farmers in the United States and internationally, see William Harbaugh, "Twentieth-Century Tenancy and Soil Conservation: Some Comparisons and Questions," in Helms and Bowers, *The History of Agriculture and the Environment,* 95–119.

40. Ayres, *Soil Erosion and Its Control,* 327.

41. Dingle, *Nothing but Conservation,* 160.

42. Cohee, "Erosion and Land Utilization in the Driftless Area of Wisconsin," 253.

43. Dingle, *Nothing but Conservation,* 86.

44. Helms, "Coon Valley, Wisconsin," 51–53.

45. U.S. Department of Agriculture Soil Conservation Service, *Soil and Water Conservation in Wisconsin* (1964), 4.

46. See for example, U.S. Department of Agriculture Soil Conservation Service, *Soil and Water Conservation in Wisconsin* (1959), 3; and the slightly revised U.S. Department of Agriculture Soil Conservation Service, *Soil and Water Conservation in Wisconsin,* 3.

47. Neil Maher, "A New Deal Body Politic: Landscape, Labor, and the Civilian Conservation Corps," *Environmental History* 7, no. 3 (2002): 435–61.

48. Quoted in Johnson, *Soil Conservation in Wisconsin,* 54.

49. Ibid., 56–57.

50. Dingle, *Nothing but Conservation*, 155.

51. Ibid., 155–56. Emphasis in the original.

52. Ayres, *Soil Erosion and Its Control*, 70.

53. For an overview of research on soil erosion see L. Donald Meyer and William C. Moldenhauer, "Soil Erosion by Water: The Research Experience," in *The History of Soil and Water Conservation*, ed. Douglas Helms and Susan L. Flader (1985), 90–102.

54. In 1931, the University of Wisconsin–Madison, together with the U.S. Department of Agriculture, established the Upper Mississippi Valley Erosion Control Experiment Station at Grand Dad's Bluff, near La Crosse, Wisconsin. Hays and Clark analyzed data from the station for nine years, beginning in 1931. See Orville E. Hays and Noble Clark, *Cropping Systems That Help Control Erosion* (1941).

55. This is the argument of the Wisconsin State Soil Conservation Committee in *Why Should I Be Interested in Soil Conservation?* 6.

56. Hays and Clark, *Cropping Systems That Help Control Erosion*, 21. The authors used data to estimate soil losses on plats 72 feet long with a 16 percent slope.

57. Chris L. Christensen, "Soil Management: Does Soil Conservation Pay? It Did Here!" in *What's New in Farm Science: Annual Report of the Director, Agricultural Experiment Station, University of Wisconsin, Madison* (1943), 63–64.

58. Randall A. Kramer and Sandra S. Batie, "Cross Compliance Concepts in Agricultural Programs: The New Deal to the Present," in Helms and Flader, *The History of Soil and Water Conservation*, 192–93; Sandra S. Batie, "Soil Conservation in the 1980s: A Historical Perspective," in Helms and Flader, *The History of Soil and Water Conservation*, 6–7.

59. Quoted in Sampson, *For Love of the Land*, 20.

60. This act created still deeper conflicts with the states and their cooperative extension services. U.S. Department of Agriculture Secretary Wallace felt that the extension services were too independent of the secretary—that the U.S. Department of Agriculture could not count on them to implement national soil conservation policy. For their part, Extension resented being bypassed and the states felt the act was too coercive at the farm level. See Kramer and Batie, "Cross Compliance Concepts in Agricultural Programs: The New Deal to the Present," 193–201.

61. For a brief description of how President Roosevelt tried to leverage cooperation from state governors, see Cletus Howard, *Putting Soil Conservation to Work: Manual 2 Legislation . . . town—county—state—federal . . . for Soil Conservation District Supervisors* (1960), 31.

62. In 1937, the state of Wisconsin provided for soil conservation districts with passage of Chapter 92. The first districts were small, ineffective, and poorly integrated into local institutions. Consequently they floundered in their early efforts to organize. A 1939 amendment making conservation district boundaries coterminous with county boundaries gave the districts new life, providing a powerful base of support in terms of county financial resources, official county involvement in soil conservation, and local acceptance of district projects. For an early history of conservation districts in Wisconsin, see Wisconsin State Soil and Water Conservation Committee, *Twenty-Five Years with the Soil and Water Conservation Districts in Wisconsin;* for a general history of districts in the nation, see Sampson, *For Love of the Land*.

63. Vernon County was one of the first to organize into a district. By 1956, all Wisconsin counties had completed the process. Wisconsin State Soil and Water Conservation Committee, *Twenty-Five Years with the Soil and Water Conservation Districts in Wisconsin*, 7–9.

64. In Vernon County, only two townships adopted zoning prior to the 1990s. Dingle, *Nothing but Conservation*, 161. On township zoning in Vernon County, see Kerry D. Vandell and Pat J. Connolly, *Analyses of Real Estate Market Dynamics in the Kickapoo River Valley* (1998), 112.

65. I cite the details of this undated study from Johnson, *Soil Conservation in Wisconsin*, 131. Unfortunately, neither the Leopold nor the Hickey papers in the University of Wisconsin–Madison Archives has an original copy of the report. Clearly related to the study, however, is a three-page unpublished manuscript that may be either a short separate essay or an introduction to Leopold and Hickey's larger study. See Aldo Leopold and Joseph Hickey, "Cows and Contours: The Problem of Steep Farms in Southwest Wisconsin" (no date), University of Wisconsin–Madison, Department of Wildlife Ecology files, Unpublished Manuscripts.

66. Leopold and Hickey, "Cows and Contours," 3.

67. Ibid., 2.

68. Ibid., 2–3.

69. Johnson, *Soil Conservation in Wisconsin*, 131.

70. Leopold, "Coon Valley," 48.

71. The Preemption Act of 1841 and the Homestead Act of 1862 were two of the most influential federal laws of this sort. They established processes by which speculators, land companies, and settlers could lay claim to land, and by which the federal government could give claimants legal title. Many scholars have observed that distribution of land was concentrated rather than even and highly unfavorable to the small farmer. See Hildegard Binder Johnson, *Order upon the Land: The U.S. Rectangular Land Survey and the Upper Mississippi Country* (1976), 64–66. For overviews of federal land policy see Benjamin Horace Hibbard, *A History of the Public Land Policies* (1924); and Paul W. Gates, *History of Public Land Law Development* (1978).

72. Johnson, *Order upon the Land*, 66–67.

73. For a more detailed summary of the bundle of rights theory of property, see Harvey M. Jacobs, Preface, in Jacobs, *Who Owns America?* x–xii; also Keith D. Wiebe, Abebayehu Tegene, and Betsey Kuhn, "Land Tenure, Land Policy, and the Property Rights Debate," in Jacobs, *Who Owns America?* 79–81.

74. Public land also has private dimensions. See Charles Geisler, "Property Pluralism," in Geisler and Daneker, *Property and Values*, 65–87; and Joseph William Singer, "Property and Social Relations: From Title to Entitlement," in Geisler and Daneker, *Property and Values*, 6.

75. Dingle, *Nothing but Conservation*, 169.

76. See Wisconsin State Soil Conservation Committee, *Inter-Agency Agreement for Planning and Developing Community Watersheds in Wisconsin* (1961).

77. Some soil scientists were openly hostile to capability maps. They took exception to the SCS's negative approach, which focused on environmental limitations rather than soil systems and their potential. Another problem for soil scientists was the way capability maps emphasized engineering, such as contour strip cropping,

rather than soil management. This, of course, was part of Leopold's larger complaint. For the technical disagreements and the parallel institutional conflicts see Gardner, *The National Cooperative Soil Survey*, 181–90.

78. Wisconsin State Soil and Water Conservation Committee, *Twenty-Five Years with the Soil and Water Conservation Districts in Wisconsin,* 15.

79. E. O. Baker to O. R. Zeasman, August 9, 1955, Otto R. Zeasman Papers, box 1, University of Wisconsin–Madison Archives.

80. O. R. Zeasman to E. O. Baker, August 11, 1955, Zeasman Papers, box 1.

81. Quoted in Anderson and Hembre, "The Coon Valley Watershed Project," 184.

82. Rasmussen, "History of Soil Conservation, Institutions, and Incentives," 11.

83. The conversions often involved planting trees, but a lot of land reverted to forests via old field succession as well.

84. R. C. Buse and R. N. Brown Jr., *The Conservation Reserve in Wisconsin, 1956–1959* (1961), 42–44, 56.

85. Ibid., 56.

86. Unfortunately, the precise numbers for my study townships (Liberty, Stark, and Clinton) are impossible to come by. The Vernon County office of the Agricultural Stabilization and Conservation Service destroyed individual records long ago (their policy was to keep farm-level records of the Acreage Reserve and Conservation Reserve programs of the Soil Bank for only ten years). Nor did the agricultural censuses of the era track land in the Soil Bank at either the county or township levels. Total acres by county in Wisconsin are available for the years 1956–59 in the bulletin by Buse and Brown. Vernon and Crawford Counties (where the majority of the Kickapoo Valley lies) had 9,353 acres in the Soil Bank, while the four-county region encompassing the entire Valley had 18,486 acres enrolled. This represents a significant undercount of total enrollment because the Soil Bank did not end until 1965. What's more, rates paid per acre increased, providing further incentives for enrollment in the years after 1959. See R. C. Buse and R. N. Brown Jr., *The Conservation Reserve in Wisconsin 1956–1959* (1961), 60–61.

87. David B. Danbom, *Born in the Country: A History of Rural America* (1995), 245.

88. Ibid., 25.

89. Ingolf Vogeler takes a different yet highly critical look at the Soil Bank. He sees catastrophic problems with the program: absentee owners bought land solely for the payments; landlords evicted their tenants by enrolling land in the program (taking land out of production but reducing poor tenant farmers to hunger); and the very richest corporate farmers received the highest subsidies. These issues were not as prominent in the Kickapoo Valley during the Soil Bank era, primarily because the Valley did not have corporate farms of the scale Vogeler documents for other parts of the country. Nonetheless, the Kickapoo Valley did experience social fallout from the program. See Vogeler, *The Myth of the Family Farm: Agribusiness Dominance of U.S. Agriculture,* 168–76.

Chapter 2. A Midwestern Ranch

1. Generalizations and stereotypes about what landowner behavior *might* be do not always correspond to what landowner behavior will be. While many ownership

surveys correlate environmental attitudes and values to socioeconomic characteristics, they do not follow through with ecological outcomes on the ground. Lyle P. Schertz and Gene Wunderlich, two well-known agricultural economists, acknowledged the problem, saying, "Such assertions, however reasonable, are more often assumed than demonstrated to be true." They then posed two questions: "Are these traditional ways of identifying owners adequate for predicting the way land is used? If not, are there better ways of classifying owners?" See Schertz and Wunderlich, "Structure of Farming and Landownership in the Future: Implications for Soil Conservation," in *Soil Conservation Policies, Institutions, and Incentives,* ed. Harold G. Halcrow, Earl O. Heady, and Melvin L. Cotner (1982), 173–74; and Peter J. Nowak, "A Discussion," in Halcrow, Heady, and Cotner, *Soil Conservation Policies, Institutions, and Incentives,* 193–97.

2. Robert G. Healy and James Short, "Rural Lands: Market Trends and Planning Implications," *Journal of the American Planning Association* 45, no. 3 (1979): 305–17.

3. Walter Ebling et al., *A Century of Wisconsin Agriculture, 1848–1948* (1948).

4. Field notes from my assistants, Matt Dahlen and Ben Gramling, July 9, 1996, author's personal files.

5. Personal communication, May 23, 2001.

6. John Brinckerhoff Jackson pioneered contemporary scholarship on the vernacular landscape in all its myriad forms and meanings. See especially, *Discovering the Vernacular Landscape* (1984) and *A Sense of Place, A Sense of Time* (1994).

7. See for example, *La Farge Epitaph,* "Absentee Land Ownersip [*sic*] in the Kickapoo Valley," September 24, 1980.

8. J. L. Barto, "Experience of Barto Family Coming to Cherry Valley," in Grace Gilmore Hocking, *The Memorable Kickapoo Valley* (1976), 96. In 1861, the Barto family settled in Cherry Valley near the villages of West Lima and Viola (which lies partly in the township of Liberty).

9. Melville H. Cohee, "Erosion and Land Utilization in the Driftless Area of Wisconsin," 251.

10. Aldo Leopold and Joseph Hickey, "Cows and Contours," 3.

11. The Wisconsin Crop and Livestock Reporting Service, County series (Steenbock Memorial Agriculture Library, University of Wisconsin–Madison), is a treasure trove of historical agricultural information by county. For a profile of Vernon County, I relied on Walter Ebling, *Vernon County, Wisconsin Agricultural Statistics Bulletin No. 202, County series no. 18* (1940); and Ebling et al., *A Century of Wisconsin Agriculture.*

12. U.S. Department of Agriculture Soil Conservation Service, *Wisconsin Soil and Water Conservation Needs Inventory* (1970), 119.

13. Howard W. Lull and Kenneth G. Reinhart, *Forests and Floods in the Eastern United States* (1972).

14. Department of Natural Resources Vernon County Forester Robert V. Roach to Mr. Irving E. Ludlow, August 11, 1965. Correspondence between agents and landowners is archived in the township files of the Vernon County DNR Forestry Office.

15. DNR Forester Alan C. Jones to Robert Holman, August 4, 1972, township files, Vernon County DNR Forestry Office.

16. DNR Forester Don R. Streiff to Jerald W. Ahrens, January 14, 1981, township files, Vernon County DNR Forestry Office.

17. J. H. Stoeckler, *Trampling by Livestock Drastically Reduces Infiltration Rate of Soil in Oak and Pine Woods in Southwestern Wisconsin* (1959).

18. Leopold and Hickey, "Cows and Contours," 2.

19. Dingle, *Nothing but Conservation*, v.

20. Trout Unlimited actively promoted stream rehabilitation in the Kickapoo Valley, but its methods were not coercive. The group worked with willing landowners.

21. Teresa Miller, "Can Trout and Cows Coexist?" *Natural Resources Report* 8, no. 3 (1997): 4–5.

22. Laura Paine to Wisconsin's Environmental Decade, printed in *The Defender* 30, no. 2 (April 2000).

23. Leo M. Walsh, "Assessment of Soil Erosion Problems and Control Strategies in Wisconsin," in *Proceedings of a Conference on Public Policy Issues in Soil Conservation*, ed. Sherrie Beyer and Leonard C. Johnson (1982), 10.

24. Ibid., 7.

25. Stanley W. Trimble, "Decreased Rates of Alluvial Sediment Storage in the Coon Creek Basin, Wisconsin, 1975–93," *Science* 285, no. 5431 (1999): 1244–46. See also Stanley W. Trimble and Steven W. Lund, *Soil Conservation and the Reduction of Erosion and Sedimentation in the Coon Creek Basin, Wisconsin* (1982); M. Scott Argabright et al., *Historical Changes in Soil Erosion, 1930–1992: The Northern Mississippi Valley Loess Hills* (1996).

26. Quoted in an essay, accompanying Trimble's *Science* article, by James Glanz, "Sharp Drop Seen in Soil Erosion Rates," *Science* 285, no. 5431 (1999): 1187–89. Trimble critiques D. Pimentel et al., "Environmental and Economic Costs of Soil Erosion and Conservation Benefits," *Science* 267, no. 5201 (1995): 1117–23; and Frederick Steiner, *Soil Conservation in the United States: Policy and Planning* (1990). Trimble's critics question how typical Coon Creek is of the midwestern or eastern United States. With respect to the low rates of erosion in Trimble's study relative to the high rates in other studies, the discrepancy turns on how reliable sediment yields are in modeling long-term trends in erosion. Trimble says that sediment yields "lead to erroneous conclusions." In Coon Creek, sediment yields have remained high and constant, for many complicated reasons having to do with watershed dynamics and time lags. Trimble also measures sediment fluxes—changes in sediment sources, amounts, and storage. These indicate a dramatic decline in rates of erosion since the 1930s. See also, J. Douglas Helms et al., "National Soil Conservation Policies: A Historical Case Study of the Driftless Area," *Agricultural History* 70, no. 2 (1996): 377–94. Helms et al. saw dramatic decreases in erosion since 1930 in five Driftless Area counties, including Vernon and Crawford, home to most of the Kickapoo Valley. They estimate that about 80 percent of the reduction in erosion came from soil conservation efforts between the years 1930 and 1982.

27. Sandra S. Batie, "Soil Conservation in the 1980s: A Historical Perspective," 16–17, 19.

28. Carolyn Merchant speaks to the latter perspective when she suggests restoration as a means to use our power to alter nature "responsibly and ethically by going back in time to heal what has been changed or damaged. But this very act, even as in some ways it reaches into the past, also creates a new future." "Restoration and Reunion with Nature," in *Learning to Listen to the Land* (1991), 206. Nancy Langston

provides concrete ideas about the potential and limitations of restoration ecology to reintroduce valuable ecological processes and patterns into degraded landscapes. *Forest Dreams, Forest Nightmares: The Paradox of Old Growth in the Inland West* (1995).

Chapter 3. What the Real Estate Ads Don't Tell You

1. *Chicago Tribune,* Friday, June 1, 1990.
2. *Minneapolis Star Tribune,* Sunday, September 1, 1991.
3. *Chicago Tribune,* Friday, June 1, 1990.
4. *Minneapolis Star Tribune,* Sunday, August 18, 1991.
5. See State of Wisconsin Before the Real Estate Board, In the Matter of Disciplinary Proceedings Against Thomas D. White, Respondent, Final Decision and Order 92 REB 325, February 22, 1996, Department of Regulation and Licensing, Division of Enforcement files; State of Wisconsin Before the Real Estate Board, In the Matter of Disciplinary Proceedings Against James W. Smith, Respondent, Final Decision and Order 92 REB 325, February 22, 1996, Department of Regulation and Licensing, Division of Enforcement files; State of Wisconsin Before the Real Estate Board, In the Matter of Disciplinary Proceedings Against Woodland Farms Real Estate Company, Final Decision and Order 92 REB 325, Respondent, February 22, 1996, Department of Regulation and Licensing, Division of Enforcement files.
6. Susan Lampert Smith, "Cashing in on Land Sales," *Wisconsin State Journal,* September 28, 1992.
7. Ibid.
8. Ibid.
9. The State of Wisconsin maintains a database for the benefit of individual circuit courts around the state, the Circuit Court Automation Program, or CCAP. This only extends back to the early 1990s, so for earlier cases researchers must still go to the court.
10. Susan Lampert Smith, "Couple Win Land Deal Case," *Wisconsin State Journal,* February 28, 1993.
11. Barbara L. Hayes, Plaintiff, v. James W. Smith and Thomas D. White, individually and d/b/a American Investment Company, Woodland Farms Real Estate Company and Univest Company of Wisconsin, and Unknown Other Trade names, Defendants. United States District Court For the Northern District of Illinois, Eastern Division, Memorandum Opinion and Order, September 4, 1992.
12. Lampert Smith, "Couple Win Land Deal Case."
13. Ibid.
14. Personal communication, Andrea Baker, former Woodland Farms client, June 2000.
15. Lampert Smith, "Cashing in on Land Sales."
16. Susan Lampert Smith, "State Asked to Reopen Woodland Farms Case," *Wisconsin State Journal,* October 1, 1992.
17. Personal communication, Andrea Baker, June 2000.
18. This was their slogan.
19. Personal communication, Andrea Baker, June 2000.

20. "Things to Know before You Buy," *Wisconsin State Journal,* September 27, 1992.

21. Ibid.

22. For this and other quotes from Lampert Smith, personal communication, May 23, 2001, and June 20, 2001.

23. Susan Lampert Smith, "Land Dealers Lose Licenses; Complaints and False Ads Bring on Fines of $37,500, Too," *Wisconsin State Journal,* February 29, 1996.

24. Lampert Smith, "State Asked to Reopen Case."

25. Ibid.

26. "Smudge on Reputation," *Wisconsin State Journal,* October 5, 1992.

27. William Cronon, *Nature's Metropolis: Chicago and the Great West.*

28. Bureau of the Census, 1950, 1970, 1990. By the 1990s, absentee owners controlled 70 percent of the land in Liberty.

29. The State of Wisconsin recently revised its rules governing septic systems, allowing new above-ground types on sites where they were once off-limits. Law and technology have united, so that what had been impossible in many places is now possible, potentially altering the face of rural Wisconsin once again. We will have to wait to see what those old fields in Liberty become—second homes, regenerated forests, or something entirely unforeseen.

30. Wisconsin courts do provide relief to stranded landowners in the form of "easements of convenience."

31. This and other quotes from Eddi Blakley, personal communication, August 1, 1998.

32. This and other quotes from Joel Swanson, personal communication, August 13, 1998.

33. Personal communication, June 20, 1996.

34. From the June 25, 1996, field report of my assistant Matt Dahlen.

35. For a similar analysis of the relationship between land turnover and logging in Ohio, see Kimberly E. Medley, Christine M. Pobocik, and Brian W. Okey, "Historical Changes in Forest Cover and Land Ownership in a Midwestern U.S. Landscape," *Annals of the Association of American Geographers* 93, no. 1 (2003): 104–20.

36. La Crosse County is one of only two counties in Wisconsin that require landowners to file formal intents to harvest timber. Robert A. Haukereid, *The Relationship between Timber Sales and Real Estate Transfers for La Crosse and Oneida Counties (1992–1994)* (1995).

37. There are greater profits and fewer hassles for a logger who harvests a large single-owner forest. This is part of the frustration you'll see expressed in the newsletter and journal of the Society of American Foresters: that so much private land is in small ownerships, and that many of those owners have little interest in intensive harvesting (agreeing to a timber sale is more spontaneous). For their part, many logging firms have little interest in light, selective logging.

38. A large part of a Wisconsin state forester's job is to enroll landowners in a range of public forestry programs. In exchange for implementing long-term forestry plans, owners receive tax breaks and cost sharing for planting trees. These plans always involve some schedule of timber harvests approved by the county forester.

39. Personal communication, June 22, 2001.

40. Oak-hickory refers to a central hardwood forest consisting of white oak (*Quercus alba*), black oak (*Quercus velutina*), shagbark hickory (*Carya ovata*), bitternut hickory (*Carya cordiformis*), white pine (*Pinus strobus*), black cherry (*Prunus serotina*), and red maple (*Acer rubrum*). Common associates in a maple-basswood (northern hardwood) forest are sugar maple (*Acer saccharum*), basswood (*Tilia americana*), white ash (*Fraxinus americana*), American hornbeam (also ironwood—*Carpinus caroliniana*), and on rich sites, yellow birch (*Betula alleghaniensis*). The most comprehensive empirical description available on forest communities and habitat types in southern Wisconsin is John Kotar and Timothy L. Burger, *A Guide to Forest Communities and Habitat Types of Central and Southern Wisconsin* (1996).

41. Craig Lorimer, "The Oak Regeneration Problem: New Evidence on Causes and Possible Solutions," *Forest Resource Analyses* 8 (1989).

42. Craig G. Lorimer, "Causes of the Oak Regeneration Problem," in *Oak Regeneration: Serious Problems, Practical Recommendations* (1993), 14–39.

43. Craig G. Lorimer, Jonathan W. Chapman, and William D. Lambert, "Tall Understorey Vegetation as a Factor in the Poor Development of Oak Seedlings beneath Mature Stands," *Journal of Ecology* 82, no. 2 (1994): 227–37; B. McCune and G. Cottam, "The Successional Status of a Southern Wisconsin Oak Woods," *Ecology* 66 (1985): 1270–78; J. J. Zaczek, J. W. Groninger, and J. W. Van Sambeek, "Stand Dynamics in an Old-Growth Hardwood Forest, in Southern Illinois, USA," *Natural Areas Journal* 22, no. 3 (2002): 211–19; S. L. Dodge, "Successional Trends in a Mixed Oak Forest on High Mountain, New Jersey," *Journal of the Torrey Botanical Society* 124, no. 4 (1997): 312–17.

44. Dan M. Pubanz and Craig G. Lorimer, *Oak Regeneration Experiments in Southwestern Wisconsin: Two-Year Results,* Agricultural Bulletin R3552, Research Division of the College of Agriculture and Life Sciences, University of Wisconsin–Madison (1992); M. A. Jenkins and G. R. Parker, "Composition and Diversity of Woody Vegetation in Silvicultural Openings of Southern Indiana Forests, *Forest Ecology and Management* 109, nos. 1–3 (1998): 57–74.

45. With lots of sunlight and little immediate competition from maples, the conditions in old fields should be excellent for oak regeneration. Personal Communication, Eric Kruger, forest ecologist, Department of Forest Ecology and Management, University of Wisconsin–Madison.

46. Copies of the firms' Articles of Organization or Articles of Incorporation, as well as Wisconsin Domestic Corporation Annual Reports, are available in the microfiche archives of the Wisconsin Department of Financial Institutions, Office of the Secretary of State of Wisconsin.

47. See State of Wisconsin Before the Real Estate Board, In the Matter of Disciplinary Proceedings Against Thomas D. White, Respondent, Final Decision and Order 92 REB 325, February 22, 1996, Department of Regulation and Licensing, Division of Enforcement files; State of Wisconsin Before the Real Estate Board, In the Matter of Disciplinary Proceedings Against James W. Smith, Respondent, Final Decision and Order 92 REB 325, February 22, 1996, Department of Regulation and Licensing, Division of Enforcement files; State of Wisconsin Before the Real Estate Board, In the Matter of Disciplinary Proceedings Against Woodland Farms Real Estate Company, Final Decision and Order 92 REB 325, Respondent, February 22, 1996, Department of Regulation and Licensing, Division of Enforcement files.

It is interesting that the state only investigated newspaper advertisements from Minnesota or Wisconsin newspapers. Official reports did not include advertisements out of the *Chicago Tribune,* even though the majority of Woodland Farms customers were from Illinois, and even though that newspaper had an abundance of Woodland Farms advertisements. I cannot speak for the investigators, but perhaps they were sensitive to the idea that Illinois buyers—frequently derided tourists in the state—might not garner the same public sympathy as fellow Minnesotans and Wisconsinites.

48. Ibid.

49. "Woodland Farms Penalties Too Late," *Wisconsin State Journal,* March 1, 1996.

50. Willie E. Garrette, Investigator, Division of Enforcement, to John P. Ebben, Attorney for Thomas White and Woodland Farms, October 13, 1993, Department of Regulation and Licensing, Division of Enforcement files.

51. Woodland Farms Attorney John P. Ebben to Willie E. Garrette, October 27, 1993, Department of Regulation and Licensing, Division of Enforcement files.

52. "Real-Estate Mogul Guilty of Mail Fraud," *Wisconsin State Journal,* February 26, 1997.

53. Quoted in Marv Balousek, "Realtor Sentenced to 14 Months in Prison; Also Fined $62,000 After Pleading Guilty to Mail Fraud," *Wisconsin State Journal,* May 7, 1997.

54. Susan Lampert Smith, "Woodland Farms Co-Founder Faces Civil Suit Over Alleged Sex Assault," *Wisconsin State Journal,* June 17, 1995; and also "Woodland Executive Prevails in Suit," *Wisconsin State Journal,* June 21, 1995.

55. Susan Lampert Smith, "Fugitive, Wife Face Charges; Real-Estate Empire Founder Indicted for Perjury in Sex Trial," *Wisconsin State Journal,* October 30, 1997.

56. "Escapee Probably in Tropics, U.S. Says," *Wisconsin State Journal,* March 14, 2000.

57. Ted Steinberg's provocative book, *Slide Mountain,* investigates the inverse relationship between ever-more-complicated property law and ever-more-simplified views of the natural world. My research in the Kickapoo Valley was underway when I first encountered *Slide Mountain,* but I came to see it as a ballast to this study. Steinberg probes the extremes of property law, while I probe the ordinary interiors of landscapes. See *Slide Mountain: Or the Folly of Owning Nature* (1996), 18.

58. "Absentee Land Ownership in the Kickapoo Valley," *La Farge Epitaph,* September 24, 1980.

59. Personal communication, June 17, 2004.

60. Personal communication, June 12, 2003.

Chapter 4. Outsiders

1. Gideon A. Miller, "The Town of Clinton Amish History," in *Vernon County Heritage,* ed. Vernon County Historical Society (1994), 156. The Vernon County Historical Museum holds Gideon Miller's original typewritten manuscript.

2. The "plain" Amish dress is at once a symbol of their identity and unity as well as their separation from the larger society around them. Noted Amish and Anabaptist

scholar John A. Hostetler says that plain dressing signifies both obedience to God and a clear protest to the rest of the world. Donald B. Kraybill calls Amish attire the "garb of humility." See Hostetler, *Amish Society* (1963; reprint, 1993), 237–40; and Kraybill, *The Riddle of Amish Culture* (1989), 49–60.

3. The Anabaptists trace their roots to Switzerland and to the upheavals of the Protestant Reformation, during which they were persecuted for their resistance to the Protestant hierarchy, and particularly for their refusal to accept infant baptism. It was their practice of adult baptism that earned them the name rebaptisers, or Anabaptists. The Johns Hopkins University Press has published the definitive works to date on Amish history and culture by leading Anabaptist scholars. Whether readers are interested in general background or a more detailed treatment of the complexities and contradictions of Amish life, they would do well to begin with Donald B. Kraybill, *The Riddle of Amish Culture;* and John A. Hostetler, *Amish Society.* Another fertile place to begin is Steven M. Nolt, *The History of the Amish* (1992).

4. Menno M. Hershberger, "Cashton, WI History," in *Wisconsin, Minnesota, and Montana Amish Directory 2002* (2002). See also Harvey M. Jacobs and Ellen M. Bassett, *The Amish: A Literature Review* (1995); Elizabeth Place, "Land Use," in *The Amish and the State,* ed. Donald B. Kraybill (1993).

5. Miller, "Town of Clinton Amish History," 156.

6. 1964–69 is the period in which dairy farms declined 6.6 percent. Douglas Jackson-Smith, *Wisconsin Agriculture in Historical Perspective: Economic and Social Changes, 1959–1995* (1996), 2–4; also, Douglas Jackson-Smith, "Understanding the Microdynamics of Farm Structural Change: Entry, Exit, and Restructuring among Wisconsin Family Farmers in the 1980s," (1995).

7. Jackson-Smith, *Wisconsin Agriculture in Historical Perspective,* 9–10.

8. "Absentee Land Ownership in the Kickapoo Valley," *La Farge Epitaph,* September 24, 1980.

9. The rates of entry into, and exit from, farming can be more important than the overall net loss of farms. As Jackson-Smith points out, they reflect the actual number of farms leaving agriculture in a given year. For a variety of reasons, fewer people in the Kickapoo Valley and Wisconsin were going into farming even as increasing numbers of farmers were leaving agriculture. From 1978 to 1982, for example, Wisconsin's annual rate of entry was 3.7 percent, whereas from 1982 to 1987 the rate dropped to 2.4 percent. This was the steepest decline of any state in the country. Jackson-Smith, *Wisconsin Agriculture in Historical Perspective,* 4–5.

10. Ibid., 16–18.

11. The growing townships all had Amish settlements.

12. Hostetler puts the average number of live births per Amish couple at seven. Average family size increased in the twentieth century as improved medical care helped lower infant mortality. *Amish Society,* 99–101.

13. Miller, "Town of Clinton Amish History," 156.

14. Population estimates for the Amish in the Kickapoo Valley go as high as five thousand. I am grateful to John Cross for providing me with his calculations for Amish communities in Wisconsin and for directing me to an excellent source: *Wisconsin, Minnesota, and Montana Amish Directory.*

15. Quoted in David Luthy, "Appendix: Amish Migration Patterns: 1972–1992," in

The Amish Struggle with Modernity (1994), 249; also, Jacobs and Bassett, *The Amish: A Literature Review,* 9.

16. "Complaints Heard of Road Damage from Cleated Amish Horseshoes," *Epitaph-News,* June 27, 1983; and "Road Damage and Horseshoes—Town of Clinton Tries to Talk It Out," *Epitaph-News,* July 21, 1983.

17. "Complaints Heard of Road Damage from Cleated Amish Horseshoes," *Epitaph-News.*

18. "Road Damage and Horseshoes—Town of Clinton Tries to Talk It Out," *Epitaph-News.*

19. As part of their separation from society and the state, the Amish do not hold public office or vote in public elections. This can create problems of governance in places like Clinton where the Amish make up the majority.

20. The local newspaper chronicled these meetings much as a secretary taking meeting minutes. Unless otherwise noted this is the material I rely on for quotes and for conveying the back-and-forth nature of the debate over Amish horseshoes. See "Complaints Heard of Road Damage from Cleated Amish Horseshoes," *Epitaph-News;* and "Road Damage and Horseshoes—Town of Clinton Tries to Talk It Out," *Epitaph-News.*

21. The following year (1984) Rude's southwestern Wisconsin district elected him to the Wisconsin State Senate.

22. Bill McAuliffe, "Uneasy Neighbors: Amish Aid—Irritate—Community," *Minneapolis Star Tribune,* December 26, 1988.

23. The case of slow-moving-vehicle signs on Amish buggies has been a persistent one in the country, with legal and social ramifications for balancing the free exercise of religion against compelling governmental interests. In addition to Fillmore County, Minnesota, Amish communities have tussled with authorities in Kentucky, Ohio, Michigan, and New York over mandatory use of slow-moving-vehicle signs. In Fillmore County, Gideon Hershberger went to jail for seven days after he refused to pay a fine for violating Minnesota law. His case followed a circuitous route in which the Minnesota Supreme Court ruled in his favor, saying that the law did infringe on rights guaranteed in the free exercise clause of the First Amendment to the United States Constitution. The United States Supreme Court then vacated the Minnesota Supreme Court decision and sent the case back for consideration in light of another of its rulings, *Smith,* the famous peyote case. (In that case the Court ruled that the First Amendment did not free one to violate a law forbidding the use of something a religious belief mandates.) Finally, the Minnesota Supreme Court ruled once more in favor of the Amish, but not on First Amendment grounds. Instead, it found that the Minnesota Constitution provides greater protection to religious freedom than the U.S. Constitution. For an excellent review of the complex cultural and legal issues surrounding slow-moving-vehicle signs and the Amish (including *State v. Hershberger* and *Minnesota v. Hershberger*), see Lee J. Zook, "Slow-Moving Vehicles," in *The Amish and the State,* ed. Donald B. Kraybill (1993), 145–62.

24. Jason Strait, "Amish Will Be Charged to Repair Roads," *Kalamazoo Gazette,* July 12, 2002.

25. "When Hatred Meets Silence," *Milwaukee Journal Sentinel,* March 13, 1998; Peter Maller, "Blanket of Secrecy Covers Crimes against Amish: Investigators' Obstacles

Include Victims' Belief That Persecution Is a Part of Life," *Milwaukee Journal Sentinel,* March 2, 1998; Meg Jones, "Violence against Amish on the Rise: Buggy Theft, Burning Bring Other Incidents to Light," *Milwaukee Journal Sentinel,* November 7, 1997.

26. Carrie Loranger Gaska, "Vandalism Arrests in Amish Country: One Resident Says He Doubts These Were Hate Crimes," *Wisconsin State Journal,* November 9, 1997; Ed Treleven, "4 Face Hate Crime Charges," *Wisconsin State Journal,* November 11, 1997.

27. Maller, "Blanket of Secrecy Covers Crimes against Amish," *Milwaukee Journal Sentinel.*

28. In addition to the cases that follow, see also "Attacks on Amish Give Town in Indiana a Scare," *Minneapolis Star Tribune,* February 16, 1996; "Police in Buggies Try to Curb Violence against Amish," *Milwaukee Journal Sentinel,* September 20, 1998; "Amish Farmers' Animals Are Killed in Missouri," *St. Louis Post-Dispatch,* November 7, 1997.

29. Dan Fesperman, "Values Unite Amish after Arsons: Community Rebuilds from Ashes of Barn-Burnings," *Minneapolis Star Tribune,* March 24, 1992; also Randall Balmer, "Cultures Collide in Plain Tragedy: 'I know I feel better than the guy who did this,'" *Minneapolis Star Tribune,* June 2, 1993.

30. For arson against the Hutterites in Montana, see Amy Beth Hanson, "Sect is Unpopular in Montana Farm Country: Vandals Have Been Preying on the Communal Hutterites, Who Have Succeeded at Farming Where Others Failed," *Associated Press,* May 9, 1998; and "Some Montana Farmers Feel Squeezed by Flourishing Hutterite Communities: FBI Investigates Burning of Colony's Lumber Shed," *St. Louis Post-Dispatch,* August 2, 1998.

31. "Some Montana Farmers Feel Squeezed by Flourishing Hutterite Communities," *St. Louis Post-Dispatch.*

32. Hanson, "Sect Is Unpopular in Montana Farm Country," *Associated Press.*

33. Ibid.

34. The Monroe County District Attorney's criminal complaint filed against Vieth quoted his confession to county police. Not surprisingly the case received wide media coverage. See Maxene Renner, "Amish Rape Suspect Arrested," *Wisconsin State Journal,* November 5, 1995; "Amish Rape Suspect to Face Trial," *Capital Times,* December 1, 1995; "Man Gets 60 Years for Attacks on Amish," *Minneapolis Star Tribune,* March 26, 1996; and Maller, "Blanket of Secrecy Covers Crimes against Amish," *Milwaukee Journal Sentinel.*

35. Personal communication, August 14, 1998.

36. Garrison Keillor, *Lake Wobegon Days* (1985).

37. Zachary Cooper, "Two Black Settlements in Wisconsin," *Wisconsin Academy Review* 27 (June, 1981): 10; also, Zachary Cooper, *Black Settlers in Rural Wisconsin* (1977; reprint, 1994); Zachary L. Cooper and Emilie Tari, *Coming Together, Coming Apart: Black Settlers in Rural Wisconsin Teacher's Manual* (1983).

38. In biographies of residents from the township of Forest (home of the Cheyenne Valley settlement), the 1884 *History of Vernon County* does not specify race. Because residents themselves contributed material, this, too, could be a sign of the prosperity and integration that African Americans had achieved. See *History of Vernon County, Wisconsin* (1884), 508–15.

39. Wisconsin historian James Knox Phillips made a strong connection between Cheyenne Valley's initial spatial integration on the landscape and its consequent economic and social integration. Phillips felt that one of his important contributions to Wisconsin history was in helping to bring this "Lost Community" to light, a project that first interested him in the late 1930s but did not come to fruition for three more decades. James Knox Phillips, "Negro-White Integration in a Midwestern Farm Community," *Negro Heritage* 7, nos. 5/6 (February/March 1968): 55–58, 62–65.

40. Census records for Forest Township in 1870 and 1880 are located in Vernon County Historical Museum files. Native Americans also intermarried with a few of these families. There is no mention of their tribe or band of origin, but it is possible they were Winnebago.

41. For the popular accounts that followed Phillips's research on Cheyenne Valley (which Phillips called "Morning Valley" in his 1960s-era articles, to protect residents who were fearful about exposing their ancestry), see Jack Houston "Wisconsin's Rural Negro Settlement," *La Crosse Tribune*, March 20, 1971; Reverend William Blake, "Celebrate Our Heritage," *Dimensions*, June 1982; Ken Brekke, "Valley Once Attracted Black Pioneers," *La Crosse Tribune*, October 6, 1985; Susan Lampert Smith, "Blacks Were Just Fellow Farmers," *Wisconsin State Journal*, May 18, 1999; and Lon Reuter, "What's So Special Bout Us?" unpublished interview, Vernon County Historical Museum files.

42. Clarence T. Yoder, "Hillsboro, WI," *The Budget*, October 10, 2001.

43. I had begun my research in the Kickapoo Valley when the Air National Guard announced its plans, so I followed the events firsthand.

44. Kraybill, "Negotiating with Caesar," in *The Amish and the State*, ed. Donald B. Kraybill (1993), 3–22.

45. Kraybill, *The Riddle of Amish Culture*, 2.

46. Ibid., 141.

47. Joseph Cook, "Politics as Unusual: Amish Become Active to Oppose Highway Proposal," *Minneapolis Star Tribune*, September 25, 1987.

48. Roger Snell, "Reclusive Amish Go Public in Ohio in Effort to Block $25M Incinerator," *USA Today*, April 12, 1988.

49. Frank Allen, "Plain Talk: Pennsylvania Dutch Act to Shield Farms from the Subdividers," *Wall Street Journal*, April 17, 1990.

50. Jeff Taylor, "Jet Maneuvers May Intrude upon Amish Life," *Houston Chronicle*, October 28, 1995.

51. James Walsh, "A Struggle to Keep the Peace: A Wisconsin Amish Community Fears a Proposed Military Flyover Route Could Threaten Its Way of Life," *Minneapolis Star Tribune*, July 23, 1995.

52. Ibid.; also Susan Lampert Smith, "Kickapoo Valley Leads Assault on Flight Plan: Listing of Guard's Opponents Is Varied, Lengthy," *Wisconsin State Journal*, October 8, 1995.

53. See for example, Taylor, "Jet Maneuvers May Intrude upon Amish Life," *Houston Chronicle;* Rogers Worthington, "Peaceful Valley in Wisconsin Fears Proposed Air Maneuvers," *Chicago Tribune*, June 12, 1995.

54. Air National Guard, *Final Environmental Impact Statement Addressing the Hardwood Range Expansion and Associated Air Space Actions, Volume 3—Other Related Correspondence* (November 2000), 1–37.

55. Ibid., 2–247.

56. Chris Stark to the Air National Guard, March 18, 1995, author's personal files.

57. Air National Guard, *Final Environmental Impact Statement Addressing the Hardwood Range Expansion and Associated Air Space Actions, Volume 3—Other Related Correspondence,* 2–289.

58. James Walsh, "Air National Guard Drops Proposal for Low-Flight Path over Wisconsin, Iowa," *Minneapolis Star Tribune,* April 17, 1996.

59. Ibid.

60. Personal communication, Ken Stark, August 13, 1998.

61. Gideon A. Miller, "Town of Clinton Amish History," 156.

Chapter 5. An Amish Environment

1. Eugene P. Ericksen, Julia A. Ericksen, and John A. Hostetler, "The Cultivation of the Soil as a Moral Directive: Population Growth, Family Ties, and the Maintenance of Community Among the Old Order Amish," *Rural Sociology* 45, no. 1 (1980): 49–68.

2. Gertrude E. Huntington, "Ideology, History, and Agriculture: Examples from Contemporary North America," *Culture and Agriculture,* nos. 45–46 (1993): 21–25.

3. Hershberger, "Cashton, WI History," 68.

4. Ibid.

5. Hostetler, *Amish Society,* 15.

6. Warren A. Johnson, Victor Stoltzfus, and Peter Craumer, "Energy Conservation in Amish Agriculture," *Science* 198, no. 4315 (1977): 373–78.

7. Hostetler, *Amish Society,* 119.

8. Hershberger, "Cashton, WI History," 68.

9. The Hutterites, by contrast, have settled on the Great Plains rather than in the eastern or midwestern United States. Their reasons speak to long-standing differences between the two Anabaptist sects. In their origins in the Protestant Reformation, and in some of the core Christian beliefs both hold, the Hutterites and Amish are alike. These similarities manifest themselves in their physical plainness, their deliberate separation from a larger society, and also in their geographic sensitivity to the world around them. The Amish and Hutterites differ, however, in their social organization. The Amish cluster together in communities, but they farm individually on privately owned land. Hutterites live communally in large colonies, and they farm on a very large scale using all the technologies available through industrial agriculture, including complex irrigation systems. Such a profound difference in socioeconomic organization helps explain their vastly different choices of physical landscapes. According to Ericksen, Ericksen, and Hostetler, "the Hutterite emphasis on community responsibility for individual lifestyles is adapted to the wide open spaces of the Great Plains. Such areas necessitate modern farming technology and allow for the development of strict isolated communes and a rapid rate of population increase." "The Cultivation of the Soil as a Moral Directive: Population Growth, Family Ties, and the Maintenance of Community among the Old Order Amish," 65. Johnson, Stoltzfus, and Craumer say, by contrast, that the Amish "are not likely to spread into the Great

Plains because that region is not conducive to the labor-intensive, unirrigated agriculture at which the Amish are so skilled." "Energy Conservation in Amish Agriculture," 373–78.

10. CROPP is based in La Farge, Wisconsin, which itself is in Stark, one of my three study townships.

11. This holds true of other Amish communities as well, as shown in Katharine V. Blake et al., "Modern Amish Farming as Ecological Agriculture," *Society and Natural Resources* 10 (1997): 143–59; P. R. Craumer, "Farm Productivity and Energy Efficiency in Amish and Modern Dairying." *Agriculture and Environment* 4 (1979): 281–89; David G. Sommers and Ted L. Napier, "Comparisons of Amish and Non-Amish Farmers: A Diffusion/Farm-Structure Perspective," *Rural Sociology* 58, no. 1 (1993): 130–45.

12. Blake et al. tried to identify the ways in which Amish farming in northern New York fit or did not fit the theoretical concept of "ecological agriculture." Ecological agriculture, according to the authors, emphasizes farm methods that are both sustainable and organic. "Modern Amish Farming as Ecological Agriculture," 144.

13. For an excellent account of the role ecological ideas have played in alternative and ecological agriculture, see Randall S. Beeman and James A. Pritchard, *A Green and Permanent Land: Ecology and Agriculture in the Twentieth Century* (2001).

14. Blake et al., "Modern Amish Farming as Ecological Agriculture," 143–59; Sommers and Napier, "Comparisons of Amish and Non-Amish Farmers: A Diffusion/Farm-Structure Perspective," 130–45; Deborah H. Stinner, M. G. Paoletti, and B. R. Stinner, "In Search of Traditional Farm Wisdom for a More Sustainable Agriculture: A Study of Amish Farming and Society," *Agriculture, Ecosystems, and Environment* 27 (1989): 77–90; and Craumer, "Farm Productivity and Energy Efficiency in Amish and Modern Dairying," 281–89.

15. For the connection between land, politics, and the concentration of power in this country, begin with John Gaventa, *Power and Powerlessness: Quiescence and Rebellion in an Appalachian Valley* (1980); and more recently, "The Political Economy of Land Tenure: Appalachia and the Southeast," in Jacobs, *Who Owns America?* 227–44. See also Chuck Hassebrook, "Saving the Family Farm," *Forum for Applied Research and Public Policy* 14, no. 3 (Fall 1999): 55–60. For the developing world, see S. P. Reyna, "The Emergence of Land Concentration in the West Africa Savanna," *American Ethnologist* 14, no. 3 (1987): 523–41; and A. Hall, "Agrarian Crisis in Brazilian Amazonia: The Grande Carajas Programme," *Journal of Development Studies* 23, no. 4 (1987): 522–52.

16. Blake et al. found a similar diversity of agriculture in an Amish community that relocated to northern New York in the 1970s. "Modern Amish Farming as Ecological Agriculture." Ericksen, Ericksen, and Hostetler describe such mixed farms as typical of the Amish. "The Cultivation of the Soil as a Moral Directive," 49–68.

17. Johnson, Stoltzfus, and Craumer, "Energy Conservation in Amish Agriculture," 373–78; also Craumer, "Farm Productivity and Energy Efficiency in Amish and Modern Dairying," 281–99. Kickapoo Valley resident Jean Lang interviewed Victor Stoltzfus about the research in "Energy Use in Amish-style Farming Studied," *La Farge Epitaph,* November 2, 1977.

18. Craumer, "Farm Productivity and Energy Efficiency in Amish and Modern Dairying," 281–99; Lee Zook, "The Amish Farm and Alternative Agriculture: A Comparison," *Journal of Sustainable Agriculture* 4, no. 4 (1994): 21–30.

19. G. K. Grahn and R. G. Wingate, "The Wisconsin Hill and Valley Cheese Factory: A Joint Venture Between Amish and Non-Amish," *Wisconsin Geographer* 4 (1988): 65–71; Maxine Renner, "Past Meets Present: Cashton Cheese Factory Finds Success While Providing an Outlet to Amish Dairy Farmers," *La Crosse Tribune,* October 15, 1995.

20. Kraybill, *The Riddle of Amish Culture,* 155–58. Lee Zook says that two crucial questions must be answered satisfactorily before a community will decide on a new technology: "Is this new technology or innovation appropriate for our Amish way of life? How will it influence our community and the way we live together?" If an irreconcilable difference arises over a decision, one part of the community may decide to leave and settle elsewhere. "The Amish Farm and Alternative Agriculture: A Comparison," 22.

21. John A. Cross, "Changes in America's Dairyland," *Geographical Review* 91, no. 4 (2001): 710.

22. Melvin Miller, "Viroqua, WI Rising Sun," *The Budget,* December 26, 2001.

23. Cashton Produce Auction, 14306 Melody Rd., Cashton, WI 54619.

24. Melvin Miller, "Viroqua, WI Rising Sun," *The Budget,* March 6, 2002.

25. Catherine Trevison, "Self-Sufficiency Isn't Easy, but Some Still Make the Effort," *La Crosse Tribune,* May 13, 1990.

26. Melvin Miller, "Viroqua, WI Rising Sun," *The Budget,* February 20, 2003.

27. Marc A. Olshan, "Modernity, the Folk Society, and the Old Order Amish: An Alternative Interpretation," *Rural Sociology* 46, no. 2 (1981): 297–309. Steven Stoll suggests that the Amish may even be postmodern. See Stoll's thoughtful examination of Amish farmer David Kline's farm in *Larding the Lean Earth: Soil and Society in Nineteenth-Century America* (2002), 215–26.

28. Ericksen, Ericksen, and Hostetler, "The Cultivation of the Soil as a Moral Directive," 49–68.

29. Romans 12:2 and 2 Corinthians, *The NIV Study Bible* (Grand Rapids, MI: Zondervan Publishing House, 1995).

30. Laura Kusnetzky et al., "In Search of the Climax Community: Sustainability and the Old Order Amish," *Culture and Agriculture* 50 (1994), 14.

31. Julia Ericksen and Gary Klein, "Women's Roles and Family Production among the Old Order Amish," *Rural Sociology* 46, no. 2 (1981): 295–96. Readers interested in more personal stories of Amish women who find space for their intellect and creativity will enjoy Louise Stoltzfus, *Amish Women* (1994).

32. Genesis 1:28–31, *The NIV Study Bible.*

33. David Kline, "God's Spirit and a Theology for Living," in *Creation and the Environment: An Anabaptist Perspective on a Sustainable World,* ed. Calvin Redekop (2000), 61.

34. Hostetler, *Amish Society,* 89–90, 114.

35. Thomas Finger, "An Anabaptist/Mennonite Theology of Creation," in Redekop, *Creation and the Environment: An Anabaptist Perspective on a Sustainable World,* 155.

36. Hostetler, "A New Look at the Old Order." *The Rural Sociologist* 7 (1987): 278–92; also Zook, "The Amish Farm and Alternative Agriculture," 28.

37. Olivia Wu, "Secret Amish Hideaway Yields a Treasure Trove of Produce," *Chicago Sun-Times,* October 11, 1995.

38. Quoted in Kline, "God's Spirit and a Theology for Living," 67.

39. Through their theoretical framework of the "foodshed," Jack Kloppenburg Jr., John Hendrickson, and G. W. Stevenson call for a renewed emphasis on a moral economy in which food is "more than a commodity to be exchanged through a set of impersonal market relationships or a bundle of nutrients required to keep our body functioning." A focus on the moral economy, they say, may offer the framework and the action necessary to direct the market forces of food production toward human needs and the environment rather than "the economist's narrow 'effective demand.'" "Coming in to the Foodshed," in *Rooted in the Land* (1996), 115.

40. Huntington makes a special point of showing the ways in which the Amish appreciate lovely scenery (many go so far as the Grand Canyon to visit one of God's special wonders) as well as the nature in their own backyards. She suggests that the Amish orientation toward nature and agriculture is in part a historical carryover from the eighteenth century, a time when it was common to look on nature "as expressive of God." "Ideology, History, and Agriculture: Examples from Contemporary North America," 21–25; also Hostetler, *Amish Society,* 87–90.

41. Clarence Yoder, "Hillsboro, WI," *The Budget,* September 5, 2001.

42. Clarence Yoder, "Hillsboro, WI," *The Budget,* October 17, 2001.

43. The Amish began withdrawing their children from public schools in the 1920s, unhappy with the trend toward school consolidation and with the increasing length of time their children were away from home. A number of court struggles ensued, and the Amish won the right to establish their own K-8 schools, at which time their children's formal education stops. The Amish may be said to represent the vanguard of more recent trends in society toward school choice and home schooling. For the Amish and schooling, see Thomas J. Meyers, "Education and Schooling," in Kraybill, *The Amish and the State,* 87–108. Quote from Aldo Leopold, *A Sand County Almanac,* 223–24.

44. Leopold, *A Sand County Almanac,* 223–24.

45. I take my cue from Amish farmer and author David Kline. Kline uses this quote from Leopold to frame the life of his and his wife's farm: "This balance of utility and beauty that I strive for on the farm, my wife achieves so well in the garden, a delightful blend of the domestic and wild." David Kline, "An Amish Perspective," in *Rooted in the Land* (1996), 38–39. For Leopold's quote see Susan L. Flader and J. Baird Callicott, eds., *The River of the Mother of God* (1991), 326.

46. Melvin Miller, "Viroqua, WI Rising Sun," *The Budget,* May 30, 2001.

47. Personal communication, Laura Hewitt, Upper Midwest Conservation Director, Trout Unlimited.

48. Sommers and Napier, "Comparisons of Amish and Non-Amish Farmers," 130–45. The Amish vary in their attitudes and actual land use as much as any other group of farmers.   49. Terry Noble, "County Avoiding Amish 'Outhouse War,'" *La Crosse Tribune,* October 13, 1994.

50. Numerous studies have documented the same dissociation from government programs. Many Amish are reluctant to consult with conservation agencies at all. Conservative Amish settlements such as the one in Clinton upheld this more strictly than some other communities. See Place, "Land Use," 191–210; Sommers and Napier, "Comparison of Amish and non-Amish Farmers," 130–45; Blake et al., "Modern

Amish Farming as Ecological Agriculture," 143–59; and Zook, "The Amish Farm and Alternative Agriculture," 21–30.

51. The conversation was in response to my queries about Amish land use and whether or not the agents found Amish farmers approachable.

52. Mary Jackson, "Amish Agriculture and No-Till: The Hazards of Applying the USLE to Unusual Farms," *Journal of Soil and Water Conservation* 43 (1988): 483–86.

53. Rogers Worthington, "Amish Are Survivors in the Drought of '88," *La Crosse Tribune,* August 9, 1988.

54. Among in-depth case studies of specific Amish farms, only Stinner, Paoletti, and Stinner allude to forest management when they say, "Our case-study Amish farmer has a saw mill on his farm and sells hardwood lumber." "In Search of Traditional Farm Wisdom for a More Sustainable Agriculture: A Study of Amish Farming and Society," 84. So far I have not found significant attention to the Amish and forest ecosystems in the scientific or social scientific literature.

55. Clarence T. Yoder, "Hillsboro, WI," *The Budget,* March 20, 2002.

56. Personal communication, William (Bill) Kempf, August 14, 1998.

57. Our field survey of Amish sawmills in Clinton is consistent with an Amish directory, in which the Cashton settlement lists twenty-nine sawmill owners. It is important to realize, however, that Amish sawmill activity is fluid. *Wisconsin, Minnesota, and Montana Amish Directory 2002,* 80–128.

58. This and other quotes from Rosanne Boyett, personal communication, July 1, 2002.

59. The occupational structure of the Amish has been the source of several studies examining the impact on Amish communities of work in nonfarm sectors, including carpentry, sawmills, furniture making, and tourism. See Donald B. Kraybill and Steven M. Nolt, *Amish Enterprise: From Plows to Profits* (1995); George M. Kreps, Joseph F. Donnermeyer, and Marty W. Kreps, "The Changing Occupational Structure of Amish Males," *Rural Sociology* 59, no. 4 (1994): 708–19; and George M. Kreps et al., "The Impact of Tourism on the Amish Subculture: A Case Study," *Community Development Journal* 32, no. 4 (1997): 354–67.

60. Steve Cahalan, "Plowing New Ground: Some Coulee Region Amish Turn to Nonfarm Income Sources," *La Crosse Tribune,* March 23, 1998.

61. Forest scientists and policy analysts at the University of Wisconsin–Madison Department of Forest Ecology and Management likewise saw a dearth of harvesting statistics, mainly because state and local agencies do not collect information on sales (e.g., location of the harvest, board feet harvested, sale price, etc., all of which would be useful for assessing logging patterns across landscapes).

62. For a description of the ecological methods and data analysis used in this study, see Heasley, "Shifting Boundaries on a Wisconsin Landscape: Can GIS Help Historians Tell a Complicated Story?"

63. The study also accounted for the influence of slope on forest patterns and trends in the townships. As one would expect, flatter land suitable for agriculture and housing had the smallest area in forests over time.

64. Wendell Berry, "Seven Amish Farms," in *The Gift of Good Land: Further Essays Cultural and Agricultural* (1981), 257–58.

65. David Kline, "God's Spirit and a Theology for Living," 63.

66. David Kline, *Great Possessions: An Amish Farmer's Journal* (1990), xxi.

67. Heather Ann Ackley Bean, "Toward an Anabaptist/Mennonite Environmental Ethic," in *Creation and the Environment: An Anabaptist Perspective on a Sustainable World,* ed. Calvin Redekop (2000), 196–97.

68. Wes Jackson, *New Roots for Agriculture* (1980), 11.

69. This would be nothing new to the Amish. Historically, they have never been free of scrutiny from the larger societies that have surrounded them.

70. Personal communication, June 22, 2001.

71. Donald Worster, *Dust Bowl: The Southern Plains in the 1930s* (1979), 238. *Dust Bowl* remains one of the most powerful interrogations of American agriculture ever written. His larger ideas about nature, culture, and agriculture in that book, as well as in *The Wealth of Nature* and "Nature and the Disorder of History," have informed my place-specific analysis of Amish agriculture.

72. Personal communication, August 14, 1998.

Chapter 6. A Dam for New Times

1. For a description of the 1907 flood see Kickapoo Valley History Project, *Kickapoo Pearls: A Collection of Kickapoo History and Folkways,* vol. 1, no. 4 (1979), 4–5.

2. According to one local history, the 1935 floods "ravaged the valley from its source to its mouth." See Eber Huston, *Kickapoo* (1959), 97, Vernon County Historical Society files.

3. "Sharing Hardships of Flood Victims in Western Wisconsin; Towns, Roads, and Rails are Submerged," *Milwaukee Journal,* August 7, 1935.

4. Hocking, *The Memorable Kickapoo Valley,* 97.

5. Raymond H. Merritt, *Creativity, Conflict, and Controversy: A History of the St. Paul District U.S. Army Corps of Engineers* (1979), 414; Bernice Schroeder, "The Legacy of the Kickapoo: A People Betrayed," in *Vernon County Heritage* (1994), 148.

6. Congress passed two flood control acts in 1917 and 1928. Those were not national in scope but focused on flood control on the lower Mississippi River. For elaboration on these acts see U.S. Army Corps of Engineers, *The History of the U.S. Army Corps of Engineers* (1998), 10, 51; U.S. Army Corps of Engineers, *Essayons (Let Us Try)* (1991), 3, 50–51. For an important account of the great Mississippi River flood of 1927—the political aftermath of which came to shape small rivers like the Kickapoo through the twentieth century—see John M. Barry, *Rising Tide: The Great Mississippi Flood of 1927 and How It Changed America* (1997).

7. U.S. Army Corps of Engineers, *Water Resources People and Issues: Interview with Gilbert F. White* (1993), 7.

8. These were the so-called "308" reports, the last of which the Corps completed in 1937. Merritt, *Creativity, Conflict, and Controversy,* 49.

9. *Flood Act of 1936. U.S. Statutes at Large* 49 (1936): 1570.

10. U.S. Army Corps of Engineers, *Water Resources People and Issues,* 15, 18.

11. The Corps submitted its results in 1940. Stephen M. Born, "Generalized Chronology of Key Events and Events Related to Provision of S&T Information in the Kickapoo Dam Controversy," in *The Kickapoo Dam (A Case Study in the Application*

of Scientific and Technologic Information to Executive Branch Decision-Making in Wisconsin) (1978); Jeffrey Smoller, "Engineer Corps Gets Kickapoo Blame," *Capital Times,* April 26, 1971.

12. Todd Shallat, *Structures in the Stream: Water, Science, and the Rise of the U.S. Army Corps of Engineers* (1994), 4. Shallat's compelling history starts with the Corps's view of itself as an impartial technical agency. He looks to the Corps's earliest history in the eighteenth century—and the competing intellectual traditions of the time from which it emerged—to detail the connection of political power to science and technology.

13. White served on the National Resources Committee and the National Resources Planning Board from 1934 to 1940. From 1940 to 1942 he was a member of the Bureau of Budget in the Executive Office of the President. See U.S. Army Corps of Engineers, *Water Resources People and Issues,* ix.

14. Ibid., 18.

15. Gilbert F. White, *Human Adjustment to Floods: A Geographical Approach to the Flood Problem in the United States* (1945); also U.S. Army Corps of Engineers, *Water Resources People and Issues,* 26–28, 38, 52.

16. The Corps formally took on a civil works mission as part of the General Survey Act of 1824. The act authorized the Corps to consider the national importance of its work from a commercial perspective as well as a military one. See U.S. Army Corps of Engineers, *The History of the U.S. Army Corps of Engineers.*

17. Amelia Janes, "Weather Hazards," in *Wisconsin's Past and Present,* ed. The Wisconsin Cartographer's Guild (1998), 46; and Bernice Schroeder, "The Legacy of the Kickapoo: A People Betrayed," in *Vernon County Heritage,* 148.

18. U.S. Army Engineer District, St. Paul, *Report on Survey of Kickapoo River, Wisconsin, for Flood Control* (1962). Congress approved the Corps plan in the *Flood Control Act of 1962. U.S. Statutes at Large* 76 (1962): 1173.

19. Max Anderson Associates, *Background of the La Farge Lake Project,* Kickapoo Area Planning Study, Working Paper Number Two (1973); also Merritt, *Creativity, Conflict, and Controversy,* 414.

20. Donald J. Pisani, "A Conservation Myth: The Troubled Childhood of the Multiple-Use Idea," *Agricultural History* 76, no. 2 (2002): 154–71; U.S. Army Corps of Engineers, *The History of the U.S. Army Corps of Engineers,* 50–51, 129–37; U.S. Army Corps of Engineers, *Water Resources People and Issues,* 9–10; and Merritt, *Creativity, Conflict, and Controversy,* 117–19. The standard reference for this transitional era is Samuel P. Hays, *Beauty, Health, and Permanence: Environmental Politics in the United States, 1955–1985* (1987).

21. When critics portray the agency as monolithic, Corps historians point to its decentralized organization. Merritt describes the Corps of Engineers as "a complex, decentralized, multipurpose, pragmatic, quasi-military, quasi-civilian federal agency comprising boards, commissions, divisions, districts, special projects, educational institutions, international organizations and intergovernmental programs." Merritt, *Creativity, Conflict, and Controversy,* 38.

22. The St. Paul District currently covers parts of Minnesota, North Dakota, South Dakota, Iowa, Wisconsin, and Michigan. Its boundaries give the district jurisdiction over federal water projects on three of the continent's largest drainage systems:

the Mississippi River; Lake Superior, draining the Great Lakes through the St. Lawrence River and ultimately to the Atlantic; and the Red River, a system reaching down to Hudson Bay.

23. Merritt, *Creativity, Conflict, and Controversy,* 119.

24. For a small sample of the high hopes Valley residents had for a better economic future, see Schroeder, "The Legacy of the Kickapoo: A People Betrayed," 148; also "Dam Proponents Rally at La Farge," *Kickapoo Scout,* April 24, 1970; and "Lake Kickapoo More of an Asset," *Viroqua Broadcaster-Censor,* May 7, 1970.

25. U.S. Army Corps of Engineers, *La Farge Reservoir Flood Control Project Kickapoo River, Wisconsin: Questions and Answers Concerning the Acquisition of Your Real Estate by the Government* (1968).

26. Ibid., 10.

27. Personal communication, Brian and Clifford Turner, June 22, 2001.

28. U.S. Army Corps of Engineers, *The History of the U.S. Army Corps of Engineers,* 10.

29. Passage of the Flood Control Act of 1938 included discussions over land acquisition—whether easements, fee simple purchases, or condemnation were more appropriate. The Corps ended up with a great deal of discretion. U.S. Army Corps of Engineers, *Water Resources People and Issues,* 16–17.

30. U.S. Army Corps of Engineers, *Essayons (Let Us Try),* 9.

31. *National Environmental Policy Act of 1969. U.S. Statutes at Large* 83 (1970): 852.

32. For instance: *Clean Water Restoration Act of 1966. U.S. Statutes at Large* 80 (1966): 1246; *Clean Air Amendments of 1970. U.S. Statutes at Large* 84 (1970): 1676; *Endangered Species Act of 1973. U.S. Statutes at Large* 87 (1973): 884.

33. *National Environmental Policy Act of 1969,* Section 2.

34. *National Environmental Policy Act of 1969,* Section 102(2)(C).

35. Ibid.

36. Martin Reuss, *Shaping Environmental Awareness: The United States Army Corps of Engineers Environmental Advisory Board 1970–1980* (1983), 4–5.

37. Shallat, *Structures in the Stream.*

38. U.S. Army Corps of Engineers, *Engineer Memoirs: Lieutenant General Ernest Graves* (1997), 131. Dr. Frank N. Schubert, chief of joint operational history in the Joint History Office (Joint Chiefs of Staff), conducted the interview with Graves in 1985. The interview was part of the U.S. Army Corps of Engineers *Engineer Memoirs* series, published by the Office of History as part of its Oral History Program.

39. U.S. Army Corps of Engineers, *Engineer Memoirs,* 131.

40. Galen L. Buterbaugh, Acting Assistant Regional Director, Fish and Wildlife Service, to Lt. Colonel Rodney E. Cox, District Engineer, U.S. Army Engineer District, St. Paul, November 15, 1971, in U.S. Army Engineer District, St. Paul, *Final Environmental Statement: La Farge Lake, Kickapoo River, Vernon County, Wisconsin* (1972). See also, U.S. Army Engineer District, St. Paul, *Revised Environmental Statement: La Farge Lake, Kickapoo River, Wisconsin* (1971).

41. Robert H. Meyers, Acting Regional Director, Bureau of Outdoor Recreation, to the District Engineer, U.S. Army Engineer District, St. Paul, November 9, 1971, in U.S. Army Engineer District, St. Paul, *Final Environmental Statement: La Farge Lake, Kickapoo River, Vernon County, Wisconsin* (1972).

42. Ibid.

43. U.S. Army Corps of Engineers, *Engineer Memoirs,* 184.

44. Ibid.

45. Ibid., 140.

46. Jeff Smoller, "Engineer Corps Gets Kickapoo Blame," *Capital Times,* April 26, 1971; Whitney Gould, "Dam Is a Biological Disaster," *Capital Times,* April 26, 1971.

47. The Sierra Club filed a lawsuit in District Court in June of 1971, and Judge James E. Doyle dismissed the case. Judge Doyle dismissed the Sierra Club's second suit as well in 1972. The Circuit Court of Appeals upheld his judgment in 1973. Opinion and Order, District Judge James E. Doyle, June 2, 1972, 345 F., Supp. 440; Opinion and Order, U.S. Court of Appeals for the Seventh Circuit, October 2, 1973, 72-1833; also refer to Whitney Gould, "Doyle Is Asked to Stop Kickapoo River Project," *Capital Times,* June 4, 1971; "Doyle Refuses to Halt La Farge Dam Project," *Wisconsin State Journal,* May 4, 1972; "Environmental Groups Appeal Doyle's Dam Project Ruling," *Wisconsin State Journal,* September 1, 1972.

48. U.S. Army Corps of Engineers, *Engineer Memoirs.*

49. Merritt, *Creativity, Conflict, and Controversy,* 415.

50. U.S. Army Corps of Engineers, *Engineer Memoirs,* 179.

51. Ibid., 148.

52. U.S. Army Engineer District, St. Paul, *Final Environmental Statement,* 2.

53. Robert W. Smith to Rodney E. Cox, Corps of Engineers District Engineer, October 15, 1971, in U.S. Army Engineer District, St. Paul, *Final Environmental Statement.*

54. Rodney E. Cox to Robert W. Smith, October 19, 1971, in U.S. Army Engineer District, St. Paul, *Final Environmental Statement.*

55. Graves said this when he faced tough questions about the La Farge dam from the Wisconsin press. Jeff Smoller, "Engineer Corps Gets Kickapoo Blame," *Capital Times,* April 26, 1971.

56. U.S. Army Corps of Engineers, *Engineer Memoirs,* 178.

57. Ibid.

58. A number of important scholarly critiques of the Corps have belied its self-held image. They show how actively it has sought to aggrandize its political influence. This is a more sweeping indictment than Gilbert White's concern with project planning and decision making. Political scientist Arthur Maas undertook one of the earliest and best-known critiques of the Corps, portraying it as a federal agency that enjoyed a dangerous level of autonomy and political influence. Following Maas was Samuel P. Hays, who portrayed the Corps as a ruthless agency when it came to protecting its own pork-barrel interests. Since Hays, historians have pursued the Corps's influence over national water policy into other eras. See Arthur Maas, *Muddy Waters: The Army Engineers and the Nation's Rivers* (1951); Samuel P. Hays, *Conservation and the Gospel of Efficiency: The Progressive Conservation Movement, 1890–1920* (1959); Otis L. Graham Jr., *Toward a Planned Society: From Roosevelt to Nixon* (1976); and also Marc Reisner's environmental critique in *Cadillac Desert: The American West and Its Disappearing Water* (1986). A few histories have shown how skillfully some Corps districts navigated regional and local politics, most recently Jared Orsi, *Hazardous Metropolis: Flooding and Urban Ecology in Los Angeles* (2004).

59. *Environmental Guidelines for the Civil Works Program of the Corps of Engineers,* ER 1165-2-500 (Nov. 30, 1970); see also Reuss, *Shaping Environmental Awareness,* 11–12.

60. *Environmental Guidelines,* 5–6; Reuss, *Shaping Environmental Awareness,* 11.

61. Quoted in Reuss, *Shaping Environmental Awareness,* 12.

62. Quoted in Reuss, *Shaping Environmental Awareness,* 20.

63. U.S. Army Corps of Engineers, *Engineer Memoirs,* 182.

64. Quoted in Reuss, *Shaping Environmental Awareness,* 20.

65. Steven Lee Meyers, "Army Corps Falsified Data for Project," *New York Times,* December 7, 2000; Michael Grunwald, "Engineers of Power Inside the Army Corps," *Washington Post,* September 10, 2000.

66. U.S. Army Corps of Engineers, *Engineer Memoirs,* 135.

67. National Park Service, "National Register of Historical Places Registration Form: La Farge Reservoir and Lake Dam" (1999), section 8, 25.

68. U.S. Army Engineer District, St. Paul, *Final Environmental Statement,* 38.

69. Ibid., 29.

70. Ibid., 44.

71. Ibid., 29.

72. National Park Service, "National Register of Historical Places Registration Form," section 8, 26.

73. Reuss, *Shaping Environmental Awareness,* 23–24, 26–28.

74. U.S. Army Corps of Engineers, *Engineer Memoirs,* 179.

75. Institute for Environmental Studies, *Environmental Analysis of the Kickapoo River Impoundment* (1974).

76. U.S. Army Corps of Engineers, *Review of Alternatives for Flood Damage Reduction on the Kickapoo River, Wisconsin* (1975). The cost-benefit problems and cost overruns brought the La Farge dam to the attention of the Carter administration, who placed it on its "hit list" of public works projects to stop. See also U.S. Army Corps of Engineers, *Engineer Memoirs,* 166–74.

77. Institute for Environmental Studies, *Environmental Analysis of the Kickapoo River Impoundment,* ix.

78. Guy D. Phillips, *Environmental Assessment of the Kickapoo River Impoundment II: An Assessment of Economic Impact* (1977), 12, 45–47; National Park Service, "National Register of Historical Places Registration Form," section 7, 2.

79. National Park Service, "National Register of Historical Places Registration Form," section 8, 30.

80. Hocking, *The Memorable Kickapoo Valley,* 41.

81. Virgil Munns, "Ballad of the Kickapoo," Miscellaneous Box, Vernon County Historical Museum (misspellings in original).

82. Robert P. Vosen to Colonel M. Noah, St. Paul District Army Corps of Engineers, February 10, 1975, La Farge Dam files, Vernon County Historical Society (misspellings in original).

83. Biographical Directory of the United States Congress, "Nelson, Gaylord Anton."

84. Johnson, *Soil Conservation in Wisconsin,* 246–47.

85. Biographical Directory of the United States Congress, "Proxmire, William." For Proxmire's own views on congressional appropriations see William Proxmire, *The Fleecing of America* (1980).

86. Johnson, *Soil Conservation in Wisconsin*, 247.

87. U.S. Army Engineer District, St. Paul, *Information Base for Further Evaluation of La Farge Lake and Channel Improvement, Wisconsin* (1977), 10–11; "Halt on Kickapoo Dam Asked by U.S. Agency," *La Crosse Tribune*, December 19, 1974.

88. U.S. Army Engineer District, St. Paul, *Information Base for Further Evaluation*, 10–11. Also, Patrick J. Lucey, Governor, to Colonel Max W. Noah, District Engineer, St. Paul District, Corps of Engineers, May 1, 1975, author's personal files.

89. *Minneapolis Star Tribune*, September 22, 1975; also quoted in Merritt, *Creativity, Conflict, and Controversy*, 416–17.

90. Quoted in Merritt, *Creativity, Conflict, and Controversy*, 416.

91. U.S. Army Corps of Engineers, *Alternatives for Flood Reduction and Recreation in the Kickapoo River Valley, Wisconsin: Special Report* (1977), 70.

92. U.S. Army Corps of Engineers, *Alternatives for Flood Reduction*, 8; also Merritt, *Creativity, Conflict, and Controversy*, 416.

93. Roy Dingle, *Nothing but Conservation*, 340, 328.

94. Lynne Heasley and Raymond P. Guries, "Forest Tenure and Cultural Landscapes: Environmental Histories in the Kickapoo Valley," in Jacobs, *Who Owns America?* 193.

95. U.S. Army Corps of Engineers, *Engineer Memoirs*, 180.

96. Among numerous university studies on regional, recreational, and economic development in the Kickapoo Valley, see Thomas Lamm, *Forest Resources in the Kickapoo Valley: Issues and Opportunities* (1981); John Leatherman, *Input-Output Analysis of the Kickapoo River Valley* (1994); P. H. Lewis and Thomas Lamm, *Recreation and Tourism Resources in the Kickapoo Valley* (1981); D. Marcouiller, A. Anderson, and W. C. Norman, *Trout Angling in Southwestern Wisconsin and Implications for Regional Development* (1995); Fahriye Sancar et al., *Development of an Action Plan for the Kickapoo River Valley of Southwestern Wisconsin: New Visions for the Kickapoo, Regional Design Proposals for Future Development* (1992).

97. "The Kickapoo Floods: Worst Flood on Record Devastates Valley," *La Farge Epitaph*, July 7, 1978.

Chapter 7. Deer Unlimited

1. "People Are People Are People," *La Farge Epitaph*, December 12, 1979.

2. For a scientific description of the distribution of forest herbs under a variety of site conditions, see John Kotar and Timothy L. Burger, *A Guide to Forest Communities and Habitat Types of Central and Southern Wisconsin* (1996).

3. In 1996, the Corps recorded $10,000 in damage to the reserve from recreational vehicles. U.S. Army Engineer District, St. Paul, *Issue Paper: La Farge Lake, Kickapoo River, Wisconsin: Management, Monitoring, Damage Repair, and Enforcement Requirements on Project Lands* (November 17, 1997).

4. Robert Pogue Harrison, *Forests: The Shadow of Civilization* (1992), 63.

5. For another historical examination of forest outlawry in medieval England, including the real-life roots of Robin Hood, see Simon Schama, *Landscape and Memory* (1995), 142–53.

6. Rudolph, a so-called white supremacist, set off bombs that killed people at the 1996 Summer Olympics in Atlanta and an abortion clinic in Alabama. He eluded authorities until 2003. Many local residents admired his skill and tenacity and probably aided him on occasion.

7. Personal communication, John Anfinson, Chief, Cultural Resources, St. Paul District Army Corps of Engineers, June 23, 2000.

8. Harrison, *Forests*, 63.

9. Hardin inspired an entire project in tenure scholarship to rebut an essay that was only six pages long. Each new generation of critics has felt obliged to debunk Hardin on at least two grounds. First is Hardin's definition of common property. The distinction between common property and open access land tenure regimes has become a foundation of property theory. A second quarrel is with the way Hardin treated the world's people and their environmental problems. When he said "we," he meant them—those "herders," those breeders in the world's poorest regions. He chose not to turn his gaze on the social and environmental problems that have arisen from private property regimes in wealthy regions. Nor did he address the rise of large-scale "corporate herders" exploiting ocean, groundwater, and land resources. To the contrary, he posited private property as solution to the tragedy of the commons. For useful surveys on common property, see Bonnie J. McCay and James M. Acheson, eds., *The Question of the Commons: The Culture and Ecology of Communal Resources* (1987); and Camilla Toulmin and Julian F. Quan, eds., *Evolving Land Rights, Policy, and Tenure in Africa* (2000). One of the finest entry points into tenure theory at large is Daniel W. Bromley, *Environment and Economy: Property Rights and Public Policy* (1991). A path-breaking, historical interrogation of Hardin's essay is Arthur McEvoy's environmental history, *The Fisherman's Problem: Ecology and Law in the California Fisheries* (1986); Brian Donahue initiated a modern project to establish a sustainable commons in suburban New England, recounted in *Reclaiming the Commons: Community Farms and Forests in a New England Town* (1999). And finally, Garrett Hardin, "The Tragedy of the Commons," *Science* 162 (December 1968), 1243–48.

10. The period was 1968–70. From 1971–73 absentee owners purchased 76 percent of all land sold. See Phillips, *Environmental Assessment of the Kickapoo River Impoundment II*, 37.

11. By the early 1970s, the real estate market had become much more complex than just a decade earlier. Prime farmland had once commanded the premium prices, but by 1973 recreational land had caught up and price per acre was no longer highly correlated to good soils. See Phillips, *Environmental Assessment of the Kickapoo River Impoundment II*, 23–40.

12. T. P. Rooney and D. M. Waller, "Direct and Indirect Effects of White-Tailed Deer in Forest Ecosytems," *Forest Ecology and Management* 181 (2003): 165–76; D. M. Waller and W. S. Alverson, "The White-Tailed Deer: A Keystone Herbivore," *Wildlife Society Bulletin* 25, no. 2 (1997): 217–26.

13. Rebecca A. Christoffel and Scott R. Craven, "Effect of Deer Harvest Strategy on Intensity of Deer Herbivory," unpublished manuscript (1998).

14. To game management specialists, carrying capacity represents a deer-centric exercise in modeling deer populations as they go up and down in particular categories of landscapes and climate zones. For an easy-to-read explanation of the concept as

applied to deer, see Wisconsin Department of Natural Resources, *Wisconsin's Deer Management Program: The Issues Involved in Decision-Making* (1998), 17.

15. Personal communication, August 23, 1996.

16. T. P. Rooney et al., "Biotic Impoverishment and Homogenization in Unfragmented Forest Understory Communities," *Conservation Biology* 18, no. 3 (2004): 787–98; S. B. Horsley, S. L. Stout, and D. S. DeCalesta, "White-Tailed Deer Impact on the Vegetation Dynamics of a Northern Hardwood Forest," *Ecological Applications* 13, no. 1 (2003): 98–118; C. P. Balgooyen and D. M. Waller, "The Use of *Clintonia borealis* and Other Indicators to Gauge Impacts of White-Tailed Deer on Plant Communities in Northern Wisconsin," *Natural Areas Journal* 15, no. 4 (1995): 308–18; W. S. Alverson, D. M. Waller, and S. L. Solheim, "Forests Too Deer: Edge Effects in Northern Wisconsin," *Conservation Biology* 2, no. 4 (1988): 348–56.

17. Rebecca A. Christoffel and Scott R. Craven, "Effect of Deer Harvest Strategy on Intensity of Deer Herbivory," unpublished manuscript (1998); also Rebecca A. Christoffel, "Ecological and Sociological Aspects of White-Tailed Deer Herbivory in South Central Wisconsin."

18. Craig G. Lorimer, "The Oak Regeneration Problem: New Evidence on Causes and Possible Solutions," *Forest Resource Analyses* (1989).

19. D. R. Foster, S. Clayden, D. A. Orwig, B. Hall, and S. Barry, "Oak, Chestnut and Fire: Climatic and Cultural Controls of Long-Term Forest Dynamics in New England, USA," *Journal of Biogeography* 29, nos. 10/11 (2002): 1359–79; J. L. Fuller, D. R. Foster, J. S. McLachlan, and N. Drake, "Impact of Human Activity on Regional Forest Composition and Dynamics in Central New England," *Ecosystems* 1 (1998): 76–95; Hazel R. Delcourt and Paul A. Delcourt, "Pre-Columbian Native American Use of Fire on Southern Appalachian Landscapes," *Conservation Biology* 11, no. 4 (1997): 1010–14; Craig G. Lorimer, "The Role of Fire in the Perpetuation of Oak Forests," *Proceedings of Challenges in Oak Management and Utilization, Madison, Wisconsin, March 28–29, 1985* (1985).

20. On Winnebago Indians and their interactions with oak-hickory forest landscapes, I have benefited from the insights of Beatrice A. Bigony, "The Interrelationships between Winnebago Folk Tales and Winnebago Habitat: A Working Paper," unpublished manuscript (1978).

21. M. D. Abrams, "Where Has All the White Oak Gone?" *Bioscience* 53, no. 10 (2003): 927–39; J. J. Zaczek, J. W. Groninger, and J. W. Van Sambeek, "Stand Dynamics in an Old-Growth Hardwood Forest, in Southern Illinois, USA," *Natural Areas Journal* 22, no. 3 (2002): 211–19; P. C. Goebel and D. M. Hix, "Changes in Composition and Structure of Mixed-Oak, Second-Growth Forest Ecosystems during the Understory Reinitiation Stage of Stand Development," *Ecoscience* 4, no. 3 (1997): 327–39; S. L. Dodge, "Successional Trends in a Mixed Oak Forest on High Mountain, New Jersey," *Journal of the Torrey Botanical Society* 124, no. 4 (1997) 312–17; B. McCune and G. Cottam, "The Successional Status of a Southern Wisconsin Oak Woods," *Ecology* 66 (1985), 1270–78.

22. Craig G. Lorimer, "The Oak Regeneration Problem," 2.

23. My team examined the rate and extent of succession on a landscape scale over six decades. Hix and Lorimer found the same trend at the stand level, in which oak forests converted to other species after commercial timber harvests. Hix and

Lorimer, "Early Stand Development on Former Oak Sites in Southwestern Wisconsin," 169–93.

24. According to Pubanz and Lorimer, by the time mature stands are logged, oak seedlings may already be too few and small to compete with other species in the understory. See Dan M. Pubanz and Craig G. Lorimer, *Oak Regeneration Experiments in Southwestern Wisconsin: Two-Year Results* (1992); also Craig G. Lorimer, Jonathan W. Chapman, and William D. Lambert, "Tall Understorey Vegetation as a Factor in the Poor Development of Oak Seedlings beneath Mature Stands," *Journal of Ecology* 82 (1994): 227–37.

25. Abrams, "Where Has All the White Oak Gone?" 927–39; Jenkins and Parker, "Composition and Diversity of Woody Vegetation in Silvicultural Openings of Southern Indiana Forests," 57–74; Craig G. Lorimer, "Causes of the Oak Regeneration Problem," 14–39; S. B. Horsley and D. A. Marquis, "Interference by Weeds and Deer with Allegheny Hardwood Reproduction," *Canadian Journal of Forest Research* 13, no. 1 (1983): 61–69. The ecological impact of deer herbivory has received national media coverage. See, for example, Andrew C. Revkin, "Out of Control, Deer Send Ecosystem into Chaos," *New York Times,* November 12, 2002, and "States Seek to Restore Deer Balance," *New York Times,* December 29, 2002.

26. Lorimer points out that other promising treatments to facilitate oak regeneration involving herbicide applications and high-quality nursery seedlings will likely be too expensive and labor intensive for small, private landowners to widely adopt. Lorimer, "The Oak Regeneration Problem," 19.

27. Burton L. Dahlberg and Ralph C. Guettinger, "The White-Tailed Deer in Wisconsin," Technical Wildlife Bulletin 14, Wisconsin Conservation Department (1956).

28. Joyce McVey Blackmore, "The Story of Rockton," *Vernon County Broadcaster,* April 19, 1945.

29. Aldo Leopold, "Coon Valley Erosion Project—Vernon County" (November 14, 1933), Aldo Leopold Papers, Box 8, University of Wisconsin–Madison Archives.

30. *Geer v. Connecticut,* 16 Sup. Ct. 600 (1896).

31. *Hughes v. Oklahoma,* 99 Sup. Ct. 1727 (1979).

32. Roderick Frazier Nash, *American Environmentalism: Readings in Conservation History* (1990).

33. From the late nineteenth century through the early twentieth century, the establishment of new hunting policies caused bruising conflicts between local subsistence hunters and wealthy recreational hunters, a conservation story told brilliantly by Louis S. Warren in *The Hunter's Game: Poachers and Conservationists in Twentieth-Century America* (1997).

34. T. A. Heberlein and T. Willebrand, "Attitudes Toward Hunting across Time and Continents: The United States and Sweden," *Gibier Faune Sauvage, Game Wildlife* 15, no. 3 (1998): 1071–80.

35. Wisconsin Department of Natural Resources, *Wisconsin's Deer Management Program,* 4.

36. Personal communication, Dave Matheys, Vernon County DNR Wildlife Biologist, July 6, 2000; see also R. A. Christoffel and S. R. Craven, "Attitudes of Woodland Owners Toward White-Tailed Deer Herbivory in Wisconsin," *Wildlife Society Bulletin* 28, no. 1 (2000): 227–34.

37. Dingle, *Nothing but Conservation*, 326.

38. Personal communication, July 6, 2000.

39. Environmental sociologist Thomas Heberlein has shown that in northwestern Wisconsin the density of deer hunters can be as small as four hunters per square mile, whereas in southern Wisconsin, the density reaches thirty to fifty hunters per square mile. The inevitable result, according to Heberlein, is that hunters in areas with high hunter densities "reported much more interference" and crowding. Thomas A. Heberlein, "Attitudes and Environmental Management," *Journal of Social Issues* 45, no. 1 (1989): 37–57.

40. "Nine Days," *La Farge Epitaph*, November 29, 1978.

41. Wisconsin *Statutes* (1983), section 29.889.

42. Wisconsin Department of Natural Resources, *2001 Wildlife Damage Abatement and Claims Program Annual Report to the Legislature.*

43. *Wisconsin Act 451, Trespass to Land* (1995); Wisconsin *Statutes* (1995), section 943.13. For a detailed analysis of Act 451, see Mark C. Patronsky, *Trespass to Land (1995 Wisconsin Act 451)* (1996).

Chapter 8. (Re)Enter the Ho-Chunk

1. U.S. Army Corps of Engineers, *Nation Builders* (circa 1989), 5.

2. Drafting Committee of the Kickapoo Valley Advisory Committee, *A Proposal for the Kickapoo River Community Reserve and Center for Rural Sustainability* (circa 1993); also Susan Lampert Smith, "Kickapoo Valley Hopes to Rise Above Past," *Wisconsin State Journal*, September 19, 1993.

3. Readers interested in how the federal government disposes of property should consult U.S. General Services Administration, *Governmentwide Review of Real Property Disposal Policy* (1997); and General Services Administration, *How to Acquire Federal Property* (no date).

4. Personal communication, Mary Francis Repko, environmental liaison, office of U.S. Senator Russell Feingold, July 11, 2000.

5. Quoted in Susan Lampert Smith, "Kickapoo Valley Hopes to Rise Above Past," *Wisconsin State Journal.*

6. Wisconsin *Statutes*, 15.07(1)(b) 18, Kickapoo Valley Governing Board, November 23, 1993.

7. Robert H. Horwich, *Proposal for the Kickapoo Community Sanctuary and Museum of Sustainability* (1992); also Susan Lampert Smith, "Kickapoo Valley Hopes to Rise Above Past," *Wisconsin State Journal.*

8. Out of a population of 3,539 Ho-Chunk in Wisconsin as of 1996, 8 individuals lived in Vernon County and another 8 in Crawford County, which together encompassed most of the Kickapoo Valley. Those people did not necessarily live in the Valley itself. Helen J. Kahn, *A Comparative Study of Tribal Implementations of Geographical Information Systems in Wisconsin* (1997), 32.

9. As part of the La Farge dam project, the Corps of Engineers and the National Park Service contracted with the Wisconsin Historical Society for a series of archeological studies of the reservoir area. Among these were William M. Hurley, "Archaeological

Research in the Projected Kickapoo Reservoir, Vernon County, Wisconsin," *The Wisconsin Archeologist* 46 (1965): 3–14; John R. Halsey, "The Markee Site (47-VE-195): An Early-Middle Archaic Campsite in the Kickapoo River Valley," *The Wisconsin Archeologist* 55 (1974): 42–73; Philip H. Salkin, "The Rose II Rockshelter (47-Ve-146): An Effigy Mound Component in the Kickapoo Valley," *The Wisconsin Archeologist* 56, no. 1 (1975): 55–71; Barbara Mead, *Archeological Investigations in the Lower Pool Area of the La Farge Lake Project Area* (1976). For a site outside the reservoir area but still in the Kickapoo Valley, see Barbara Mead, "The Rehbein I Site (47-Ri-81); A Multicomponent Site in Southwestern Wisconsin," *The Wisconsin Archeologist* 60 (1979): 91–182.

10. Treaty with the Sioux, Etc., 1825, which fixed boundaries among the Sioux, Chippewa, Sauk, Fox, Menominee, Ioway, Ottawa, Potawatomie, and Winnebago; followed by the Treaty with the Chippeway, Menominee and Winnebago Tribes, 1827. In George E. Fay, *Treaties between the Winnebago Indians and the United States of America, 1817–1865* (1967).

11. The Winnebago/Ho-Chunk Nation is part of the Siouan linguistic family. Radin dated their entry into Wisconsin to the "second of the Siouan migrations" out of four moving west. Winnebago/Ho-Chunk trace their own origins to Green Bay, Wisconsin, or Red Banks, where Jean Nicolet, agent for Governor Champlain, found them on the southern shore of Green Bay in 1634. Over the next 175 years they made war and negotiated with other tribes in Wisconsin, they made war and negotiated with the French, the English, and the Americans too, and they suffered, then rebounded, from the diseases that took hold after their first contact with Europeans. By the nineteenth century, forty Winnebago bands occupied the area included in the 1825 and 1827 treaties. See Paul Radin, *The Winnebago Tribe* (1923; reprint, 1970), 1–5, 28–30; Helen Hornbeck Tanner, *Atlas of Great Lakes Indian History* (1987); Mark Diedrich, *Winnebago Oratory: Great Moments in the Recorded Speech of the Hochungra, 1742–1887* (1991), 13, 20.

12. Diedrich, *Winnebago Oratory,* 23.

13. Ibid., 27.

14. For a fine essay on the lead-mining region see Michael Conzen, "The European Settling and Transformation of the Upper Mississippi Valley Lead Mining Region," in *Wisconsin Land and Life* (1997), 163–96; also, Robert E. Bieder, *Native American Communities in Wisconsin, 1600–1960: A Study of Tradition and Change* (1995), 125–28, 145–46.

15. Fay, *Treaties,* Article 1.

16. For the chronology, terms, and historical context of the treaties in the following discussion, I rely on: Fay, *Treaties;* Tanner, *Atlas;* Diedrich, *Winnebago Oratory; The HoChunk Nation: A Brief History* (circa 1995); Zoltán Grossman, "The Ho-Chunk and Dakota Nations," in *Wisconsin's Past and Present: A Historical Atlas* (1998).

17. Diedrich, *Winnebago Oratory,* 22–36. During this period tensions were high between the Winnebago and miners, as well as between the Winnebago and Objibwe, who were allied with the American military. At the behest of his tribe, Winnebago leader Red Bird made war on the Americans, killing two members of a family and three other settlers near Prairie du Chien, along the Mississippi River in southwestern Wisconsin. This uprising ensured rapid U.S. action to clinch the first treaty of cession. Red Bird, along with other Winnebago members, surrendered to the American government. Though Red Bird died in prison less than a year later, the confinement

of the others provided the U.S. government with a valuable bargaining chip in negotiating for the lead mining region and beyond. For a graphic Eurocentric account of
the Red Bird affair see *History of Vernon County Wisconsin* (1884), 92–95.

18. Caleb Atwater, "A Sequel to the Great American Indian Treaty," in *History of
Vernon County Wisconsin*, 333–34.

19. Richard White, *The Middle Ground: Indians, Empires, and Republics in the Great
Lakes Region, 1650–1815* (1991), 508.

20. In his 1833 account of the battle, John A. Wakefield put the number of Black
Hawk's followers killed at four hundred people. *History of Vernon County Wisconsin*,
375–79.

21. Diedrich, *Winnebago Oratory*, 43–45.

22. This would have been part of a typical Indian subsistence pattern in oak-
hickory landscapes of southeastern Minnesota, southern Wisconsin, and southern
Michigan. Beatrice A. Bigony, "The Interrelationships between Winnebago Folk Tales
and Winnebago Habitat: A Working Paper," unpublished manuscript; Tanner, *Atlas;*
and W. T. Sterling, interviewed by Frazier and Poff, *The Kickapoo Valley*, 20–21.

23. Halsey, "The Markee Site (47-VE-195) An Early-Middle Archaic Campsite in
the Kickapoo River Valley"; Salkin, "The Rose II Rockshelter (47-Ve-146): An Effigy
Mound Component in the Kickapoo Valley," 55–71.

24. Hocking, *The Memorable Kickapoo Valley*, 19.

25. Diedrich, *Winnebago Oratory*, 52–53.

26. In 1865, the Winnebago ceded land in the Dakota Territory in return for part
of the Omaha Reservation in Nebraska. The group that moved to the reservation
became established as the Nebraska Winnebago. See treaties of 1846, 1855, 1859, and
1865 in Fay, *Treaties*.

27. Grossman, "The Ho-Chunk and Dakota Nations," 9.

28. *History of Vernon County Wisconsin*, 389.

29. Francis Stover, "The Valley of the Wandering Kickapoo" (no date), Miscellaneous Box, Vernon County Historical Museum.

30. See Karojosephataka, in *The Winnebago Indians of Wisconsin: Their History*
(1879), 8.

31. Diedrich, *Winnebago Oratory*, 99.

32. Nancy Oestreich Lurie and Helen Miner Miller, *Historical Background of the
Winnebago People* (1964; revised, 1965), 1–2; Bieder, *Native American Communities in
Wisconsin*, 170–72.

33. Frazier and Poff, *The Kickapoo Valley*, 20.

34. Though historians and geographers must be wary of drawing parallels between
vastly different places and cultures, regional comparisons can offer important insights,
in this case on notions of property and territory. For African examples on the importance of being first (as well as an oft-overlooked adaptation of Frederick Jackson
Turner's frontier thesis), see Igor Kopytoff, *The African Frontier: The Reproduction of
Traditional African Societies* (1987); also, Lynne Heasley and James Delehanty, "The
Politics of Manure: Resource Tenure and the Agropastoral Economy in Southwest-
ern Niger," in *Society and Natural Resources* 9, no. 1 (1996): 31–46. Frederick Jackson
Turner, "The Significance of the Frontier in American History," in *Rereading Frederick
Jackson Turner*, ed. John Mack Faragher (1893, reprint, 1998), 31–60.

35. Nancy Oestreich Lurie, "Wisconsin: A Natural Laboratory for North American Indian Studies," *Wisconsin Magazine of History* 53, no. 1 (1969): 2–20; Bieder, *Native American Communities in Wisconsin*, 205–6.

36. Lurie and Miller, *Historical Background of the Winnebago People*, 6.

37. As Secretary of the Wisconsin Winnebago Business Committee in 1961, Whiterabbit was writing to the Bureau of Indian Affairs. See Mitchell Whiterabbit to The Task Force, Bureau of Indian Affairs, U.S. Government, March 27, 1961, Wisconsin Historical Society pamphlet collection, 89-4815.

38. Lurie and Miller, *Historical Background of the Winnebago People*, 7.

39. Winnebago was a name Algonquian peoples had given the Ho-Chunk by the arrival of Jean Nicolet. From that time forward European settlers knew them as Winnebago, even though they called themselves *Hocak*. See "Winnebago Return to Traditional Name 'Ho Chunk Nation,'" *News from Indian Country*, Mid-December 1994; and "Ho-Chunk Nation Rediscover Heritage through Language," *News from Indian Country: The Nations Native Journal*, Mid-September 1995. For earlier debates over the origin and meaning of the name see Radin, *The Winnebago Tribe*, 5.

40. Address by Mrs. Helen L. Peterson to the Wisconsin Winnebago General Council Meeting on December 9, 1961, author's personal files.

41. *Cal. v. Cabazon Band of Mission Indians*, 107 Sup. Ct. 1083 (1987); *California v. Cabazon Band of Mission Indians*, 107 Sup. Ct. 867 (1987).

42. Their success in opening large casinos came at a high price. Conflict erupted within the Ho-Chunk Nation as different leadership factions sought control over gambling operations and the large amounts of money involved in running them. For a sample of the disputes as they appeared in *News from Indian Country*, see "Wisconsin Winnebago Discord Causes Potential Closing of Gaming Halls," Mid-December 1990; "Riot Erupts as 'Six Pack' Supporters Attempt to Retake Closed Bingo Hall at Lake Delton," Late July 1991; "Political Scraps Weaken Wisconsin Winnebago Tribe, Overtures Come after Week in Which Two Are Shot, Bingo Is Torched," Mid-February 1992; "Former Ho-Chunk Chair Denies Ordering Fire," Mid-June 1997.

43. "Wisconsin Winnebago Propose Cultural Heritage Park," *News from Indian Country*, Late July 1993; Pat Carome, "Artifacts Validate Ho-Chunk Legend," *News from Indian Country*, Late February 1999.

44. Personal communication, Glen Reynolds, Ho-Chunk attorney, May 11, 2000.

45. Personal communication, Mary Francis Repko, environmental liaison, office of U.S. Senator Russell Feingold, July 11, 2000.

46. Personal communication, Glen Reynolds, May 11, 2000.

47. Richard W. Jaeger, "Senate OKs Transfer of Federal La Farge Dam Project Land to State: Tribe Would Get Acreage as Part of Agreement," *Wisconsin State Journal*, July 12, 1996.

48. *Water Resources Development Act of 1996*. U.S. *Statutes at Large* 110 (1996): 3658, section 361, Kickapoo River, Wisconsin, paragraph (B).

49. *National Historic Preservation Act of 1966*. U.S. *Statutes at Large* 80 (1966): 915. The *American Indian Religious Freedom Act* also required the Corps to consider sacred sites in its planning.

50. Memoranda for the Record: La Farge: April 11 and May 21 Interagency and Tribal Meetings (1997), author's personal files. Various documents—memoranda,

minutes, notes, programmatic agreement, and management plan—cited in the current chapter are from a collection in my personal files obtained from the St. Paul District through a freedom of information act request (FOIA).

51. Memorandum for the Record, Meeting on La Farge, Wisconsin, Land Transfer (December 30, 1996), author's personal files.

52. This complaint was one sign of internal divisions within the Ho-Chunk Nation. In January of 1997, at the time the tribe was gearing up to negotiate on the land, Chloris Lowe was removed as president at a general council meeting by a close vote. Over time, the tribal officers assigned to the Kickapoo Reserve negotiations changed as well, another sign of the importance of this deal and the internal struggles within the tribe. See "Ho-Chunk Oust Lowe as President," *News from Indian Country,* Late January 1997; also Memorandum for the Record, Meeting on La Farge, Wisconsin, Land Transfer, at the Ho-Chunk Nation (January 30, 1997); and Memorandum: La Farge: April 11 Interagency and Tribal Meeting (1997), author's personal files.

53. Memorandum: La Farge: April 11 Interagency and Tribal Meeting (1997), author's personal files. The Ho-Chunk returned to the definition of significant archeological sites in a July 2 meeting reiterating that even a single flake might be significant.

54. Memorandum for the Record, Meeting on La Farge, Wisconsin, Land Transfer (December 18, 1996), author's personal files.

55. Memoranda: La Farge: May 30, June 13, July 2, July 23 Interagency and Tribal Meetings (1997), author's personal files; also, personal communication with Glenn Reynolds, Ho-Chunk attorney, May 11, 2000.

56. Memorandum: La Farge Lake Project: Memorandum of Understanding Negotiating Team Meeting: Ho-Chunk Nation and State of Wisconsin (August 18, 1997), author's personal files. An alternative set of minutes to those of John Anfinson's specifically talked about the concerns of local residents over Ho-Chunk ownership. Kickapoo Valley Governing Board Minutes, February 15, 1996, author's personal files.

57. Programmatic Agreement Among the United States Army Corps of Engineers, St. Paul District, the Bureau of Indian Affairs, the Advisory Council on Historic Preservation, and the Wisconsin State Historic Preservation Officer, Regarding the Transfer of Land at the La Farge Lake Vernon County, Wisconsin (October 29, 1997), author's personal files.

58. Memorandum: La Farge Lake Project: Memorandum of Understanding Negotiating Team Meeting: Ho-Chunk Nation and State of Wisconsin (October 10, 1997), author's personal files.

59. Memorandum of Understanding between the Ho-Chunk Nation and the State of Wisconsin (1997), 2–3, author's personal files.

60. Ibid., Appendix B: Joint Management Plan between the Ho-Chunk Nation and the State of Wisconsin for the La Farge Lake Project Land Transfers (1997), Summary, author's personal files.

61. Personal communication, May 9, 2000.

62. Personal communication, June 23, 2000.

63. Personal communication, Marcy West, Executive Director, Kickapoo Valley Reserve, June 26, 2000.

Conclusion: Claims on Paradise

1. Nuzum, *Here on the Kickapoo,* chapter 2, no page number.
2. Ibid.
3. Josie Churchill, *Among the Hills* (1984), 179.
4. Ben Logan, *The Land Remembers: The Story of a Farm and Its People* (1985 [1975]), 7.
5. Robert E. Gard and Dale O'Brien, *Down in the Valleys: Wisconsin Back Country Lore and Humor* (1971), no page number.

Bibliography

Archives

Wisconsin Historical Society, Madison, Wisconsin
    Government Information and Records Collection
    Maps and Atlas Collection
    Pamphlet Collection
    Social Action Collections
    Wisconsin Land Economic Inventory
State of Wisconsin, Department of Regulation and Licensing, Madison, Wisconsin
University of Wisconsin–Madison Archives
    Aldo Leopold Papers
    Government Records
    Joseph J. Hickey Papers
    Otto R. Zeasman Papers
University of Wisconsin–La Crosse, Special Collections and Area Research Center,
    Murphy Library
    Rare Books
    Wisconsiana
    Wisconsin Historical Society Archives
U.S. Army Corps of Engineers, St. Paul District, St. Paul, Minnesota
    Civil Works Project Files, Kickapoo River
Vernon County Historical Society, Vernon County Museum, Viroqua, Wisconsin
    La Farge Dam files
    Miscellaneous files
    Ralph Nuzum Collection
    Township, village, and county files

Maps and Photos

Ayres Associates. "Digital Orthophotography for Vernon County, Wisconsin." Duluth, MN: Ayres Associates, 1995.

Finley, Robert W. *Map of the Original Vegetation of Wisconsin.* Compiled from notes on the original vegetation cover of Wisconsin. Transcribed by Finley (1951) from information recorded in the original government land survey. St. Paul, MN: North Central Forest Experiment Station, USDA Forest Service, 1976.

Ho-Chunk Nation. "Kickapoo Reserve Ho-Chunk Nation 1200 Acre Designation." Memorandum of Understanding Between the Ho-Chunk Nation and the State of Wisconsin. St. Paul, MN: St. Paul District, U.S. Army Corps of Engineers, 1997.

Ice, John R., and Berlie Moore. *Assessor's Map: Clinton Township, Vernon County.* Viroqua, WI, 1931.

———. *Assessor's Map: Stark Township, Vernon County.* Viroqua, WI, 1931.

———. *Assessor's Map: Liberty Township, Vernon County.* Viroqua, WI, 1931.

Rockford Map Publishers. *Land Atlas and Plat Book: Vernon County, Wisconsin.* Rockford, IL: Rockford Map Publishers, 1955.

———. *Land Atlas and Plat Book: Vernon County, Wisconsin.* Rockford, IL: Rockford Map Publishers, 1965.

———. *Land Atlas and Plat Book: Vernon County, Wisconsin.* Rockford, IL: Rockford Map Publishers, 1978.

———. *Land Atlas and Plat Book: Vernon County, Wisconsin.* Rockford, IL: Rockford Map Publishers, 1995.

Wisconsin Land Economic Inventory Field Maps. *Small Scale Land Cover Maps, Large Scale Land Cover Maps.* Madison: State of Wisconsin, 1929–47.

Publications

Abrams, M. D. "Where Has All the White Oak Gone?" *Bioscience* 53, no. 10 (2003): 927–39.

Air National Guard. *Final Environmental Impact Statement Addressing the Hardwood Range Expansion and Associated Airspace Actions, Volume III—Other Related Correspondence.* Andrews Air Force Base, MD: Air National Guard, National Guard Bureau, November 2000.

Alig, Ralph J., Karen J. Lee, and Robert J. Moulton. *Likelihood of Timber Management on Nonindustrial Private Forests: Evidence from Research Studies.* Asheville, NC: USDA Forest Service, Southeastern Forest Experiment Station, GTR-SE-60, 1990.

Alverson, W. S., D. M. Waller, and S. L. Solheim. "Forests Too Deer: Edge Effects in Northern Wisconsin." *Conservation Biology* 2, no. 4 (1988): 348–56.

Anderson, H. O., and I. O. Hembre. "The Coon Valley Watershed Project—A Pioneer Venture in Good Land Use." *Journal of Soil and Water Conservation* 10, no. 4 (1955): 180–84.

Appalachian Land Ownership Task Force. *Who Owns Appalachia? Land Ownership and Its Impact.* Lexington: University Press of Kentucky, 1983.

Argabright, M. Scott, Roger G. Cronshey, J. Douglas Helms, George A. Pavelis, H. Raymond Sinclair Jr. *Historical Changes in Soil Erosion, 1930–1992: The Northern Mississippi Valley Loess Hills.* Washington, D.C.: USDA Natural Resources Conservation Service, Historical Notes Number 5, 1996.

Arnold, Ron, and Alan Gottlieb. *Trashing the Environment: How Runaway Environmentalism Is Wrecking America.* Bellevue, WA: Merril Press, 1993.

Ayres, Quincy Claude. *Soil Erosion and Its Control.* New York: McGraw-Hill, 1936.

Balgooyen, C. P., and D. M. Waller. "The Use of *Clintonia borealis* and Other Indicators to Gauge Impacts of White-Tailed Deer on Plant Communities in Northern Wisconsin." *Natural Areas Journal* 15, no. 4 (1995): 308–18.

Barker, Kenneth, ed. *The NIV Study Bible.* Grand Rapids, MI: Zondervan Publishing House, 1995.

Barry, John M. *Rising Tide: The Great Mississippi Flood of 1927 and How It Changed America.* New York: Touchstone, 1997.

Barto, J. L. "Experience of Barto Family Coming to Cherry Valley." In *The Memorable Kickapoo Valley* (Grace Gilmore Hocking, ed.). Richland Center, WI: Richland County Publishers, 1976.

Bates, C. G., and O. R. Zeasman. *Soil Erosion—A Local and National Problem.* Madison: Agricultural Experiment Station, University of Wisconsin, Madison, Research Bulletin 99, 1930.

Batie, Sandra S. "Soil Conservation in the 1980s: A Historical Perspective." In *The History of Soil and Water Conservation* (Douglas Helms and Susan L. Flader, eds.), 5–21. Berkeley: University of California Press, 1985.

Bean, Heather Ann Ackley. "Toward an Anabaptist/Mennonite Environmental Ethic." In *Creation and the Environment: An Anabaptist Perspective on a Sustainable World* (Calvin Redekop, ed.), 183–206. Baltimore: Johns Hopkins University Press, 2000.

Beeman, Randal S., and James A. Pritchard. *A Green and Permanent Land: Ecology and Agriculture in the Twentieth Century.* Lawrence: University Press of Kansas, 2001.

Bennett, Hugh Hammond, and W. R. Chapline. *Soil Erosion: A National Menace.* U.S. Department of Agriculture Circular 33, 1928.

Berry, Wendell. "Seven Amish Farms." In *The Gift of Good Land: Further Essays Cultural and Agricultural* (Wendell Berry, ed.), 249–63. San Francisco: North Point Press, 1981.

Bieder, Robert E. *Native American Communities in Wisconsin, 1600–1960: A Study of Tradition and Change.* Madison: University of Wisconsin Press, 1995.

Bigony, Beatrice A. "The Interrelationships between Winnebago Folk Tales and Winnebago Habitat: A Working Paper." Unpublished manuscript. Menomonie: University of Wisconsin–Stout, 1978.

Birch, Thomas W., and Nancy A. Pywell. *Communicating with Nonindustrial Private Forest-Land Owners: Getting Programs on Target.* Upper Darby, PA: USDA Forest Service, Northeastern Forest Experiment Station, NE-RP-593, 1986.

Blake, Katharine V., Enrico A. Cardamone, Steven D. Hall, Glenn R. Harris, Susan M. Moore. "Modern Amish Farming as Ecological Agriculture." *Society and Natural Resources* 10 (1997): 143–59.

Blanchard, W. O. *The Physical Geography of Southwestern Wisconsin.* Madison: Wisconsin Geological and Natural History Survey Bulletin no. 65, 1924.

Born, Stephen M. *The Kickapoo Dam (A Case Study in the Application of Scientific and Technologic Information to Executive Branch Decision-Making in Wisconsin).* Madison: State Science, Engineering, and Technology Project Center for Study of Public Policy and Administration, University of Wisconsin–Madison, 1978.

Bromley, Daniel W. *Environment and Economy: Property Rights and Public Policy.* Oxford: Blackwell, 1991.

———. "Regulatory Takings: Coherent Concept or Logical Contradiction?" *Vermont Law Review* 17, no. 3 (1993): 647–82.

———. "Rousseau's Revenge: The Demise of the Freehold Estate." In *Who Owns America? Social Conflict Over Property Rights* (Harvey M. Jacobs, ed.), 19–28. Madison: University of Wisconsin Press, 1998.

Buse, R. C., and R. N. Brown Jr. *The Conservation Reserve in Wisconsin, 1956–1959.* Madison: Agricultural Experiment Station, University of Wisconsin–Madison, 1961.

Carpenter, E. M. *Ownership Change and Timber Supply on Non-Industrial Private Forest Land.* St. Paul, MN: USDA Forest Service, NC-265, 1985.

Christensen, Chris L. "Soil Management: Does Soil Conservation Pay? It Did Here!" In *What's New in Farm Science: Annual Report of the Director, Agricultural Experiment Station, University of Wisconsin, Madison,* 62–69. Madison: Agricultural Experiment Station, University of Wisconsin, 1943.

Christman, John. *The Myth of Property: Toward an Egalitarian Theory of Ownership.* Oxford: Oxford University Press, 1995.

Christoffel, Rebecca Ann. "Ecological and Sociological Aspects of White-Tailed Deer Herbivory in South Central Wisconsin." Master's thesis, University of Wisconsin–Madison, 1998.

Christoffel, R. A., and S. R. Craven. "Attitudes of Woodland Owners Toward White-Tailed Deer Herbivory in Wisconsin." *Wildlife Society Bulletin* 28, no. 1 (2000): 227–34.

Churchill, Josie. *Dirt Roads: A Collection of Stories.* Westby, WI: Josie Churchill, 1981.

———. *Among the Hills.* Richland Center, WI: Josie Churchill, 1984.

Classen, Larry. *Fool's Wisdom: An Analysis of the Anti-Conservation Movement in the Midwest.* Madison: Wisconsin's Environmental Decade Institute, 1996.

Cohee, Melville H. "Erosion and Land Utilization in the Driftless Area of Wisconsin." *Journal of Land and Public Utility Economics* 10, no. 3 (1934): 243–53.

Conzen, Michael P. "The European Settling and Transformation of the Upper Mississippi Valley Lead Mining Region." In *Wisconsin Land and Life* (Robert C. Ostergren and Thomas R. Vale, eds.), 163–96. Madison: University of Wisconsin Press, 1997.

Cooper, Zachary. *Black Settlers in Rural Wisconsin.* Madison: State Historical Society of Wisconsin, 1994. First published 1977.

———. "Two Black Settlements in Wisconsin." *Wisconsin Academy Review* 27 (1981): 9–13.

Cooper, Zachary L., and Emilie Tari. *Coming Together, Coming Apart: Black Settlers in Rural Wisconsin, Teacher's Manual.* Madison: Wisconsin Department of Public Instruction, Bulletin no. 3254, 1983.

Craumer, P. R. "Farm Productivity and Energy Efficiency in Amish and Modern Dairying." *Agriculture and Environment* 4 (1979): 281–99.

Cronon, William. *Changes in the Land: Indians, Colonists, and the Ecology of New England.* New York: Hill and Wang, 1983.

———. *Nature's Metropolis: Chicago and the Great West.* New York: W. W. Norton, 1991.

Cross, John A. "Change in America's Dairyland." *Geographical Review* 91, no. 4 (2001): 702–14.

Cullon, Joseph F. "Landscapes of Labor and Leisure: Common Rights, Private Property and Class Relations along the Boise Brule River, 1870 to 1940." Master's thesis, University of Wisconsin–Madison, 1995.

Curtis, John T. *The Vegetation of Wisconsin: An Ordination of Plant Communities.* Madison: University of Wisconsin Press, 1987. First published in 1959.

Dahlberg, Burton L., and Ralph C. Guettinger. "The White-Tailed Deer in Wisconsin." Technical Wildlife Bulletin 14, Wisconsin Conservation Department, 1956.

Danbom, David B. *Born in the Country: A History of Rural America.* Baltimore: Johns Hopkins University Press, 1995.

Delcourt, Hazel R., and Paul A. Delcourt. "Pre-Columbian Native American Use of Fire on Southern Appalachian Landscapes." *Conservation Biology* 11, no. 4 (1997): 1010–14.

Diedrich, Mark. *Winnebago Oratory: Great Moments in the Recorded Speech of the Hochungra, 1742–1887.* Rochester, MN: Coyote Books, 1991.

Dingle, Roy H. *Nothing but Conservation.* Richland Center, WI: Roy H. Dingle, 1993.

Dodge, S. L. "Successional Trends in a Mixed Oak Forest on High Mountain, New Jersey." *Journal of the Torrey Botanical Society* 124, no. 4 (1997): 312–17.

Donahue, Brian. *Reclaiming the Commons: Community Farms and Forests in a New England Town.* New Haven: Yale University Press, 1999.

Drafting Committee of the Kickapoo Valley Advisory Committee. *A Proposal for the Kickapoo River Community Reserve and Center for Rural Sustainability.* Kickapoo Valley, WI: Kickapoo Valley Project, 1993.

Duncan, Colin A. M. "Legal Protection for the Soil of England: The Spurious Context of Nineteenth-Century 'Progress.'" In *The History of Agriculture and the Environment* (Douglas Helms and Douglas E. Bowers, eds.), 75–94. Berkeley: University of California Press, 1994.

Ebling, Walter. *Vernon County, Wisconsin Agricultural Statistics.* Madison: Wisconsin Crop and Livestock Reporting Service, Bulletin no. 202, County Series no. 18, 1940.

Ebling, Walter, C. D. Caparoon, E. C. Wilcox, and C. W. Estes. *A Century of Wisconsin Agriculture, 1848–1948.* Madison: Wisconsin Crop and Livestock Reporting Service, Bulletin no. 290, 1948.

Ely, James W. Jr. *The Guardian of Every Other Right: A Constitutional History of Property Rights.* New York: Oxford University Press, 1992.

Epstein, Richard. *Takings: Private Property and the Power of Eminent Domain.* Cambridge, MA: Harvard University Press, 1985.

Ericksen, Eugene P., Julia A. Ericksen, and John A. Hostetler. "The Cultivation of the Soil as a Moral Directive: Population Growth, Family Ties, and the Maintenance of Community among the Old Order Amish." *Rural Sociology* 45, no. 1 (1980): 49–68.

Ericksen, Julia, and Gary Klein. "Women's Roles and Family Production among the Old Order Amish." *Rural Sociology* 46, no. 2 (1981): 282–96.

Fay, George E. *Treaties between the Winnebago Indians and the United States of America, 1817–1865.* Greeley, CO: Museum of Anthropology Miscellaneous Series, no. 1, 1967.

Field, D. R., P. R. Voss, T. K. Kuczenski, R. B. Hammer, and V. C. Radeloff. "Reaffirming Social Landscape Analysis in Landscape Ecology: A Conceptual Framework." *Society and Natural Resources* 16, no. 4 (2003): 349–61.

Finger, Thomas. "An Anabaptist/Mennonite Theology of Creation." In *Creation and the Environment: An Anabaptist Perspective on a Sustainable World* (Calvin Redekop, ed.), 154–69. Baltimore: Johns Hopkins University Press.

Flader, Susan, and J. Baird Callicott, eds. *The River of the Mother of God.* Madison: University of Wisconsin Press, 1991.

Force, Jo Ellen, Gary E. Machlis, Lianjun Zhang, and Anne Kearney. "The Relationship between Timber Production, Local Historical Events, and Community Social Change: A Quantitative Case Study." *Forest Science* 39 (1993): 722–42.

Fortmann, Louise. "Introduction: Bonanza! The Unasked Questions: Domestic Land Tenure through International Lenses." In *Who Owns America? Social Conflict Over Property Rights* (Harvey M. Jacobs, ed.), 3–15. Madison: University of Wisconsin Press, 1998.

Foster, David R. "Land-Use History (1730–1900) and Vegetation Dynamics in Central New England, USA." *Journal of Ecology* 80 (1992): 753–72.

Foster, D. R., S. Clayden, D. A. Orwig, B. Hall, and S. Barry. "Oak, Chestnut, and Fire: Climatic and Cultural Controls of Long-Term Forest Dynamics in New England, USA." *Journal of Biogeography* 29, nos. 10/11 (2002): 1359–79.

Frazier, Gertrude, and Rose Poff. *The Kickapoo Valley: The Gem of Wisconsin.* No city: Frazier and Poff, 1896.

Freyfogle, Eric T. "The Owning and Taking of Sensitive Lands." *UCLA Law Review* 77 (1995): 77–138.

———. *Bounded People, Boundless Lands: Envisioning a New Land Ethic.* Washington, D.C.: Island Press, 1998.

Fuller, J. L., D. R. Foster, J. S. McLachlan, and N. Drake. "Impact of Human Activity on Regional Forest Composition and Dynamics in Central New England." *Ecosystems* 1 (1998): 76–95.

Gard, Robert E., and Dale O'Brien. *Down in the Valleys: Wisconsin Back Country Lore and Humor.* Madison: Wisconsin House, 1971.

Gardner, David Rice. *The National Cooperative Soil Survey of the United States.* Washington, D.C.: U.S. Department of Agriculture, Natural Resources Conservation Service, Historical Notes Number 7, 1998. Reprint of unpublished dissertation, Harvard University, 1957.

Gates, Paul W. "An Overview of American Land Policy." *Agricultural History* 50 (1976): 213–29.

———. *History of Public Land Law Development.* Washington, D.C.: Zenger, 1978.

Gaventa, John. *Power and Powerlessness: Quiescence and Rebellion in an Appalachian Valley.* Chicago: University of Illinois Press, 1980.

———. "The Political Economy of Land Tenure: Appalachia and the Southeast." In *Who Owns America? Social Conflict Over Property Rights* (Harvey M. Jacobs, ed.), 227–44. Madison: University of Wisconsin Press, 1998.

Geib, H. V. *Strip Cropping to Prevent Erosion.* United States Department of Agriculture Leaflet 85, 1931.

Geisler, Charles. "Property Pluralism." In *Property and Values: Alternatives to Public and Private Ownership* (Charles Geisler and Gail Daneker, eds.), 65–87. Washington, D.C.: Island Press, 2000.

Geisler, Charles, and Gail Daneker, eds. *Property and Values: Alternatives to Public and Private Ownership*. Washington, D.C.: Island Press, 2000.

Gilbert, Jess, and Carolyn Howe. "Beyond 'State vs. Society': Theories of the State and New Deal Agricultural Policies." *American Sociological Review* 56 (1991): 204–20.

Glanz, James. "Sharp Drop Seen in Soil Erosion Rates." *Science* 285, no. 5431 (1999): 1187–89.

Goebel, P. C., and D. M. Hix. "Changes in Composition and Structure of Mixed-Oak, Second-Growth Forest Ecosystems during the Understory Reinitiation Stage of Stand Development." *Ecoscience* 4 (1992): 327–39.

Gottlieb, Alan M., ed. *The Wise Use Agenda*. Bellevue, WA: Free Enterprise Press, 1989.

Graham, Otis L. Jr. *Toward a Planned Society: From Roosevelt to Nixon*. New York: Oxford University Press, 1976.

Grahn, G. K., and R. G. Wingate. "The Wisconsin Hill and Valley Cheese Factory: A Joint Venture between Amish and Non-Amish." *Wisconsin Geographer* 4 (1988): 65–71.

Grossman, Zoltán. "The Ho-Chunk and Dakota Nations." In *Wisconsin's Past and Present: A Historical Atlas* (Wisconsin Cartographer's Guild, ed.), 8–9. Madison: University of Wisconsin Press, 1998.

Hall, A. "Agrarian Crisis in Brazilian Amazonia: The Grande Carajas Programme." *Journal of Development Studies* 23, no. 4 (1987): 522–52.

Halsey, John R. "Gillen 9 (47-VE-177): An Archaic-Woodland Campsite in the Kickapoo River Valley." *The Wisconsin Archeologist* 55 (1974): 200–216.

————. "The Markee Site (47-VE-195): An Early-Middle Archaic Campsite in the Kickapoo River Valley." *The Wisconsin Archeologist* 55 (1974): 42–73.

Harbaugh, William. "Twentieth-Century Tenancy and Soil Conservation: Some Comparisons and Questions." In *The History of Agriculture and the Environment* (Douglas Helms and Douglas E. Bowers, eds.), 95–119. Berkeley: University of California Press, 1994.

Hardin, Garrett. "The Tragedy of the Commons." *Science* 162 (December 1968): 1243–48.

Harrison, Robert Pogue. *Forests: The Shadow of Civilization*. Chicago: University of Chicago Press, 1992.

Hassebrook, Chuck. "Saving the Family Farm." *Forum for Applied Research and Public Policy* 14, no. 3 (1999): 55–60.

Haukereid, Robert E. *The Relationship between Timber Sales and Real Estate Transfers for La Crosse and Oneida Counties (1992–1994)*. Madison: Department of Forestry, University of Wisconsin–Madison, 1995.

Hays, Orville E., and Noble Clark. *Cropping Systems That Help Control Erosion* (June). Madison: Wisconsin State Soil Conservation Committee, 1941.

Hays, Samuel P. *Beauty, Health, and Permanence: Environmental Politics in the United States, 1955–1985*. New York: Cambridge University Press, 1987.

————. *Conservation and the Gospel of Efficiency: The Progressive Conservation Movement, 1890–1920*. Cambridge, MA: Harvard University Press, 1959; Pittsburgh: University of Pittsburgh Press, 1999.

Healy, Robert G., and James Short. "Rural Lands: Market Trends and Planning Implications." *Journal of the American Planning Association* 45, no. 3 (1979): 305–17.

Heasley, Lynne. "A Thousand Pieces of Paradise: Property, Nature, and Community in the Kickapoo Valley." Ph.D. dissertation, University of Wisconsin–Madison, 2000.

———. "Shifting Boundaries on a Wisconsin Landscape: Can GIS Help Historians Tell a Complicated Story?" *Human Ecology* 31 (2003): 183–211.

Heasley, Lynne, and James Delehanty. "The Politics of Manure: Resource Tenure and the Agropastoral Economy in Southwestern Niger." *Society and Natural Resources* 9, no. 1 (1996): 31–46.

Heasley, Lynne, and Raymond P. Guries. "Forest Tenure and Cultural Landscapes: Environmental Histories in the Kickapoo Valley." In *Who Owns America? Social Conflict Over Property Rights* (Harvey M. Jacobs, ed.), 182–207. Madison: University of Wisconsin Press, 1998.

Heasley, Lynne, Keith Rice, Raymond Guries, and Hawthorne Beyer. "Claims on Paradise: Land Ownership and Landscape Dynamics in the Kickapoo Valley, Wisconsin, 1930–1995." Poster presented at the annual meeting of the American Society for Environmental History, Houston, Texas, March 16–20, 2005.

Heat-Moon, William Least. *Prairy Erth.* Boston: Houghton Mifflin, 1991.

Heberlein, Thomas A. "Attitudes and Environmental Management." *Journal of Social Issues* 45, no. 1 (1989): 37–57.

Heberlein, T. A., and T. Willebrand. "Attitudes Toward Hunting across Time and Continents: The United States and Sweden." *Gibier Faune Sauvage, Game Wildlife* 15, no. 3 (1998): 1071–80.

Helms, Douglas. "Coon Valley, Wisconsin: A Conservation Success Story." In *Readings in the History of the Soil Conservation Service,* 51–53. Washington, D.C.: Soil Conservation Service, 1992.

Helms, J. Douglas, George A. Parvelis, Scott Argabright, Roger G. Cronshey, H. Raymond Sinclair Jr. "National Soil Conservation Policies: A Historical Case Study of the Driftless Area." *Agricultural History* 70, no. 2 (1996): 377–94.

Hershberger, Menno M. "Cashton, WI History." In *Wisconsin, Minnesota, and Montana Amish Directory 2002.* Millersburg, OH: Abana Books, 2002.

Hibbard, Benjamin Horace. *A History of the Public Land Policies.* New York: The Macmillan Company, 1924.

History of Vernon County, Wisconsin. Springfield, IL: Union Publishing Company, 1884.

Hix, David M., and Craig G. Lorimer. "Early Stand Development on Former Oak Sites in Southwestern Wisconsin." *Forest Ecology and Management* 42 (1991): 169–93.

———. "Growth-Competition Relationships in Young Hardwood Stands on Two Contrasting Sites in Southwestern Wisconsin." *Forest Science* 36 (1990): 1032–49.

HoChunk Nation. *The HoChunk Nation: A Brief History.* [Wisconsin]: The Ho-Chunk Nation, circa 1995.

Hocking, Grace Gilmore. *The Memorable Kickapoo Valley.* Richland Center, WI: Richland County Publishers, 1976.

Horsley, S. B., and D. A. Marquis. "Interference by Weeds and Deer with Allegheny Hardwood Reproduction." *Canadian Journal of Forest Research* 13, no. 1 (1983): 61–69.

Horsley, S. B., S. L. Stout, and D. S. DeCalesta. "White-Tailed Deer Impact on the Vegetation Dynamics of a Northern Hardwood Forest." *Ecological Applications* 13, no. 1 (2003): 98–118.

Horwich, Robert H. *Proposal for the Kickapoo Community Sanctuary and Museum of Sustainability.* Gays Mills, WI: Community Conservation Consultants, 1992.

Hostetler, John A. *Amish Society.* Baltimore: Johns Hopkins University Press, 1993. First published 1963.

———. "A New Look at the Old Order." *The Rural Sociologist* 7 (1987): 278–92.

Howard, Cletus. *Putting Soil Conservation to Work: Manual 2 Legislation . . . town—county—state—federal . . . for Soil Conservation District Supervisors* (July). Madison: State Soil Conservation Committee and University of Wisconsin, College of Agriculture, Agricultural Extension Service, 1960.

Huntington, Gertrude. "Ideology, History, and Agriculture: Examples from Contemporary North America." *Culture and Agriculture* 45–46 (1993): 21–25.

Hurley, William M. "Archaeological Research in the Projected Kickapoo Reservoir, Vernon County, Wisconsin." *The Wisconsin Archeologist* 46 (1965): 1–114.

———. "The Wisconsin Effigy Mound Tradition." Ph.D. dissertation, University of Wisconsin–Madison, 1970.

Institute for Environmental Studies. *Environmental Analysis of the Kickapoo River Impoundment.* Madison: Institute for Environmental Studies, University of Wisconsin–Madison, IES Report no. 28, 1974.

Jackson, John Brinckerhoff. *Discovering the Vernacular Landscape.* New Haven: Yale University Press, 1984.

———. *A Sense of Place, A Sense of Time.* New Haven: Yale University Press, 1994.

Jackson, Mary. "Amish Agriculture and No-Till: The Hazards of Applying the USLE to Unusual Farms." *Journal of Soil and Water Conservation* 43 (1988): 483–86.

Jackson, Wes. *New Roots for Agriculture.* Berkeley, CA: North Point Press, 1980.

Jackson-Smith, Douglas. "Understanding the Microdynamics of Farm Structural Change: Entry, Exit, and Restructuring among Wisconsin Family Farmers in the 1980s." Ph.D. dissertation, University of Wisconsin–Madison, 1995.

———. *Wisconsin Agriculture in Historical Perspective: Economic and Social Changes, 1959–1995.* Madison: Agricultural Technology and Family Farm Institute, University of Wisconsin–Madison, ATFFI Technical Report no. 4, 1996.

Jacobs, Harvey M. "The Anti-Environmental 'Wise Use' Movement in America." *Land Use Law and Zoning Digest* 47 (1995): 3–8.

———. "The 'Wisdom,' but Uncertain Future, of the Wise Use Movement." In *Who Owns America? Social Conflict Over Property Rights* (Harvey M. Jacobs, ed.), 29–44. Madison: University of Wisconsin Press, 1998.

———, ed. *Who Owns America? Social Conflict Over Property Rights.* Madison: University of Wisconsin Press, 1998.

Jacobs, Harvey M., and Ellen M. Bassett. *The Amish: A Literature Review.* Madison: School of Natural Resources, College of Agriculture and Life Sciences, University of Wisconsin–Madison, 1995.

Janes, Amelia. "Weather Hazards." In *Wisconsin's Past and Present* (Wisconsin Cartographer's Guild, ed.), 46–47. Madison: University of Wisconsin Press.

Jenkins, M. A., and G. R. Parker. "Composition and Diversity of Woody Vegetation in Silvicultural Openings of Southern Indiana Forests." *Forest Ecology and Management* 109, nos. 1–3 (1998): 57–74.

Johnson, Hildegard Binder. *Order upon the Land: The U.S. Rectangular Land Survey and the Upper Mississippi Country.* New York: Oxford University Press, 1976.

Johnson, Leonard C. *Soil Conservation in Wisconsin: Birth to Rebirth.* Madison: Department of Soil Science, University of Wisconsin–Madison, 1991.

Johnson, Warren A., Victor Stoltzfus, and Peter Craumer. "Energy Conservation in Amish Agriculture." *Science* 198, no. 4315 (1977): 373–78.

Kahn, Helen. "A Comparative Study of Tribal Implementation of Geographical Information Systems in Wisconsin." Master's thesis, University of Wisconsin–Madison, 1997.

Karojosephataka. *The Winnebago Indians of Wisconsin: Their History.* Stevens Point, WI: Gazette Book and Job Office, 1879.

Keillor, Garrison. *Lake Wobegon Days.* New York: Viking, 1985.

Kickapoo Valley History Project. *Kickapoo Pearls: A Collection of Kickapoo History and Folkways,* vol. 1, no. 4. La Crosse, WI: Kickapoo Valley History Project, 1979.

Kline, David. *Great Possessions: An Amish Farmer's Journal.* New York: North Point Press, 1990.

———. "An Amish Perspective." In *Rooted in the Land: Essays on Community and Place* (William Vitek and Wes Jackson, eds.), 35–39. New Haven: Yale University Press, 1996.

———. "God's Spirit and a Theology for Living." In *Creation and the Environment: An Anabaptist Perspective on a Sustainable World* (Calvin Redekop, ed.), 61–69. Baltimore: Johns Hopkins University Press, 2000.

Kline, Virginia M. "Dynamics of the Vegetation of a Small Watershed." Ph.D. dissertation, University of Wisconsin–Madison, 1976.

Kloppenburg, Jack Jr., John Hendrickson, and G. W. Stevenson. "Coming in to the Foodshed." In *Rooted in the Land* (William Vitek and Wes Jackson, eds.), 113–23. New Haven: Yale University Press, 1996.

Knowles, Anne Kelly, ed. "Historical GIS: The Spatial Turn in Social Science History." Special theme issue of *Social Science History* 24 (2000).

———, ed. *Past Time, Past Place: GIS for History.* Redlands, CA: ESRI Press, 2002.

Knox, James C., and Douglas J. Faulkner. *Post-Settlement Erosion and Sedimentation in the Lower Buffalo River Watershed: Final Report.* Madison: Department of Geography, University of Wisconsin–Madison, 1994.

Kopytoff, Igor. *The African Frontier: The Reproduction of Traditional African Societies.* Bloomington: Indiana University Press, 1987.

Kotar, John, and Timothy L. Burger. *A Guide to Forest Communities and Habitat Types of Central and Southern Wisconsin,* Madison: Department of Forestry, University of Wisconsin–Madison, 1996.

Kramer, Randall A., and Sandra S. Batie. "Cross Compliance Concepts in Agricultural Programs: The New Deal to the Present." In *The History of Soil and Water Conservation* (Douglas Helms and Susan L. Flader, eds.), 205–17. Berkeley: University of California Press, 1985.

Kraybill, Donald B. *The Riddle of Amish Culture.* Baltimore: Johns Hopkins University Press, 1989.

————, ed. *The Amish and the State.* Baltimore: Johns Hopkins University Press, 1993.

Kraybill, Donald B., and Steven M. Nolt. *Amish Enterprise: From Plow to Profits.* Baltimore: Johns Hopkins University Press, 1995.

Kreps, George M., Joseph F. Donnermeyer, and Marty W. Kreps. "The Changing Occupational Structure of Amish Males." *Rural Sociology* 59, no. 4 (1994): 708–19.

Kreps, George M., Joseph F. Donnermeyer, Charles Hurst, Robert Blair, and Marty Kreps. "The Impact of Tourism on the Amish Subculture: A Case Study." *Community Development Journal* 32, no. 4 (1997): 354–67.

Kuczenski, T. K., D. R. Field, P. R. Voss, V. C. Radeloff, and A. E. Hagen. "Integrating Demographic and Landsat (TM) Data at a Watershed Scale." *Journal of the American Water Resources Association* 36, no. 1 (2000): 215–28.

Kusnetzky, Lara, Jeffrey Longhofer, Jerry Floersch, Kristine Latta. "In Search of the Climax Community: Sustainability and the Old Order Amish." *Culture and Agriculture* 50 (1994): 12–14.

Lamm, Thomas. *Forest Resources in the Kickapoo Valley: Issues and Opportunities.* Madison: Environmental Awareness Center, University of Wisconsin–Madison, 1981.

Langston, Nancy. *Forest Dreams, Forest Nightmares: The Paradox of Old Growth in the Inland West.* Seattle: University of Washington Press, 1995.

Last, Donald. "Private Property Rights with Responsibilities: What Would Thomas Jefferson Say about the 'Wise Use' Movement?" In *Who Owns America? Social Conflict Over Property Rights* (Harvey M. Jacobs, ed.), 45–53. Madison: University of Wisconsin Press, 1998.

Laycock, William A. "The Conservation Reserve Program—How Did We Get Where We Are and Where Do We Go From Here?" In *The Conservation Reserve—Yesterday, Today, and Tomorrow.* Symposium Proceedings, U.S. Department of Agriculture Forest Service, Rocky Mountain Forest and Range Experiment Station. General Technical Report RM-203 (1991): 1–6.

Leatherman, John C. *Input-Output Analysis of the Kickapoo River Valley.* Staff Paper 94.2. Madison: Center for Community Economic Development, University of Wisconsin–Madison/Extension, 1994.

Leopold, Aldo. *A Sand County Almanac.* New York: Oxford University Press, 1968. First published 1949.

————. "Coon Valley: An Adventure in Cooperative Conservation." In *For the Health of the Land: Previously Unpublished Essays and Other Writings* (J. Baird Callicott and Eric T. Freyfogle, eds.), 47–54. Washington, D.C.: Island Press, 1999. First published 1935.

Leopold, Aldo, and Joseph Hickey. "Cows and Contours: The Problem of Steep Farms in Southwest Wisconsin," unpublished manuscript. Madison: Department of Wildlife Ecology, University of Wisconsin–Madison, no date.

Lewis, P. H., and Thomas Lamm. *Recreation and Tourism Resources in the Kickapoo Valley.* Madison: Environmental Awareness Center, University of Wisconsin–Madison, 1981.

Locke, John. *Two Treatises of Government, Student Edition,* ed. Peter Laslett. Cambridge: Cambridge University Press, 1988.

Logan, Ben. *The Land Remembers: The Story of a Farm and Its People.* Minocqua, WI: Heartland Press, 1985. First published 1975.

Lorimer, Craig G. "The Role of Fire in the Perpetuation of Oak Forests." In *Proceedings of Challenges in Oak Management and Utilization, Madison, Wisconsin, March 28–29, 1985*. Madison: University of Wisconsin–Extension, 1985.

——. "The Oak Regeneration Problem: New Evidence on Causes and Possible Solutions." In *Forest Resource Analyses* no. 8. Madison: Department of Forestry, School of Natural Resources, College of Agricultural and Life Sciences, University of Wisconsin–Madison, 1989.

——. "Causes of the Oak Regeneration Problem." In *Oak Regeneration: Serious Problems, Practical Recommendations* (D. L. Loftis and C. E. McGee, eds.), 14–39. Washington, D.C.: USDA Forest Service General Technical Report, SE-84, 1993.

Lorimer, Craig G., Jonathan W. Chapman, and William D. Lambert. "Tall Understorey Vegetation as a Factor in the Poor Development of Oak Seedlings beneath Mature Stands." *Journal of Ecology* 82, no. 2 (1994): 227–37.

Lull, Howard W., and Kenneth G. Reinhart. *Forests and Floods in the Eastern United States*. Upper Darby, PA: U.S. Department of Agriculture, Northeastern Forest Experiment Station, Forest Service Research Paper NE-226, 1972.

Lurie, Nancy Oestreich. "Wisconsin: A Natural Laboratory for North American Indian Studies." *Wisconsin Magazine of History* 53, no. 1 (1969): 2–20.

Lurie, Nancy Oestreich, and Helen Miner Miller. *Historical Background of the Winnebago People*. Wisconsin Winnebago Business Committee, 1965.

Luthy, David. "Appendix: Amish Migration Patterns: 1972–1992." In *The Amish Struggle with Modernity* (Donald B. Kraybill and Marc A. Olshan, eds.), 243–59. Hanover, NH: University Press of New England, 1994.

Maas, Arthur. *Muddy Waters: The Army Engineers and the Nation's Rivers*. Cambridge, MA: Harvard University Press, 1951.

Maher, Neil. "A New Deal Body Politic: Landscape, Labor, and the Civilian Conservation Corps." *Environmental History* 7, no. 3 (2002): 435–61.

Marcouiller, David, A. Anderson, and W. C. Norman. *Trout Angling in Southwestern Wisconsin and Implications for Regional Development*. Madison: Center for Community Economic Development, University of Wisconsin–Madison/Extension, 1995.

Marquis, D. A., P. L. Eckert, and B. A. Roach. *Acorn Weevils, Rodents, and Deer All Contribute to Oak Regeneration Difficulties in Pennsylvania*. Upper Darby, PA: USDA Forest Service Research Paper NE-356, Northeast Forest Experiment Station, 1976.

Marsh, George Perkins. *Man and Nature; or, Physical Geography as Modified by Human Action*, ed. David Lowenthal. Seattle: University of Washington Press, 2003. First published 1864.

Martin, Lawrence. *The Physical Geography of Wisconsin*. Madison: University of Wisconsin Press, 1965. First published 1939.

Max Anderson Associates. *Background of the La Farge Lake Project*. Kickapoo Area Planning Study, Working Paper Number Two, 1973.

McCay, Bonnie J., and James M. Acheson, eds. *The Question of the Commons: The Culture and Ecology of Communal Resources*. Tucson: University of Arizona Press, 1987.

McClaughry, John. "The New Feudalism." *Environmental Law* 5 (1975): 675–702.

McCune, B., and G. Cottam. "The Successional Status of a Southern Wisconsin Oak Woods." *Ecology* 66 (1985): 1270–78.

McDonald, Angus. *Early American Soil Conservationists.* Washington, D.C.: U.S. Department of Agriculture, Miscellaneous Publication 449, 1941.

McEvoy, Arthur F. *The Fisherman's Problem: Ecology and Law in the California Fisheries.* New York: Cambridge University Press, 1986.

———. "Markets and Ethics in U.S. Property Law." In *Who Owns America? Social Conflict Over Property Rights* (Harvey M. Jacobs, ed.), 94–113. Madison: University of Wisconsin Press, 1998.

McGarigal, Kevin, and Barbara J. Marks. *FRAGSTATS: Spatial Pattern Analysis Program for Quantifying Landscape Structure.* Portland, OR: USDA Forest Service General Technical Report PNW-GTR-351, 1995.

Mead, Barbara E. *Archeological Investigations in the Lower Pool Area of the La Farge Lake Project Area.* Madison: State Historical Society of Wisconsin, 1976.

———. "The Rehbein I Site (47-Ri-81): A Multicomponent Site in Southwestern Wisconsin." *The Wisconsin Archeologist* 60 (1979): 91–182.

Medley, Kimberly E., Christine M. Pobocik, and Brian W. Okey. "Historical Changes in Forest Cover and Land Ownership in a Midwestern U.S. Landscape." *Annals of the Association of American Geographers* 93, no. 1 (2003): 104–20.

Merchant, Carolyn. "Restoration and Reunion with Nature." In *Learning to Listen to the Land* (Bill Willers, ed.), 206–11. Washington, D.C.: Island Press, 1991.

Merritt, Raymond H. *Creativity, Conflict, and Controversy: A History of the St. Paul District U.S. Army Corps of Engineers.* Washington, D.C.: U.S. Government Printing Office, 1979.

Meyer, L. Donald, and William C. Moldenhauer. "Soil Erosion by Water: The Research Experience." In *The History of Soil and Water Conservation* (Douglas Helms and Susan L. Flader, eds.), 90–102. Berkeley: The University of California Press, 1985.

Meyers, Peter C. "Future Costs and Benefits of Conservation Reserve Lands." In *The Conservation Reserve—Yesterday, Today, and Tomorrow.* Symposium Proceedings, U.S. Department of Agriculture Forest Service, Rocky Mountain Forest and Range Experiment Station. General Technical Report RM-203 (1991): 43–45.

Meyers, Thomas J. "Education and Schooling." In *The Amish and the State* (Donald B. Kraybill, ed.), 87–108. Baltimore: Johns Hopkins University Press.

Miller, Char, and V. Alaric Sample. "Gifford Pinchot and the Conservation Spirit." In *Breaking New Ground* (Char Miller and V. Alaric Sample, eds.), xi–xvii. Washington, D.C.: Island Press, 1998.

Miller, Gideon A. "The Town of Clinton Amish History." In *Vernon County Heritage* (Vernon County Historical Society, ed.), 156. Dallas, TX: Taylor Publishing Company, 1994.

Miller, Teresa. "Can Trout and Cows Coexist?" *Natural Resources Report: A Newsletter for Natural Resource Managers and Researchers* 8, no. 3 (1997): 4–5.

Mladenoff, David J. "Vegetation Change in Relation to Land Use and Ownership on the Gogebic Iron Range, Wisconsin." Master's thesis, University of Wisconsin–Madison, 1979.

Nash, Roderick Frazier. *American Environmentalism: Readings in Conservation History.* New York: McGraw-Hill, 1990.

National Park Service. "National Register of Historical Places Registration Form: La Farge Reservoir and Lake Dam." Washington, D.C.: Administrative Services Division, National Park Service, NPS Form 10-900 (Rev. 10-90), 1999.

National Resources Board. *A Report on National Planning and Public Works in Relation to Natural Resources and Including Land Use and Water Resources with Findings and Recommendations.* Washington, D.C.: National Resources Board, 1934.

Nature Conservancy. *A Future for the Kickapoo River Watershed.* Madison: Wisconsin Chapter of the Nature Conservancy, 1989.

Nolt, Steven M. *A History of the Amish.* Intercourse, PA: Good Books, 1992.

Nowak, Peter J. "A Discussion." In *Soil Conservation Policies, Institutions, and Incentives* (Harold G. Halcrow, Earl O. Heady, and Melvin L. Cotner, eds.), 193–97. Ankeny, IA: Soil Conservation Society of America, 1982.

Nuzum, Ralph E. *Here on the Kickapoo.* Viroqua, WI: Nuzum, 1955.

Olshan, Marc A. "Modernity, the Folk Society, and the Old Order Amish: An Alternative Interpretation." *Rural Sociology* 46, no. 2 (1981): 297–309.

Orsi, Jared. *Hazardous Metropolis: Flooding and Urban Ecology in Los Angeles.* Berkeley: University of California Press, 2004.

Patronsky, Mark C. *Trespass to Land (1995 Wisconsin Act 451).* Madison: Wisconsin Legislative Council Staff, Information Memorandum 96-20, 1996.

Phillips, Guy D. *Environmental Assessment of the Kickapoo River Impoundment II: An Assessment of Economic Impact.* Madison: Institute for Environmental Studies, University of Wisconsin–Madison, IES Report no. 91, 1977.

Phillips, James Knox. "Negro-White Integration in a Midwestern Farm Community." *Negro Heritage* 7, no. 5/6 (1968): 55–58, 62–65.

Pimentel, D., C. Harvey, P. Resosudarmo, K. Sinclair, D. Kurz, M. McNair, S. Crist, L. Shpritz, L. Fitton, R. Saffouri, R. Blair. "Environmental and Economic Costs of Soil Erosion and Conservation Benefits." *Science* 267, no. 5201 (1995): 1117–23.

Pinchot, Gifford. *Breaking New Ground.* Washington, D.C.: Island Press, 1998. First published 1947.

Pisani, Donald J. "A Conservation Myth: The Troubled Childhood of the Multiple-Use Idea." *Agricultural History* 76, no. 2 (2002): 154–71.

Place, Elizabeth. "Land Use." In *The Amish and the State* (Donald B. Kraybill, ed.), 101–210. Baltimore: Johns Hopkins University Press, 1993.

Proxmire, William. *The Fleecing of America.* Boston: Houghton Mifflin, 1980.

Pubanz, Dan M., and Craig G. Lorimer. *Oak Regeneration Experiments in Southwestern Wisconsin: Two-Year Results.* Madison: Department of Forestry, School of Natural Resources, College of Agricultural and Life Sciences, University of Wisconsin–Madison, 1992.

Pyne, Stephen J. "Smokechasing: The Search for a Usable Place." *Environmental History* 6 (2001): 530–40.

Radin, Paul. *The Winnebago Tribe.* Lincoln: University of Nebraska Press, 1970. First published 1923.

———. *The Culture of the Winnebago: As Described by Themselves.* Baltimore: Waverly Press, 1949.

Rasmussen, Wayne D. "History of Soil Conservation, Institutions, and Incentives." In *Soil Conservation Policies, Institutions, and Incentives* (Harold G. Halcrow, Earl

Heady, and Melvin L. Cotner, eds.), 3–18. Ankeny, IA: Soil Conservation Society of America, 1982.

Redekop, Calvin, ed. *Creation and the Environment: An Anabaptist Perspective on a Sustainable World.* Baltimore: Johns Hopkins University Press, 2000.

Reisner, Marc. *Cadillac Desert: The American West and Its Disappearing Water.* New York: Viking, 1986.

Reuss, Martin. *Shaping Environmental Awareness: The United States Army Corps of Engineers Environmental Advisory Board, 1970–1980.* Washington, D.C.: U.S. Army Corps of Engineers, 1983.

Reyna, S. P. "The Emergence of Land Concentration in the West Africa Savanna." *American Ethnologist* 14, no. 3 (1987): 523–41.

Roberts, John C., Wayne G. Tlusty, and Harold C. Jordahl. *The Wisconsin Private Non-Industrial Woodland Owner: A Profile.* Madison: University of Wisconsin Cooperative Extension Service Occasional Paper Series no. 19, 1986.

Rooney, T. P., and D. M. Waller. "Direct and Indirect Effects of White-Tailed Deer in Forest Ecosystems." *Forest Ecology and Management* 181 (2003): 165–76.

Rooney, T. P., S. M. Wiegmann, D. A. Rogers, D. M. Waller. "Biotic Impoverishment and Homogenization in Unfragmented Forest Understory Communities." *Conservation Biology* 18, no. 3 (2004): 787–98.

Rose, Carol M. "Property as Storytelling: Perspectives from Game Theory, Narrative Theory, Feminist Theory." *Yale Journal of Law and the Humanities* 2, no. 1 (1990): 37–57.

Runge, C. Ford, M. Teresa Duchos, John S. Adams, Barry Goodwin, Judith A. Martin, Roderick D. Squires, and Alice E. Ingerson. "Public Sector Contributions to Private Land Value: Looking at the Ledger." In *Property and Values: Alternatives to Public and Private Ownership* (Charles Geisler and Gail Daneker, eds.), 41–62. Washington, D.C.: Island Press, 2000.

Salamon, Sonya. "Culture and Agricultural Land Tenure." *Rural Sociology* 58 (1993): 580–98.

Salkin, Philip H. "The Rose II Rockshelter (47-Ve-146): An Effigy Mound Component in the Kickapoo Valley." *The Wisconsin Archeologist* 56, no. 1 (1975): 55–71.

Sampson, R. Neil. *For Love of the Land: A History of the National Association of Conservation Districts.* League City, TX: National Association of Conservation Districts, 1985.

Sancar, Fahriye, H. Macari, T. Barman, K. Onaran, and G. Sargin. *Development of an Action Plan for the Kickapoo River Valley of Southwestern Wisconsin: New Visions for the Kickapoo: Regional Design Proposals for Future Development.* Madison: Department of Landscape Architecture, University of Wisconsin–Madison, 1992.

Schama, Simon. *Landscape and Memory.* New York: Alfred A. Knopf, 1995.

Schertz, Lyle P., and Gene Wunderlich. "Structure of Farming and Landownership in the Future: Implications for Soil Conservation." In *Soil Conservation Policies, Institutions, and Incentives* (Harold G. Halcrow, Earl O. Heady, and Melvin L. Cotner, eds.), 163–83. Ankeny, IA: Soil Conservation Society of America, 1982.

Schroeder, Bernice. "The Legacy of the Kickapoo: A People Betrayed." In *Vernon County Heritage* (Vernon County Historical Society, ed.), 148. Dallas, TX: Taylor Publishing Company, 1994.

Shallat, Todd. *Structures in the Stream: Water, Science, and the Rise of the U.S. Army Corps of Engineers*. Austin: University of Texas Press, 1994.

Singer, Joseph. "Property and Social Relations: From Title to Entitlement." In *Property and Values: Alternatives to Public and Private Ownership* (Charles Geisler and Gail Daneker, eds.), 3–19. Washington, D.C.: Island Press, 2000.

Sommers, David G., and Ted L. Napier. "Comparison of Amish and Non-Amish Farmers: A Diffusion/Farm-Structure Perspective." *Rural Sociology* 58, no. 1 (1993): 130–45.

Steinberg, Ted. *Slide Mountain: Or the Folly of Owning Nature*. Berkeley: University of California Press, 1996.

Steiner, Frederick R. *Soil Conservation in the United States: Policy and Planning*. Baltimore: Johns Hopkins University Press, 1990.

Stinner, Deborah H., M. G. Paoletti, and B. R. Stinner. "In Search of Traditional Farm Wisdom for a More Sustainable Agriculture: A Study of Amish Farming and Society." *Agriculture, Ecosystems, and Environment* 27 (1989): 77–90.

Stoddard, Charles H. *The Small Private Forest in the United States*. Washington, D.C.: Resources for the Future, 1961.

Stoeckler, J. H. *Trampling by Livestock Drastically Reduces Infiltration Rate of Soil in Oak and Pine Woods in Southwestern Wisconsin*. St. Paul, MN: U.S. Department of Agriculture, Lake States Forest Experiment Station, U.S. Department of Agriculture, Forest Service Technical Note 556, 1959.

Stoll, Steven. *Larding the Lean Earth: Soil and Society in Nineteenth-Century America*. New York: Hill and Wang, 2002.

Stoltzfus, Louise. *Amish Women*. Intercourse, PA: Good Books, 1994.

Tanner, Helen Hornbeck. *Atlas of Great Lakes Indian History*. Norman: University of Oklahoma Press, 1987.

Thiesenhusen, William C. *Broken Promises: Agrarian Reform and the Latin American Campesino*. Boulder, CO: Westview Press, 1995.

Tocqueville, Alexis de. *Democracy in America*, vol. 1, ed. Phillips Bradley. New York: Alfred A. Knopf, 1945. First published in 1835.

Toulmin, Camilla, and Julian F. Quan, eds. *Evolving Land Rights, Policy, and Tenure in Africa*. London: DFID/IIED/NRI, 2000.

Trimble, Stanley W. "Perspectives on the History of Soil Erosion Control in the Eastern United States." *Agricultural History* 59 (1985): 162–80.

———. "Decreased Rates of Alluvial Sediment Storage in the Coon Creek Basin, Wisconsin, 1975–93." *Science* 285 (1999): 1244–46.

Trimble, Stanley W., and Steven W. Lund. *Soil Conservation and the Reduction of Erosion and Sedimentation in the Coon Creek Basin, Wisconsin: A Study of Changes in Erosion and Sedimentation after the Introduction of Soil-Conservation Measures*. Washington, D.C.: U.S. Geological Survey, Professional Paper no. 1234, 1982.

Turner, Frederick Jackson. "The Significance of the Frontier in American History." In *Rereading Frederick Jackson Turner* (John Mack Faragher, ed.), 31–60. New Haven: Yale University Press, 1998. First published 1893.

U.S. Army Corps of Engineers. *La Farge Reservoir Flood Control Project Kickapoo River, Wisconsin: Questions and Answers Concerning the Acquisition of Your Real Estate by the Government*. Rock Island, IL: U.S. Army Engineer District, Rock Island Corps of Engineers, 1968.

———. *Environmental Guidelines for the Civil Works Program of the Corps of Engineers*. Washington, D.C.: U.S. Army Corps of Engineers, ER 1165-2-500, 1970.

———. *Evaluation of Water Quality and Environmental Setting for La Farge Lake Project on the Kickapoo River, Vernon County, Wisconsin*. St. Paul, MN: St. Paul District, U.S. Army Corps of Engineers, 1975.

———. *Review of Alternatives for Flood Damage Reduction on the Kickapoo River, Wisconsin*. St. Paul, MN: St. Paul District, U.S. Army Corps of Engineers, 1975.

———. *Alternatives for Flood Reduction and Recreation in the Kickapoo River Valley, Wisconsin: Special Report*. St. Paul, MN: St. Paul District, U.S. Army Corps of Engineers, 1977.

———. *Nation Builders*. Washington, D.C.: U.S. Army Corps of Engineers, circa 1989.

———. *Essayons (Let Us Try)*. Washington, D.C.: U.S. Army Corps of Engineers, 1991.

———. *Water Resources People and Issues: Interview with Gilbert F. White* (Martin Reuss, Interviewer). Fort Belvoir, VA: U.S. Army Corps of Engineers, 1993.

———. *Engineer Memoirs: Lieutenant General Ernest Graves* (Frank N. Schubert, Interviewer). Washington, D.C.: U.S. Army Corps of Engineers, 1997.

———. *The History of the U.S. Army Corps of Engineers*. Washington, D.C.: U.S. Army Corps of Engineers, 1998.

U.S. Army Engineer District, St. Paul. *Report on Survey of Kickapoo River, Wisconsin, for Flood Control*. St. Paul, MN: St. Paul District, U.S. Army Corps of Engineers, 1962.

———. *Revised Environmental Statement: La Farge Lake, Kickapoo River, Wisconsin*. St. Paul, MN: St. Paul District, U.S. Army Corps of Engineers, 1971.

———. *Final Environmental Statement: La Farge Lake, Kickapoo River, Vernon County, Wisconsin*. St. Paul, MN: St. Paul District, U.S. Army Corps of Engineers, 1972.

———. *Information Base for Further Evaluation of La Farge Lake and Channel Improvement, Wisconsin*. St. Paul, MN: St. Paul District, U.S. Army Corps of Engineers, 1977.

———. *Issue Paper: La Farge Lake, Kickapoo River, Wisconsin: Management, Monitoring Damage Repair, and Enforcement Requirements on Project Lands*. St. Paul, MN: St. Paul District, U.S. Army Corps of Engineers, 1997.

U.S. Bureau of the Census. *1990 Census of Population and Housing for Wisconsin*. Washington, D.C.: United States Government Printing Office, 1992.

U.S. Department of Agriculture. *Soils and Men: The 1938 Yearbook of Agriculture*. Washington, D.C.: United States Government Printing Office, 1938.

———. *Land: The 1958 Yearbook of Agriculture*. Washington, D.C.: United States Government Printing Office, 1958.

U.S. Department of Agriculture Forest Service. *The Conservation Reserve—Yesterday, Today, and Tomorrow*. Symposium Proceedings, U.S. Department of Agriculture Forest Service, Rocky Mountain Forest and Range Experiment Station. General Technical Report RM-203, 1995.

U.S. Department of Agriculture Soil Conservation Service. *Soil and Water Conservation in Wisconsin* (July). Madison, WI: USDA Soil Conservation Service, 1959.

———. *Soil and Water Conservation in Wisconsin* (July). Madison, WI: USDA Soil Conservation Service, 1964.

———. *Wisconsin Soil and Water Conservation Needs Inventory* (September). Madison, WI: USDA Soil Conservation Service, 1970.

U.S. General Services Administration. *Governmentwide Review of Real Property Disposal Policy.* Washington, D.C.: General Services Administration, Federal Property Resources Service, Office of Real Property, 1997.

———. *How to Acquire Federal Real Property.* Washington, D.C.: General Services Administration, Federal Property Resources Service, Office of Real Property, no date.

Vandell, Kerry D., and Pat J. Connolly. *Analyses of Real Estate Market Dynamics in the Kickapoo River Valley.* Madison, WI: KDV Associates, 1998.

Ventura, Stephen J. *Implementation of Land Information Systems in Local Government: Steps Toward Land Records Modernization in Wisconsin.* Madison: Wisconsin State Cartographer's Office, 1991.

Vernon County Historical Society. *Vernon County Heritage.* Dallas, TX: Taylor Publishing Company, 1994.

Vitek, William, and Wes Jackson, eds. *Rooted in the Land: Essays on Community and Place.* New Haven: Yale University Press, 1996.

Vogeler, Ingolf. *The Myth of the Family Farm: Agribusiness Dominance of U.S. Agriculture.* Boulder, CO: Westview Press, 1981.

Waller, D., and W. S. Alverson. "The White-Tailed Deer: A Keystone Herbivore." *Wildlife Society Bulletin* 25, no. 2 (1997): 217–26.

Walsh, Leo M. "Assessment of Soil Erosion Problems and Control Strategies in Wisconsin." In *Proceedings of a Conference on Public Policy Issues in Soil Conservation, Madison, Wisconsin, July 22–23, 1982* (Sherrie Beyer and Leonard C. Johnson, eds.), 5–20. Madison: Soil Conservation Society of America, Wisconsin Chapter, 1982.

Warren, Louis S. *The Hunter's Game: Poachers and Conservationists in Twentieth-Century America.* New Haven: Yale University Press, 1997.

White, Gilbert F. *Human Adjustment to Floods: A Geographical Approach to the Flood Problem in the United States.* Chicago: University of Chicago, Department of Geography, Research Paper 29, 1945.

White, Richard. *The Middle Ground: Indians, Empires, and Republics in the Great Lakes Region, 1650–1815.* New York: Cambridge University Press, 1991.

———. "'Are You an Environmentalist or Do You Work for a Living?': Work and Nature." In *Uncommon Ground: Toward Reinventing Nature* (William Cronon, ed.), 171–85. New York: W. W. Norton and Company, 1995.

Wiebe, Keith D., Abebayehu Tegene, and Betsey Kuhn. "Land Tenure, Land Policy, and the Property Rights Debate." In *Who Owns America? Social Conflict Over Property Rights* (Harvey M. Jacobs, ed.), 79–93. Madison: University of Wisconsin Press, 1998.

Wilkening, E. A., P. Wolpat, J. G. Linn, C. Geisler, and D. McGranahan. *Quality of Life in Kickapoo Valley Communities.* Madison: Institute for Environmental Studies, University of Wisconsin–Madison, IES Report no. 11, 1973.

Williams, Michael. *Americans and Their Forests: A Historical Geography.* New York: Cambridge University Press, 1989.

Wisconsin Cartographer's Guild, ed. *Wisconsin's Past and Present: A Historical Atlas.* Madison: University of Wisconsin Press, 2002.

Wisconsin Conservation Department. *Digest of the Conservation Reserve of the Soil Bank Program in Wisconsin.* Madison: Wisconsin Conservation Department, 1957.

Wisconsin Department of Natural Resources. *Wisconsin's Deer Management Program: The Issues Involved in Decision-Making.* Madison: Wisconsin Department of Natural Resources, Deer Management Program, 1998.

Wisconsin, Minnesota and Montana Amish Directory 2002. Millersburg, OH: Abana Books, 2002.

Wisconsin State Board of Soil and Water Conservation Districts. *Wisconsin's Soil, Water, and Related Natural Resources: An Appraisal.* Madison: University of Wisconsin–Extension, 1980.

———. *A Soil and Water Resources Conservation Program for Wisconsin* (April). Madison: University of Wisconsin–Extension, 1981.

Wisconsin State Soil Conservation Committee. *Soil Erosion Survey of Wisconsin.* Madison: State Soil Conservation Committee of Wisconsin, 1940.

———. *Why Should I Be Interested in Soil Conservation?* (May). Madison: State Soil Conservation Committee of Wisconsin, 1947.

———. *Inter-Agency Agreement for Planning and Developing Community Watersheds in Wisconsin.* Madison: Wisconsin State Soil Conservation Committee, 1961.

Wisconsin State Soil and Water Conservation Committee. *Twenty-Five Years with the Soil and Water Conservation Districts in Wisconsin.* Madison: Wisconsin State Soil and Water Conservation Committee, 1964.

Wisconsin's Environmental Decade. "Member Questions WED's Water Quality Position." *The Defender,* April 2000.

Worster, Donald. *Dust Bowl: The Southern Plains in the 1930s.* New York: Oxford University Press, 1979.

———. "Doing Environmental History." In *The Ends of the Earth: Perspectives on Modern Environmental History* (Donald Worster, ed.), 289–307. Cambridge: Cambridge University Press, 1988.

———. "Transformations of the Earth: Toward an Agroecological Perspective in History." *Journal of American History* 76 (1990): 1087–1106.

———. *The Wealth of Nature: Environmental History and the Ecological Imagination.* New York: Oxford University Press, 1993.

———. "Nature and the Disorder of History." In *Reinventing Nature? Responses to Postmodern Deconstruction* (Michael E. Soulé and Gary Lease, eds.), 65–86. Washington, D.C.: Island Press, 1995.

Young, Robert A., and Michael R. Reichenbach. "Factors Influencing the Timber Harvest Intentions of Nonindustrial Private Forest Owners." *Forest Science* 33 (1987): 381–93.

Zaczek, J. J., J. W. Groninger, and J. W. Van Sambeek. "Stand Dynamics in an Old-Growth Hardwood Forest, in Southern Illinois, USA." *Natural Areas Journal* 22, no. 3 (2002): 211–19.

Zeasman, O. R., and I. O. Hembre. *A Brief History of Soil Erosion Control in Wisconsin.* Madison: Wisconsin State Soil and Water Conservation Committee, 1963.

Zook, Lee J. "Slow-Moving Vehicles." In *The Amish and the State* (Donald B. Kraybill, ed.), 145–62. Baltimore: Johns Hopkins University Press, 1993.

———. "The Amish Farm and Alternative Agriculture: A Comparison." *Journal of Sustainable Agriculture* 4, no. 4 (1994): 21–30.

Newspapers

The Budget (Sugarcreek, Ohio)
The Capital Times (Madison, Wisconsin)
Chicago Sun-Times
Chicago Tribune
Denver Post
Dimensions
Epitaph-News (Viola, Wisconsin)
Houston Chronicle
Kalamazoo Gazette
Kickapoo Scout
La Crosse Tribune
La Farge Epitaph
Milwaukee Journal
Milwaukee Journal Sentinel
Minneapolis Star Tribune
New York Times
News from Indian Country
St. Louis Post-Dispatch
USA Today
Vernon County Broadcaster (Viroqua, Wisconsin)
Viroqua Broadcaster-Censor
Wall Street Journal
Wisconsin State Journal

Index